That Ambitious
Mr. Legaré

JAMES M. LEGARÉ (1823–1859) The Only Known Likeness
From a Capewell & Kimmel engraving in *The Knickerbocker Gallery*
(New York, 1855).

That Ambitious
Mr. Legaré

The Life of James M. Legaré of South Carolina,
Including a Collected Edition of His Verse

❧

CURTIS CARROLL DAVIS

UNIVERSITY OF SOUTH CAROLINA PRESS
COLUMBIA, S. C.

This book is for

LUCY G. MURCHISON
(1848–1939)
*Of "Holly Hill," near Manchester, in Cumberland County,
North Carolina*

To Doubters of the *Legenda Aurea* about "Southern Womanhood"
She Demonstrated It Could Still Happen Here

Also by CURTIS CARROLL DAVIS

*Chronicler of the Cavaliers: A Life
of the Virginia Novelist, Dr. William A. Caruthers*

*The King's Chevalier:
A Biography of Lewis Littlepage*

Editor, John Sergeant Wise's, *The End of an Era* (1899)

Editor, *Belle Boyd in Camp and Prison* (1865)

Editor, Dr. William A. Caruthers', *The Knights
of the Golden Horse-Shoe* (1841)

CONTENTS

vii

viii

APPENDIXES 289

INDEX 327

Illustrations

PREFACE

The stairway of the university library kept winding up, and up, and around. Eventually I found it, lurking under the eaves—the graduate students' reading room. On one of the shelves, cringing between taller and stouter tomes, I found also a slender volume which, having but recently been rebound, had not had time to acquire the genteel drabness of library rebindings. So the two words on its spine stared out commandingly: ORTA UNDIS. I was intrigued. Was this a travel book of adventures long ago in some quaint region? Or perchance a Utopian novel? I passed on to more serious matters.

It was not until after a couple more visitations under the eaves that I could resist no longer the stare of those unblinking syllables: ORTA UNDIS. After I had dipped into the little book, I presently gazed up and about me in the manner of Cortez at Darien. Who was this unknown—this Le-ga-ré—who had penned such charming verse? His name was as odd as his title! So I trotted over to the office of Professor Jay B. Hubbell, who knew everything about Southern literature.

"Who was J. M. Legaré, and how do you pronounce it?"

"Down there in Charleston," Professor Hubbell informed me, "they pronounce it luh-*gree,* and to tell you the truth, they don't seem to know much about him."

All this was more than a quarter-century ago. A copy of my

first published writing on James M. Legaré subsequently found
its way to me late in 1944, at an Army Air Corps fighter strip
not far from Mount Vesuvius.

Since those antique times, and amid many unrelated pursuits,
I have kept chiseling away at the wall of obscurity immuring
J. M. Legaré. Here was a Southern author whose appearance
on the New York and Philadelphia literary scenes has been
ignored by literary historians. Here was a Southern author whose
correspondence with Henry W. Longfellow constitutes a remarkable example of intersectional rapport, yet no notice has been
taken of it. Here, in sum, was a Southern author as little known
as Thomas Holley Chivers, and, wrong-headedly or no, I could
not resist the challenge of obscurity. Provided, of course, something of value promised to emerge therefrom. Before much further examination, I decided there would be.

By then I knew that Legaré had not only written some
superior verse. He had also written fiction that was widely read
in its day, and won prizes for it. He had painted, and won
prizes in painting. He had invented—experimenting, among
other things, with processes approaching the realm of discovery
that has produced our modern field of plastics—and won prizes
for his inventions. He had, in other words, proved himself as a
various and valid transmitter of the culture of his region and
period, occasionally as a rebel against it; and I thought that
this was important. (To show the continuity of the transmission
process I have presented, in some detail, new data on his unde-
servedly obscure father, John D. Legaré.)

By the time I had satisfied myself on these things I found that
I had also, such being the beneficence of humanistic studies,
acquired a liberal-arts education all over again.

The end result? I cannot claim to have snatched from Time's
maw a genius, or even a fully first-rate talent. But I think there
is a very good talent here, and an artist should be evaluated on
the evidence of his best effort. Legaré's verse is not on the same
plane as that of Lanier or Poe, but neither is it that of just

another starving poet (which he was often not far from becoming). He is, at his best, appreciably better than Paul Hamilton Hayne and certainly the equal of Henry Timrod and Edward C. Pinckney. This evidence accumulates, I feel, only with the present reprinting of his poems, over half of which have not hitherto been collected. I have collected his letters, too—frustratingly few they are!—and made of them the best use I could.

There arises a special gratification to me in Legaré's salvage —the sedate thrill of adding another chapter, however minor, to a volume still far from complete: the annals of Southern cultural history. As the Virginia politician, sportsman, and duellist John Sergeant Wise, put it about 1895: "For two hundred years New England has been writing, writing, writing continuously, until her fine industrious chirography has covered the whole page of our country's history and obscures the story of other sections."

Legaré's contribution to the culture of his section was among the fullest. In no less than three fields he produced significant work. Here is reason enough for exhuming him. Whether I have also brought him to life—the basic policy and ultimate goal of biography—is another matter.

As in all efforts at exhumation, archaeological or literary, many fellow diggers have aided the exhumator. Since their names have accumulated from the year 1940, it would be impractical to list them all. It would be impertinent not to list the following:

Aiken, S.C.—Mrs. R. Conover Bartram, historian, Saint Thaddeus' Episcopal Church, and Rev. Charles M. Seymour, Jr., its former rector. Athens, Ga.—John W. Bonner, Jr., of the University Libraries; the late Prof. Edd W. Parks of the University of Georgia. Atlanta, Ga.—Prof. Bertram H. Flanders of the local division of the University of Georgia. Augusta, Ga.— Charles G. Cordle of Augusta College; Joseph B. Cumming, Esq. Baltimore, Md.—Mrs. Charles R. Anderson (the former Mary [Pringle] Fenhagen); Mrs. Philip G. Slauson, my typist;

Prof. James W. Poulteney, Department of Classics, and Dr. Richard A. Macksey, Humanities Center, of The Johns Hopkins University (Dr. Macksey herewith offers the first known translation of Legaré's Latin poem, "Orta-Undis"). Charleston, S.C.— E. Milby Burton, director, the Charleston Museum; Mrs. Ernest W. King of "Hillsborough"; W. Allan Moore, Jr., Esq.; the late Mrs. Ernest H. Pringle; the late Prof. Granville T. Prior of The Citadel; Miss Virginia Rugheimer of the Library Society; Mrs. R. H. Simmons of the Huguenot Society. Columbia, S.C.—the late Prof. Robert L. Meriwether, former, and Dr. W. Edwin Hemphill, current editor of *The Papers of John C. Calhoun.* Durham, N.C.—Prof. Jay B. Hubbell of Duke University (who, as in so many projects touching Southern literary history, inaugurated it all). Edinburgh—J. S. Ritchie of the National Library of Scotland. New York City—Mrs. Katherine Maas, formerly with the C. Waller Barrett Collection of American Literature (now in the University of Virginia Library); the late Edward B. Morrison of the New York Public Library Manuscript Room.

At "2-A"   Curtis Carroll Davis
Baltimore
January, 1971

ABBREVIATIONS

CCD (1)   Curtis Carroll Davis, "Poet, Painter, and Inventor . . . ," *NCHR,* XXI (July, 1944), 215-31

CCD (2)   ——, "A Letter from the Muses . . . ," *NCHR,* XXVI (Oct., 1949), 417-38

CCD (3)   ——, "Fops, Frenchmen, Hidalgos, and Aztecs . . . ," *NCHR,* XXX (Oct., 1953), 524-60

CCD (4)   ——, "Mr. Legaré Inscribes Some Books . . . ," *Papers of the Bibliographical Society of America,* LVI (2nd Quarter, 1962), 219-36

JJL Coll.   The Joseph John Legaré Collection. Charleston Library Society, Charleston, S.C.

JML   James Mathewes Legaré (1823-1859), subject of the present work

NCHR   *North Carolina Historical Review* (Raleigh), quarterly (1924–)

O-U   J. M. Legaré, *Orta-Undis, and Other Poems* (Boston: William D. Ticknor & Co., M DCCC XLVIII)

THAT AMBITIOUS MR. LEGARÉ

I : LOW COUNTRY GENESIS

Pliny said there was no book but what had *some* good in it. But I think it a sin to publish one that has not a great deal of good in it—tho' I have been guilty of publications of little value myself—but I charged them to no one. Legaré's ambition is awful. You must excuse his puff of the Knicker-bocker—*he did it for bread.*

Ex-Gov. James H. Hammond
of South Carolina, Oct. 28, 1849, to William Gilmore Simms

If the external facts of the life and the personal memorials of James Matthew [*sic*] Legaré of South Carolina were not, as they apparently are, irretrievably obscured, one could imagine some future American Matthew Arnold delineating his delicate and reticent soul in such charming pages as the English critic devoted to Maurice or Eugénie Guérin. But we know next to nothing of the personality of this "quiet singer"; the Duyckinks [*sic*] knew nothing; and personal inquiries in Charleston fail to elicit any memory that has a specific flavor, a personal note.

Ludwig Lewisohn,
in *Library of Southern Literature,* VII (1909), 3,191

How the passage of just a little time can alter a man's reputa-
tion! In 1849 a Carolina politician thought that James Mathewes Legaré boasted too much "personality"; sixty years later a Carolina literary critic felt that he boasted not enough. And each was right. Legaré was ambitious, consumingly so. He was also reticent. He came by these and other characteristics as do most men, through inheritance modified by circumstance.

On both sides of his family the heritage seems to have been pretty much of a piece. It was that triad of qualities without which the invading white man could never have subdued the beckoning but obdurate environment of the New World: quenchless enthusiasm for religion, energetic effort in commerce, and passion for culture. James M. Legaré's ancestors, on both sides, were God-fearing churchgoers who spent most of their time working at secular callings, but rarely to the neglect of cultural affairs.

His mother's line, the "Matheweses"—they rang all possible changes on the spelling, often in the same family at the same period—went back in coastal Carolina at least as far as the fourth decade of the eighteenth century.[1] The *South-Carolina Gazette* of August 24, 1738, tells of a horse killed by lightning at Mrs. Matthews' stable on Church Street and refers to her home as being "over against the Baptist Meeting house." One of the few vestiges of the existence of James's grandmother Frances (Doughty) Mathews is a set of Dr. Ramsay's *The History of South Carolina* (1809), presented her by her father, Thomas Doughty. Her husband, James Mathews, of Charleston, inscribed his name in every one of the nine volumes of the Count de Buffon's *Natural History* (1785).[2] James Mathews, probably the lawyer of that name, attained the patriarchal age of nearly seventy-two years before they lowered him away in the Circular Churchyard in the autumn of 1844.[3] He had sired seven children, of whom the last, Mary Doughty Mathews, became the

[1] See *Index to Wills of Charleston County, South Carolina* (Charleston: Charleston Free Library, 1950), pp. 194–96.

[2] These titles are among the Mathews, Doughty, and Legaré association items, all with autograph inscriptions, in the JJL Coll. The subject of this book probably spelled his middle name "Mathewes." The rector of his parish church at Aiken, S.C., Rev. J. H. Cornish, spelled it under all variations. The regional authority, A. S. Salley, renders it "Mathewes" as early as 1902. JML almost invariably signed himself "J. M. Legaré," otherwise "James M. Legaré."

[3] The death notice in the Charleston *Courier,* Nov. 25, 1844, p. 2, col. 7, requests that the families of Thomas D. Mathewes and of J. D. Legaré attend the burial services. Among the witnesses to James Mathews' will, proved Dec. 12, 1844, were J. D. and James M. Legaré, probably identical with JML and his father. (Will Book XLIII, 816, Probate Court, Charleston.) Cf. also John B. O'Neall, *Biographical Sketches of the Bench and Bar of South Carolina. . .* (Charleston: S. G. Courtenay & Co., 1859), II, 602.

mother of our subject. When Mary married, she married a second cousin.

Our subject's father, John D. Legaré—son of Joseph, grandson of Isaac—stood at the fifth generation of his name in Carolina. The pater familias there, Solomon, had been born in France a dozen or so years prior to Louis XIV's revocation of the Edict of Nantes in 1685. He was taken by his parents, François (a jeweller, from a family specializing in the craft) and Anne, via England to the New World. The emigrants settled at Braintree in Massachusetts colony, and Solomon grew up to become a goldsmith. In proper course he acquired three wives.

Striking off in his early twenties, against his father's wishes, to the proprietary colony of Carolina, Solomon settled at Charleston. By the time he died there in the spring of 1760, a very wealthy man, the *South-Carolina Gazette* could announce that he had been in the colony no less than sixty-four years. This circumstance sufficed to plant Solomon's tree beyond peradventure among those of the *Ur*-Charlestonians. Local standards decree that heads of family arriving only in 1719 or thereafter —when the colony became a Royal province—qualify merely as "new" Charlestonians. If their advent postdates the American Revolution, they rate as "green." If they failed to arrive until after the War between the States, they are just visitors.

In the guillotined French that gradually evolved in the region the name was, and is, pronounced "luh-*gree*," as in "Simon Legree." By this sound the word became world property in 1852 when a New England housewife gave *Uncle Tom's Cabin* to the ages. Mrs. Stowe could have encountered the Legaré name in her chief source for the novel, and she could have been instructed in its local pronunciation by a Charleston-born friend. Whether she bestowed it upon her whip-wielding drunkard as a general castigation of Carolina Low Country cliques is a speculation that may well have intrigued at least one family group therein.[4]

[4] Though Mrs. Stowe did not visit South Carolina until after the Civil War, her *A Key to Uncle Tom's Cabin* . . . (London: T. Bosworth, 1853)

The pater familias, Solomon, had been a nonconformist refugee from his native land. Many of his descendants continued so in theirs, and the burying ground of the Independent or Congregational ("Circular") Church of Charleston is hillocked with Legaré graves, including that of our James's great-grandfather Isaac.[5] One of old Solomon's grandsons, Thomas, is said to have taken his bride in marriage partly in order to salvage the girl from the grasp of the frivolous Anglicans. Whether he did or no, the fact of Elizabeth Bassnett Legaré's conversion remained, a good fifteen years after her demise, a gratifying exemplum for a religious tract society.[6] Others of the clan merged gradually

---

frequently cites South Carolina and Charleston sources. Her acquaintance Theodore D. Weld's *American Slavery As It Is* . . . (New York: American Anti-Slavery Society, 1839), p. 171, lists Hugh Swinton Legaré as among the Charleston élite. Weld's wife, the former Angelina Grimké, derived from the same Charleston aristocracy as did the Legarés, and the two families had long known one another. Mrs. Stowe informed Mrs. Weld "that while writing *Uncle Tom's Cabin* she slept with *Slavery As It Is* under her pillow. . . ." (See Benjamin P. Thomas, *Theodore Weld: Crusader for Freedom* [New Brunswick, N.J.: Rutgers University Press, 1950], p. 223.) Mrs. Weld had helped her husband in the writing of *American Slavery As It Is*. The editor of *The Annotated Uncle Tom's Cabin* (New York: Paul S. Eriksson, Inc., 1964) writes in part as follows: "She may, of course, have used the name without being consciously aware of what she was doing. That is, she had heard the name but forgot having heard it. Anyway, it is an ingenious idea. If I had known about it, I would have referred to it in my introduction." (Philip van Doren Stern, Paris, Aug. 6, 1964, to CCD.) JML may have returned the compliment by utilizing the surname of John Van Trompe, the honest old emancipator pictured in chap. 9 of *Uncle Tom's Cabin*, for the two young van Trumps (*sic*) who figure in his stories, "Fleur de Sillery," *The Knickerbocker Magazine*, Oct.–Nov., 1854, and "The Loves of Mary Jones," in *The Knickerbocker Gallery* . . . (New York, 1855).

[5] See "Early Generations of the Legaré Family in South Carolina," *Transactions of the Huguenot Society of South Carolina*, No. 46 (Charleston, 1941), pp. 72–81, with genealogical tree by W. Allan Moore, Jr. Isaac Legaré and a son, Joseph, were trustees of the Congregational church in Christ Church Parish (see Petrona R. McIver, "Wappataw Congregational Church," *South Carolina Historical Magazine*, LVIII [Apr., 1957], 85n., 93). There is a good sketch of Solomon Legaré's career in R. Milby Burton, *South Carolina Silversmiths, 1690–1860* (Charleston, S.C.: The Charleston Museum, 1942), pp. 105–110. Reprinted Rindge, N. H., 1968.

[6] "Illness and Death of Mrs. Legare," *Publications of Virginia Religious Tract Society*, No. 6 (Harrisonburg: Theological Printing-Office, 1813),

into the established faith of the Carolina colony, becoming equally devout, if less intense, Episcopalians. The merchant Samuel Legaré, of the same generation as Episcopalian-loathing Thomas, was both warden and vestryman of Saint Michael's, the town's second oldest congregation in the Establishment.[7] John D. Legaré espoused the Presbyterian faith, but his eldest son chose Anglicanism.

Besides a firm piety the Legarés exhibited a dogged pursuit of business. One of old Solomon's sons, Solomon of Johns Island, has been rated among the most eminent merchants of the pre-Revolutionary period.[8] In the next generation Isaac—our subject's great-grandfather—a planter out in Christ Church Parish, controlled a baronial 1,400 acres and thirty-six slaves. Thomas the bride-redeemer established commercial relations with the New York firm of Beekman at least by his twentieth birthday and eventually prospered sufficiently to erect a residence which rates today among the Charleston landmarks.[9] Colonel James Legaré, of the generation of our subject's father, as partner in the cotton-factorage house of Legaré, Colcock & Co., did well enough to build (among other residences) a fine summer place in what South Carolinians still call "the Up-Country." Here he

---

pp. 18–22 (copy in the College of William and Mary Library). Thomas Legaré (1732–1801) married Elizabeth Bassnett (1734–1798) in 1753. In Joseph Johnston, M.D., *Traditions and Reminiscences Chiefly of the American Revolution in the South* (Charleston: Walker & James, 1851), pp. 370–71, are anecdotes about him.

[7] See George S. Holmes, *A Historic Sketch of the Parish Church of St. Michael, in the Province of South Carolina, from . . . 1752 to 1887 . . .* (Charleston: Walker, Evans, & Cogswell, 1887), pp. 35–36.

[8] By Richard H. Barry, *Mr. Rutledge of South Carolina* (New York: Duell, Sloane, & Pearce, [1942]), p. 60. The subject is Gov. John Rutledge, later Chief Justice of the Palmetto State. Emphasizing the supreme value to the Colony in agriculture, manufacture, and commerce of the French-descended settlers is Arthur H. Hirsch, *The Huguenots in Colonial South Carolina* (Durham: Duke University Press, 1928), p. 168. In cultural affairs he does not place them among the leaders (*ibid.,* p. 164).

[9] Samuel Chamberlain, "Living with Antiques in Charleston," *Antiques,* LXIX (Feb., 1946), 141, with photograph of fireplace. Cf. also Philip L. White (ed.), *The Beekman Mercantile Papers, 1746–1799* (New York: New-York Historical Society, 1956), I, 160.

had toiling for him, by the time of the War between the States, a good three hundred Negroes.[10]

But these Legarés were the stellar offshoots. Most of the genus flourished quietly, even obscurely, pursuing their callings at the median level and leaving little other than their names to mark their passing through the land.[11] For American history, indeed, the only one whose name echoes today was neither merchant nor planter but a deformed and recluse scholar-statesman—our James's third cousin, once removed—Hugh Swinton Legaré. In him the cultural side of old Solomon's blood first came to its crest. It was coming to another, slighter crest in the career of John D. Legaré.

Hugh Swinton Legaré attained eminence through a ruthless absorption with a single field of endeavor, humanistic inquiry (for years he studied fifteen hours a day). His cousin John D. Legaré was much more a man of the diversified first half of the nineteenth century. His activities rambled over half-a-dozen fields, and in each of them he attained a modest celebrity. By the time James, first-born of his three children, appeared in November, 1823, the parent was already well launched in one of these fields.

In 1824, as a member of the Agricultural Society of South Carolina, founded in 1785, J. D. Legaré was named to a committee to look into an invention for detaching the annular strip of bark from cotton plants.[12] The following winter, 1825,

---

[10] See botanist Henry William Ravenel's *Private Journal . . . 1859–1887*, ed. Arney R. Childs (Columbia: University of South Carolina Press, 1947), p. 115. Colonel James Legaré's dates are 1805–1883.

[11] For Civil War skirmishes occurring at "Legare's Place" in 1862 and at "Legare's, James Island" in 1864 see Jacob N. Cardozo, *Reminiscences of Charleston* (Charleston: Joseph Walker, 1866), pp. 120, 132–33. A Charleston anecdote in rhyme about the snobbery of JML's brother, Joe Legaré—for years the bookkeeper at Panknin's Drug Store, on Meeting Street—is related in *The Letters of William Gilmore Simms*, ed. Mary C. Simms Oliphant, Alfred T. Odell, and T. C. Duncan Eaves (Columbia: University of South Carolina Press, 1952–1956), II, 435n.

[12] See James Cuthbert and John D. Legaré, "Report of the Committee of the Agricultural Society of South-Carolina, on the Decorticator," dated Charleston, Oct. 19, 1824, in the pamphlet, *Original Communications Made to the Agricultural Society of South Carolina . . .* (Charleston:

at the Society's livestock show on the Old Race Course near Charleston, his bull "Hamlet," exhibited for improving the breed of milch cattle, won the Gold Medal.[13] By the summer of 1827 the Society had decided it ought to establish its own periodical. John D. Legaré, whom it now appointed its Librarian, was asked to head a committee to look into the matter. The committee's conclusion was that the Society could not successfully effect such a project. But Legaré became so taken with the idea that, after consulting various local planters—Charleston's commerce had been dwindling for years, and a rural culture was slowly dominating the city—he determined to get out the periodical himself, with the approval and patronage of the Society. He distributed a printed circular far and wide.

"It is not fit or becoming for us any longer," his opinion ran, "to sit with folded arms and wait patiently until the Manufacturers have bound us as victims to the altar; it is time that we should awake from our sleep, which unfortunately has been too long and deep . . . ."[14]

In January, 1828, with the appearance of the inaugural issue of the *Southern Agriculturist* at Charleston, their sleep was broken. John D. Legaré had produced the first important farm journal in the lower South.[15] He edited it for its first seven years, and it lasted no less than fourteen in all.

A. E. Miller, 1824), pp. 51–55 (copy in Charleston Library Society). The report is briefly noted in Chalmers S. Murray, *This Our Land: The Story of the Agricultural Society of South Carolina* (Charleston: Carolina Art Assn., 1949), p. 86. Legaré's middle name was probably Daniel, after his great-great-grandfather, who died at Charleston in 1791.

[13] Minutes, Feb. 21–22, 1825, Agricultural Society of South Carolina (Society MSS, People's Building, Charleston). The Minutes reveal that John D. Legaré was Librarian of the society from the inception of that post, Aug. 21, 1827, until its abolition, Aug. 16, 1831.

[14] A copy of this undated circular is Ac. no. 1009, Elliott–Gonzales Papers, Southern Historical Collection, University of North Carolina Library. On its verso is a letter from John S. Ashe, Charleston, July 31, 1827, to William Elliott (the Beaufort sportsman and State legislator who subsequently contributed to the *Southern Agriculturist*) doing just what "My Friend," John D. Legaré, had requested, viz., spreading the gospel.

[15] See Albert L. Demaree, *The American Agricultural Press, 1819–1860* (New York: Columbia University Press, 1941), pp. 356–58, who would

A reader knowing little of agriculture, turning the pages today of this neatly printed periodical, will be struck with how broadly the responsible men of the time conceived that central sphere of their economy. The range of articles which Legaré accepted is impressive. The Charleston physician Thomas Y. Simons, for example, offered "General Observations on the Effects of Malaria." From Georgia, Joseph Eve sent in an essay "On the Construction of Roads in the Southern States." Dr. Thomas Cooper, the economist and president of South Carolina College at Columbia, contributed a paper "On Various Processes of Manufacturing Sugar." General Robert Y. Hayne, Charleston lawyer and United States Senator, wrote the editor a special communication on the properties of indigo seed from Bengal. John R. Mathews of Edisto Island debated the subject of animal birthmarks with Dr. Samuel L. Mitchill of New York City, former editor of the *Medical Repository* there.

John D. Legaré was too busy as editor to contribute more than occasionally to his *Southern Agriculturist*. At this time he was also Recording Secretary of the Horticultural Society of Charleston—a group which included such people as the naturalist Rev. John Bachman, pastor of Saint John's Lutheran Church, and Joel R. Poinsett, who had served as the first American Minister to Mexico. Legaré was intrigued with experimentation on seeds and vegetables. At the Society's exhibition in May, 1832, at Seyle's Long-Room the editor won premiums for his samples of Swiss chard, tart rhubarb, sea kale, and white-stone turnips; and the horticulturists were publicly congratulated that one of their members had demonstrated the feasibility of raising such exotics in the Low Country climate.[16]

---

claim its primacy for the entire South; but this is to ignore John S. Skinner's *American Farmer* at Baltimore (1819–1897). Legaré's periodical is also noted by Frank L. Mott, *A History of American Magazines* (Cambridge, Mass.: Harvard University Press, 1957), I, 442n. CCD used the set in the Library of Congress, which is complete for J. D. Legaré's first editorship but broken for the New Series. The set in the University of South Carolina Library is complete.

[16] See "Proceedings of the Horticultural Society of Charleston," *Southern Agriculturist*, V (July, 1832), 366–67. Legaré's own "Notice of the

Legaré was also proud of the fact that successful cultivation, out at his farm, of the *aracacha*, an edible root from Colombia, was the first such attempt in the United States.[17]

In soliciting articles and advice for his magazine the editor journeyed up and down the coastal area, visiting such large-scale planters in Georgia as John Hamilton Couper of "Hopeton" and Thomas Spalding of Sapelo Island.[18] His interest in belles lettres moved him to accept a lengthy biographical essay about Eli Whitney and to print a five-part fiction story entitled "The Successful Planter, or Memoirs of My Uncle Ben." His range of inquiry did not disdain a contribution on "How to Clear a House of Cockroaches." (Answer: drown them in molasses-sweetened water.) He saw to it that each volume of the *Southern Agriculturist* contained an excellent topical index, and his section of "Miscellaneous Intelligence" concluding each issue is tribute to the breadth of his reading and the range of his professional acquaintance.

By the close of 1834, however, J. D. Legaré had almost worn himself out. There was too much work, too many pressing invitations for visits. For some time he had thought about retiring before his health gave way completely. In a lengthy valedictory the editor finally bade agriculture—pleasurable and reputation-making though it had been—"a long, and last *farewell.*"[19]

Floral Exhibition of the Horticultural Society of Charleston," *ibid.*, VI (June, 1833), 308, reveals that at the April exhibition in the Academy of Fine Arts he was on the Arrangements Committee together with Joseph A. Winthrop and Joel R. Poinsett.

[17] See "Result of an Attempt to Cultivate the Aracacha; by the Editor," *Southern Agriculturist*, V (Feb., 1832), 73–79, with reference to his "farm" on p. 76n.

[18] In addition to Legaré's own "Account of an Agricultural Excursion Made into the South of Georgia in the Winter of 1832 . . . ," *ibid.*, VI (March–Nov., 1833), 138, 157, 297, 358, 410, 460, and 571ff., see also Medora F. Perkerson, *White Columns in Georgia* (New York: Rinehart & Co., [1952]), p. 119, for his "Hopeton" sojourn.

[19] See "A Farewell Address of the Editor," dated Charleston, Dec. 1, 1834, in *Southern Agriculturist*, VII (Dec., 1834), 659. The bulk of this six-page article is devoted to suggestions for improving the condition of agriculture.

For six months already he had been busied with another venture—hotel-keeping.

By the end of June, 1834, Legaré had built up, almost from nothing, an attractive spa at the Grey Sulphur Springs in the mountains of Giles County in southwest Virginia. There he, as well as his guests, took the benefit of the air and the waters for the next four years, presumably in company of wife Mary and the Legaré children. (There were now three in all—James, his younger brother, Joseph John, and Frances, or Fannie.) The Philadelphia bookseller and writer on economics Philip H. Nicklin, who visited the Grey three months after its proprietor had thrown open the doors, declared approvingly: "Every thing here is conducted after the polished and agreeable manner of South Carolina; all is redolent of the Palmetto. . . ."

The chemical quality of the waters at the Grey Sulphur attracted favorable attention as far afield as Benjamin Silliman's *Journal of Science and Arts* in Connecticut. For the convenience of the patronage come to sample them, John D. Legaré had erected a brick hotel extending ninety feet in length. There were two ranges of cabins, each 162 feet long. Together with subsidiary buildings, he could accommodate anywhere from eighty to a hundred guests. Eventually he served the Number One guest of them all. In 1838 President Martin Van Buren and his party sat down "to a sumptuous dinner on the 6th [September], prepared especially for the occasion . . . ."

At this high point the hotelier chose to bow out. As a Low Country planter visiting there at the time explained it, Legaré had "kept his house well, and had been pretty well patronized at first, but the water of his Spring had so little of the Sulphur about it that people could not be persuaded that it had any tonic or healing virtues. The popularity of a Mineral Spring depends upon its nastiness, and there was very little about Mr. Legaré's spring to distinguish it from common spring water."[20]

20 "The Memoirs of Frederick Adolphus Porcher," ed. Samuel G. Stoney, *South Carolina Historical and Genealogical Magazine*, XLVII (Apr.,

Disposing of his interests in the Grey, John D. Legaré returned to Charleston.

There he took over editorship of the Agricultural Society's magazine once more. Its title was changed to the *Southern Cabinet of Agriculture* for his first year (1840), and he edited it through 1842. The Society promptly paid him the compliment of Honorary Membership;[21] and the ornithologist John James Audubon, whose sons were in the process of marrying Charleston girls, advised one of the boys that Legaré's "periodical is taken by a great number of Gents from this City and neighborhood." Under Legaré's successor, Benjamin R. Carroll, the magazine lasted until 1846. Ten years later the *South Carolina Agriculturist* at Laurensville still remembered its Charleston forerunner as "a capital Magazine—but being mainly confined to seaboard crops, its popularity and usefulness was local and its patronage necessarily limited."[22]

Half a year after manning the helm of the *Southern Cabinet* Legaré also opened an agricultural and horticultural "Repository." This store was located at 81 and 83 East Bay, "in that aristocratical quarter of trade . . . south of the exchange," as

1946), 85. For other annotation on this period of John D. Legaré's career see CCD (2), p. 419 and n. One of his books, *The Encyclopedia of Wit* (London: R. Phillips ["1804," added in pencil]), a squat 554-page volume bound in calf and stamped in gilt on the lower spine "J. D. L.," bears in ink on its title page, "Grey Sulphur Springs," and in pencil on the inside back cover, "June the 4 1837" (JJL Coll.). Copies of J. D. Legaré's own eighteen-page publicity brochure, *Account of the Medical Properties of the Grey Sulphur Springs, Virginia* (Charleston: A. E. Miller, 1836), are at the Virginia State Library and the Library of Congress.

[21] At the Anniversary Meeting, Aug. 18, 1840 (MS Minutes of the Society). Announced in the Charleston *Southern Patriot*, Aug. 25, 1840, p. 2, col. 2. In 1839–1840 one James Legaré, probably he of n. 10 above, served as treasurer of the Society. His great-granddaughter advises that "this Col. James was also a great botanist and agriculturist" (Mrs. Ernest W. King, Charleston, S.C., Apr. 6, 1942, to CCD).

[22] Quoted from Vol. I of the periodical by [W. A. Clark, W. G. Hinson, and D. P. Duncan], *History of the State Agricultural Society of South Carolina from 1839 to . . . 1861, inclusive . . .* (Columbia: R. L. Bryan Co., 1916), pp. xxi–xxii.

son James wryly labeled it in one of his later stories.[23] John D. Legaré had, in effect, become a shopkeeper. The action damaged, though it did not obliterate, his assertion of gentry status. He sold seeds, fruit trees, roots, and all kinds of farm implements. He served as agent or adviser for customers in various sections of the Low Country, such as Joel R. Poinsett up at Georgetown.[24] He became active enough in local politics to be named a committee member of the Democrats for the Charleston Congressional District in 1844. When crop failures in the Up-Country during the winter of 1845 caused much hardship, John D. Legaré was among those representing the Third Ward on the city-wide relief committee set up to send aid to the distressed.[25]

Of the few books from his personal library that have come down to us, each one carefully inscribed with his own name, the categories are divided as follows: religion, two titles; belles lettres, three; science, five.[26] In heading his little family of four, editor-merchant Legaré could find ample exercise for this balanced range of interests—the more so now that his elder son was at man's estate, and would require a proper send-off into the world.

[23] JML, "Deux Oies, Vertes," *Graham's Monthly Magazine,* XXXVIII (Apr., 1851), 304. The title may be translated, "Two Silly Geese."

[24] See J. D. Legaré to J. R. Poinsett, Esq., Charleston, Jan. 2, 1843 (Joel R. Poinsett Papers, XVI, 138, Historical Society of Pennsylvania). At this period Poinsett's interest in art, and cultural affairs generally, may be presumed to have afforded him and Legaré more than a merely agricultural point of contact (see "Art: For the People," *Newsweek,* May 10, 1965, p. 103).

[25] See the Charleston *Courier,* Dec. 24, 1845, p. 2, col. 2.

[26] Included in this last category is the dictionary, or handbook, by Stephen Elliott, Sr., *A Sketch of the Botany of South-Carolina and Georgia* (2 vols; Charleston: J. R. Schenck, 1821–1824). JJL Coll.

II: A CHARLESTON-BALTIMORE EDUCATION

Ah! Jimmy why abuse this book
With scribbling you deface its look
Refrain my *son* dont be a fool
You'r in a College, not at school—

J... Wilson

James M. Legare is a fool
and instead of college should be at school

ADJ

The true owner of this book
I should with great pains take care to look
In it no other name should be
Except the name, J M LeGaré

J M Legare

The book of James Legare or James Legare Book
Steal not this book my Hall
For fear the gallows be your all[1]

In the America of the 1830's and '40's was there any other city in which four distinct cultures—American, English, Spanish, and French—were more effectively interfused? All four laid their impress on young James Legaré.

[1] See CCD (4), p. 236, item no. 60. Schoolmates named are A. D. Jones and (probably) J. R. Wilson and Henry S. Hall, on whom see J. Harold Easterby, *A History of the College of Charleston, Founded 1770* ([Charleston: Trustees of the College of Charleston], 1935), pp. 307, 328, and 303, respectively. CCD was advised by Mrs. G. A. Middleton, Charleston, May 19, 1953, that Jones is probably Alexander David Jones (1825–

As for the most basic, the Anglo-American, the boy had been suckled on suspenseful stories about the guerrilla fighting in the Carolinas during the Revolution. His father, John D. Legaré, publicly encouraged the gathering of such regional reminiscences in order that he might preserve them in the pages of his *Southern Agriculturist*. It was in this spirit that young Legaré chose to perpetuate one of the "legends transmitted by word of mouth" about those tumultuous times.

"Among the many related to me during my childhood," he recalled, "one remains vividly stamped on my memory—the heroine of which was a great grandmother and the scene of action an estate (Yona,) in Christ Church Parish. The proper names, however, I have suppressed." Christ Church Parish lies across Charleston Harbor to the east of the city; and one of the names young Legaré suppressed was probably that of his paternal ancestress, Ann White Legaré (died 1796), wife of the planter Isaac, who was James's great-grandfather.[2] In the second earliest of his known pieces of fiction, "A Revolutionary Incident," published in the *Southern Literary Gazette* at Athens, Georgia, in September, 1848, the young author related how the mistress of Yona Hall confronted the terrible Tarleton himself, commander of the British Legion in the Carolinas in 1780. General Marion, too, hovers vaguely in the background, and both the rival soldiers appear, much more vividly, in James's lengthy narrative poem of 1845, "Du Saye."

Every Fourth of July, when James heard the bells of Saint Michael's give out with "Yankee Doodle," he knew that they had also tolled frantically at the approach of the Redcoats. Around him he could detect the lingering influence of those

1866), on whom see George Farquhar Jones (comp. and ed.), *The Jones Family of Milford, Massachusetts, and Providence, Rhode Island* (Philadelphia: Globe Printing House, 1884), p. 126.

[2] For some data on the obscure Isaac Legaré (1735–1788) see CCD (3), p. 534 and n. "Yona" is probably Youghal ("yawl") Plantation, still extant. Isaac and a son, Joseph, were trustees of the Congregational church in the parish (see Petrona R. McIver, "Wappataw Congregational Church," *South Carolina Historical Magazine,* LVIII [Apr. 1957], 85 and n., 93, citing JML's contribution to the local legendry).

Britishers in the number of gentlemen's clubs in his city, in the popularity of hunting and horse racing, and in the general fondness of the "fus' blood"—as a Negro character in one of his stories called them—for the spaciousness and serenity of a country establishment.[3] If you could afford it, that is. James's family couldn't.

The Spanish influence was almost equally pervasive. Aside from the prominence given Caribbean affairs by the local newspapers, there was the fact that, since the turn of the century, here had been the home of the largest, most cultivated community of Sephardic Jews in the United States. In the enviable wine collection of James's relation Dr. Thomas Legaré and his son John Berwick, visitors smacked their lips particularly over the Spanish sherry.[4] One of the family acquaintances, Robert de Leaumont, a notary and insurance broker who had his office at the French consulate, specialized in executing Spanish and French documents for the public.[5]

As for the Gallic aura, upon the establishment of the French Republic, back in the Nineties, there had been a city-wide celebration. Among those prominent residents greeting the new consul, Citizen Mangourit, a Legaré had of course been numbered.[6] In what other city would a person become so stirred by a French romance—which he could select, among others "just received direct from Paris," at John P. Beile's place on King Street, "The Sign of the Bible"—that the city's leading news-

---

[3] JML, "Ninety Days," *Graham's Magazine*, XXXVIII (Jan. 1851), 54, 58.

[4] See William Henry Trescot, Charleston, Aug. 10, 1846, to William Porcher Miles (W. P. Miles Papers, University of North Carolina Library). Trescot had been visiting father and son for the preceding two days.

[5] In JJL Coll. a copy of Thomas Wright (ed.), *Contemporary Narrative of the Proceedings against Dame Alice Kyteler, Prosecuted for Sorcery in 1324 . . .* (London: Camden Society, 1843) is autographed in ink, "R de L'eaumont A. M." A person of this name had received the Master of Arts degree from Saint Mary's College, Baltimore, at the commencement which certificated JML.

[6] Captain Benjamin Legaré, as of Jan. 11, 1793. See Chalmers G. Davidson, *Friend of the People: The Life of Dr. Peter Fayssoux* (Columbia: Medical Association of South Carolina, 1950), pp. 117–18.

paper would print endless rimed "Reflections" in its praise?[7] As a foreign celebrity put it, when she passed through the area at Christmas time, 1838:

> The appearance of the city is highly picturesque, a word which can apply to none other of the American towns; and although the place is certainly pervaded with an air of decay, it is a genteel infirmity, as might be that of a distressed elderly gentlewoman. It has none of the smug mercantile primness of the Northern cities, but a look of state, as of quondam wealth and importance, a little gone down in the world, yet remembering its former dignity. * * * It is . . . a far more aristocratic . . . city than any I have yet seen in America, inasmuch as every house seems built to the owner's particular taste; and in one street you seem to be in an old English town, and in another some continental city of France or Italy.

The city was Charleston, South Carolina, population (1840) 29,231—13,000 "Free White Persons," 1,558 "Free Colored Persons," 14,673 slaves. Since about the year 1830, with the advent of Hugh Swinton Legaré and the *Southern Review*, it had undergone a literary "renaissance."[8] When, therefore, a younger member of the same family indulged in his earliest known efforts at verse (quoted at the head of this chapter), about a decade thereafter, he was only adapting to his environment. At the time of the youngster's gloss to Messrs Tytler and Nares' *Universal History*—there were also profiles and full-lengths of little men, a pig with "JML" initialled across its innards, a Romanesque

[7] See the lengthy verses signed "Clarence" in the Charleston *Courier*, Aug. 23, 1839, p. 2, col. 6. The novel was J. X. B. Saintine's *Picciola*, of which enormously popular romance a New Edition (Philadelphia: Lea & Blanchard, 1847) bears in ink on the first flyleaf the signature of JML's future wife: "Annie C. Andrews. Augusta. 1847" (JJL Coll.). Succeeding quotation from Frances Anne Kemble, *Journal of a Residence on a Georgian Plantation in 1838–1839,* ed. John A. Scott (New York: Alfred A. Knopf, 1961), pp. 37–38.

[8] According to William Stanley Hoole, "The Literary and Cultural Background of Charleston" (Ph.D. dissertation, Duke University, 1934), p. 289. See also Jay B. Hubbell, "Charleston," in *The South in American Literature, 1607–1900* ([Durham]: Duke University Press, 1954), pp. 568–71.

doorway topped by a cross and identified as the "Tomb of Cyrus"—James Legaré was in his freshman year at the College of Charleston.

This was the country's first such municipal institution. In 1840–1841 total enrollment stood at barely fifty, but there was a library containing well over three thousand volumes. Young Legaré, who had come up through the Grammar and English schools, found the curriculum heavily humanistic.[9] The college freshmen were injected with solid doses of the Greek and Latin classics (though never to the neglect of algebra and Euclid), and as late as 1930 three years of Latin were mandatory for graduation. The faculty of four was headed by an unobtrusive but efficient Baptist minister, William T. Brantly, D.D., president of the college, who discoursed on moral, intellectual, and political philosophy. Irish-born William Hawkesworth, M.A., a product of Trinity College, Dublin, instructed in the ancient languages. A Charlestonian educated in France, Lewis R. Gibbes, M.D., taught mathematics and natural philosophy. Young Francis W. Capers, A.B., who had been valedictorian in the Class of 1840, assisted Dr. Gibbes as tutor in maths. All this cost the goodly sum of approximately $60 a year tuition. Fortunately there were many scholarships.

Young James Legaré probably assimilated almost as much education from his fellow students as in the more formal mode. Most of them were from representative families, and several of them would develop into outstanding men. One of these, a year or so ahead of him, James D. B. DeBow, when he had become the South's leading magazine publisher recalled that James "had even then begun to assume position" in the literary way.[10] Another future author, the planter's son, Augustin Louis Taveau

---

[9] See the pamphlet *Catalogue of the Trustees, Faculty and Students of the College of Charleston, South-Carolina, for 1841–42* (Charleston: Hayden & Burke, 1841), p. 6 (copy in the College of Charleston Library). Subsequent discussion of the regimen follows Easterby, *A History of the College of Charleston* (1935), *passim*. JML's class had twenty members. The catalogs for 1839 and 1840 do not mention him.

[10] During his review of *O-U*. See CCD (2), p. 434.

(whose aunt was a Legaré), was there too.[11] So was William Henry Trescot, future diplomatic historian and Assistant Secretary of State (he took second honors in the class of 1841). Then there were kin or connections like John Edwin Mathews and Samuel Jones Legaré, '42. Others attending the college in the early 1840's were such quintessentially Low Country offspring as Henry Samuel Dickson, son of the physician-poet who had founded the Medical College of South Carolina, Christopher P. Gadsden, and J. Ford Prioleau.

They and the other degree candidates of the Class of 1842 lined up to receive their diplomas during the commencement exercises held on Washington's Birthday at the First Presbyterian Church.[12] For this, the college's third such function as a city institution, James Legaré may or may not have been in the audience. He was preparing to depart for the North and a "finishing" year at Saint Mary's College up in Maryland.

On March 12, 1842, in the churchmanly serenity of his study, walled off from the clangor and dust of a bustling commercial center boasting in excess of one hundred and two thousand people, the Very Reverend Louis R. Deluol, S.S., Superior of all Sulpicians in the United States and professor of Hebrew at Saint Mary's College, Pennsylvania Avenue near Franklin Street, Baltimore, took up his pen. In his meticulous script Father Deluol—who had come to Baltimore from France in 1817—made note in his personal diary that the "Farenheit est à 28." (He was always particular about the temperature.[13]) Then he

[11] These facts emerge during Taveau's petition, 1848, to the Law Court of Appeals of South Carolina for admission to the bar. Two letters to Taveau (1828–1886) from his father, the planter Louis A. T. Taveau, from Clermont [island?], Jan. 15 and May 5, 1848, both concern "your aunt Legaré's house" which the elder Taveau was contemplating purchasing but thought too expensive. (A. L. Taveau Papers, Duke University.)

[12] See "Annual Commencement at the College of Charleston," Charleston *Courier*, Feb. 22, 1842, p. 2, col. 5, and "College Commencement," *ibid.*, Feb. 23, 1842, p. 2, col. 3. The valedictory oration, "On the Pleasures and Pains of Genius," was delivered by William Porcher Miles, who also composed and recited an ode for the occasion.

[13] As well as other items. On March 25, 1842, Father Deluol noted: "Le Père Ryder a preché une heure et 3 minutes." The bulk of the anno-

made a less statistical entry: "Mr James Legaré fils de John Legaré de Charleston est entré au Collège comme écolier."

As Reverend Father was to discover during the ensuing seventeen-month period, he had got a bear of a student "comme écolier." This was as well, for to send James to Saint Mary's was a thumping expense to John D. Legaré. The charges for the first six months alone were costing him $138.50. They broke down as follows: board and tuition, $100; washing and mending, $15; mattress, $8, washstand, $4, cot, $3.50; Doctor's fee, $5; paper and quills (in advance), $3.[14] When it came to be itemized on July 19, next year, the "Legaré final bill" in the institution's cash-book would total $540.45.

In exchange for this disbursal young James was exposed to the intellects of twenty-six professors and teachers, bulwarked by a library of fourteen thousand volumes. The President of the college, French-born Father Gilbert Raymond, S. S., was a widely learned priest, especially in political economy, and was noted as an inspiring teacher. The institution he headed was in process of numbering among its alumni men who were or would become leaders in American politics, the professions, and industry. Among them were Robert Walsh, founder of the first standard quarterly magazine, the Philadelphia *American Review of History and Politics;* two future governors of Maryland, Oden Bowie and Augustus W. Bradford; the civil engineer Benjamin W. Latrobe, Jr. (son of the architect); and Robert M. McLane, Congressman and ambassador to Mexico and France.[15]

James would assimilate an education, moreover, not just from books but also from his one hundred and seventy college

---

tation for this period of JML's career may be found in CCD (2), pp. 419–20n., and CCD (3), pp. 537–38n.

[14] See the MS volume labeled "Copies of Bills St. Mary's College 1836 to 1844," p. 446. Total charges ran from March 12, 1842, through July 19, 1843. (Saint Mary's Seminary, Roland Park, Baltimore, Md.)

[15] Rev. James Joseph Kortendick, "The History of Saint Mary's College, Baltimore, 1799–1852," M.A. essay, School of Library Science, Catholic University of America (Washington, D.C., 1942), p. 133.

mates, a tutelage far richer than his home-town school could have offered. Though founded and run by the teaching order of French Sulpicians, Saint Mary's was not restricted to adherents of the Church of Rome. During the 1830's and '40's, its period of richest growth, annual enrollment for all divisions of the institution averaged well above 225 pupils, of whom about half were apt to be non-Catholic. While James was a student, there was even a boy from Scotland. The Caribbean and South America were well represented. Spain and Teneriffe were heard from. On the North American continent students hailed from points as widely separated as Montreal and Mobile. The states of Louisiana and Maryland were especially strong and, among cities, Philadelphia and Baltimore. From the local metropolis the young Charlestonian rubbed shoulders with such representative families as the Bowies, the Careys, the Carrolls, the Jenkinses, the Lanahans, and the Pattersons.[16] All of them were clad in a uniform consisting of a black hat, a fine-quality blue-cloth coat with black-velvet collar and gilt buttons, blue pantaloons, and a black or buff waistcoat (in summer, trousers and vest where white). And they were all of them guided by The Rule. This formidable set of precepts—the original document was in French—regulated the conduct of the pupils in dormitory, infirmary, chapel, and playground, from dawn to dusk. Among its varied injunctions were such as these:

> The students will rise immediately, will dress promptly and modestly. In their dress, they will avoid anything that might suggest peculiarity, anything that might not be in conformity with the rules of modesty.
>
> After night prayers, everyone retires to the dormitories, in a deep silence.
>
> The customary punishment at the college are: a written work to be done in the study-hall; to be deprived of some-

[16] *The Catalogue of Saint Mary's College, for the Academical Year, 1842–43* (Baltimore: John Murphy, 1842), p. 18, lists JML as a member of the Third Senior Class, 5th year. (Copies in Saint Mary's Seminary, Baltimore, Md.)

thing at meals; to be deprived of some recreation, or of permission to go into the city; to be put into the college jail; finally, to be expelled from the college.

On Sundays, it is moreover forbidden to play ball, to fly a kite, or to play any musical instrument other than the piano. It is moreover forbidden to shout, yell, all of which is entirely contrary to the purpose for which Sundays were established.[17]

Such an environment seems merely to have stimulated James Legaré. He tore into his work. His schedule was comprised of courses in English, French, German, and Spanish; Greek and Latin (whether Cicero's *Orations,* in the Harper Stereotype Edition, or Terence's *Comoediae,* in the original); chemistry and mathematics; and fine arts. From home came such helpful presents from John D. Legaré as a Paris edition of *Faust,* in the original, and Tomás de Iriarte's popular *Fabulas Literarias.*[18] By the time Commencement rolled around, Tuesday, July 18, 1843, James was not among the six graduates, but instead received—along with classmates from Baltimore, New Orleans, and North Carolina—an Honorary Certificate. He also racked up the following record:

Astronomy —a Premium, ex-aequo with Gilbert Fetterman of Pittsburg, and R. Johnson

Fine Arts —1st Premium of diligence, in oil painting

German —a Premium in composition; Premiums ex-aequo with E. Goodwin in memory and diligence (for which James was awarded a copy of Goethe's *Werther*)

Natural History —2nd Premium, ex-aequo with George Lucas of Baltimore

[17] Kortendick, *op. cit.,* pp. 190–97 *passim.*
[18] For these and the prize volumes listed later in the text, see CCD (4), pp. 234–36.

Rhetoric —1st Premium of eminence; 1st Premium of composition, ex-aequo with George M. Robinson of Boston (James received John Aikin's *Select Works of the British Poets* and Fléchier and Bossuet's *Oraisons Funèbres*)

Spanish —Premiums in composition and in diligence, ex-aequo with G. Frederick Maddox of Saint Mary's County, Md.

Though the attainment of such a record was jeopardizing James's health, not all was scholarship at Saint Mary's. He decided to put his flair for languages to work on a little fun. Perhaps he had read how *The Book of Mormon* was dug up one day from a hillside in rural New York State, back in 1828. He had probably heard of the wonderful "Moon Hoax," perpetrated to such international furore by the newspaperman Richard A. Locke in 1835. He resolved to have a go at a spoof of his own. He concocted an elaborate one, requiring weeks in the making and nearly a year for its execution.

In his spare moments James painstakingly worked up a genealogy of the Legarés. He inaugurated the line quite loftily by having the first one on the tapis, Hubert, created Earl de L'Egare by Rollo, "or Robert," the first Duke of Normandy. This was in A.D. 912. He then listed each successor, taking even mere knights into account—paltry fellows entitled to display nothing better than a gold spur. William the Conqueror was presently brought into the picture through the device of having him deprive Fronton, the eighth earl, of his title because of a rebellion against William in A.D. 1036, when William was just a duke. This glittering chain was linked clear down to the time of Charles VII, "at present King of France, and our most just Lord; whom may it please God (Maxime optimus) with his holy saints to protect." Cyclical transmutations in the orthography of the surname were dutifully recorded. At that point, with the tree ripe for branching off to the New World, James ceased and desisted, having brought it down to Solomon Legaré. All the ramifications of the line were then "transcribed" from an ancient manuscript at the Château de la Gare. The date was September, 1654. There were three noble witnesses, one of them a chevalier, to the authenticity of the original document, plus a notary public.

The genealogist festooned his creation at the top with an impressive coronet, crest, motto—*Gare l'égaré,* or " 'Ware the Wanderer!"—and a coat of arms featuring three boars' heads. He had acquired a piece of parchment to inscribe it all on. He wrote every word of it in Latin.

For his treasure James had definite ideas as to a proper container. Sallying forth one morning before classes began—doubtless covertly, since Saint Mary's students were permitted to venture into the city proper just once a month, and then only with permission of the President—he made his way to the Monument Foundry, run by Adam Denmead, a machinist whose establishment was at the corner of Monument and North Streets, Baltimore. Later Denmead recalled what ensued:

> . . . . sometime between the 20th & 30th of May 1843 a young gentleman of light complexion, mild and gentlemanly manners, as he thinks with light or auburn hair but deponent never saw him with his hat off, about five feet eight inches in height, slender & very erect, without beard or whiskers, and as deponent judged from the tones of his voice between youth and manhood or from 18 to 20 years of age, called on deponent and gave directions for the construction of a small iron box which he stated he wanted to preserve an old family parchment in. Deponent had a box made according to the directions, but the young gentleman objected to it as too large. Deponent then had a second pattern prepared and caused the figures 1 6 8 2 to be carved thereon according to a copy furnished by the youth. The box was cast and fitted up with spring latches but without hinges by Mr. Franklin Johnson of this City, locksmith. The young man who ordered it stated that he

was from Charleston, and deponent who has been in that city conversed with him about it. From the age of the young man and his always calling in the morning at about 6 or 7 o'clock deponent thought he was at school, but the youth did not say so, nor did deponent ask his name. The box was sold to him for $4 and delivered according to this entry in deponent's books on the 30th of May 1843. The box delivered was about 9 inches long by 3 1/16 wide & 3¼ inches high divided into two compartments . . . .[19]

In his eagerness the genealogist visited Monument Foundry several times before his box was completed. At last it was done. He paid for it, then requested that the pattern be burned. (For reasons best known to himself, Denmead did not do so.) Tucking his treasure chest under his arm, James Legaré returned complacently to Saint Mary's. Months later, under strange circumstances, the chest would reappear in Charleston.

Shortly he was off to Washington City, to pay a visit to his third cousin, once removed, the most illustrious Legaré of them all.

The fact of the nearby presence of the Attorney General of the United States may have been one reason John D. Legaré had decided to send his elder son to Baltimore, for he was friendly with Hugh Swinton Legaré and his talented sister, Mary. They and their mother resided in the Count de Menou's building;[20] and since the second week of May, when Daniel

[19] Deposition sworn before P. T.(?) Merryman, J.P., Baltimore, April 6, 1844. Therein one of Denmead's clerks, John C. McElroy, testified "that the description of him [JML] there given corresponds with the recollection of this deponent except that he thinks his hair was rather dark." A briefer deposition, same date, sworn before Noah Ridgely (?), J.P., further describes the iron box and gives sketches of the spring latches whereby the lid could be lifted off. Both papers are part of a three-part letter to Colonel James Legaré, in possession of his great-granddaughter, Mrs. Ernest W. King, of Charleston, S.C.

[20] According to Linda Rhea, *Hugh Swinton Legaré: A Charleston Intellectual* (Chapel Hill: University of North Carolina Press, 1934), pp. 202, 206. In JJL Coll. both volumes of *The Writings of Hugh Swinton Legaré* . . . , ed. His Sister (Charleston, Philadelphia, New York and Boston: Burges & James, 1845–1846) carry in ink on the title page, "To

Webster withdrew from the Cabinet, Hugh S. Legaré had been serving as Secretary of State *ad interim*. To the collegian this great man's sonorous voice, as he recited the lines of Byron or Dryden, must have more than compensated for the spectacle of his paralysis-shriveled legs. James could sympathize with his senior's shyness and could only have venerated his radiant intellectual energy. He would not agree, at least not yet, with the Secretary's disdain for the mere literary man as not a full-fledged member of society.

James also got to know one of the statesman's professional and personal acquaintances, Secretary John C. Spencer, of New York, and his wife. Their residence was at 14 Jackson Place, and Spencer had recently relinquished the War portfolio for that of the Treasury. Then there were Mr. and Mrs. Anthony Morris, friends both of Mary Legaré and of Mrs. James Madison (whose son, John Payne Todd, had also attended Saint Mary's College).[21]

There were probably several such visits by James to the Secretary of State's home in the Capital. This one ended in tragedy while he was there.[22]

John D. Legare with the affte regards of the author's sister Mary S. Legaré."

[21] In his letter to Spencer, Charleston, Feb. 16, 1844, introducing "a relation and particular friend Mr J. Berwick Legaré of South Carolina," JML also offers his "respects to Mrs Spencer, and best regards to Mr and Mrs. Morris." (For repository of this and all subsequently cited letters to or from JML, see Bibliography below.) Lawyer John Berwick Legaré is identical with him of fn. 4, above; a few items by him constitute Ac. no. 1283, Southern Historical Collection, University of North Carolina Library. From Philadelphia, March 21, 1844, Mary S. Legaré wrote Mrs. Madison: "Young Morris is really a very pleasing gentlemanly person, quite handsome, & in manner & smile reminds me of Walter Davidge & my far away cousin James L'Egaré whom Mrs Morris knows." (See Allen C. Clark, *Life and Letters of Dolly Madison* [Washington, D.C.: W. F. Roberts Co., 1914], p. 335; original in Dolley Madison Papers, III [1843–1844], Manuscript Room, Library of Congress.)

[22] This fact emerges from JML to John C. Calhoun, Aiken, S.C., Sept. 14, 1847 (Calhoun Papers, Clemson College Library, Clemson, S.C.) Did JML know that his kinsman had detested what he felt to be the egregious ambitions of Calhoun? See Margaret L. Coit, *John C. Calhoun: American Portrait* (Boston: Houghton Mifflin Co. [1950]), pp. 229–30.

About June 15 Hugh Legaré had gone to Boston to join President Tyler and the rest of the Cabinet in the ceremonies at the unveiling of the new Bunker Hill monument. There, abruptly, he sickened and died on June 20. Within the week, by Presidential order, all the Navy Yards and all the ships at sea were lowering their flags to halfmast. In a little over a month the news had carried to far-off Venice, where a Carolinian could mourn the passing of "perhaps the most finished and chastest orator of the day."[23]

The news reached Baltimore by the night of Wednesday, June 21, at latest—Washington by the following day, at latest. This may explain why the former date was appended by James Legaré to the poem which he in due course composed "On the Death of a Kinsman." One of the finer elegies produced by an American, it is inconceivable that it could have been written, as it now stands, on such short notice. It is also unlikely that the young poet would, when including the piece in his volume of verse five years later, have made an error in a date so significant for family annals. It seems safest to conclude that the puzzle of James's placing "June 21st" at the end of the elegy was to recall to him the day when he first received the sad news.

A week later the *National Intelligencer* in Washington published a lengthy eulogy on the Secretary of State by some anonymous friend who must have known him well. In erecting his oratorical edifice the eulogist summoned to his aid half-a-dozen poets from three literatures, English, Persian, and Latin, and quoted three times from the last alone.[24] The next day the *Intelligencer* ran a biographical editorial on the deceased that was twice as lengthy, reaching back to *Lycidas* to lament the

[23] As the painter De Veaux wrote a friend, July 27, 1843. See Robert W. Gibbes, M.D., *A Memoir of James De Veaux, of Charleston, S. C. . . .* (Columbia: I. C. Morgan, 1846), p. 162 (CCD used the author's presentation copy to John Pendleton Kennedy, in the Peabody Library, Baltimore).

[24] W——n, "Communication. Hugh S. Legaré," *Daily National Intelligencer,* June 28, 1843, p. 2, cols. 3–4.

slitting of the statesman's thin-spun life.[25] On June 30 the rival Washington *Globe* carried in full the commemorative "Remarks" with which Mr. Justice Story had inundated his law students at Boston.[26] Amid all this, who is to say but that an obscure young kinsman's one hundred and fifty-one simple words may not remain Hugh Swinton Legaré's most telling memorial?

James returned to Baltimore.

There he attended the graduation exercises at Saint Mary's, receiving his Certificate and all his honors. Then he boarded the coastal packet for South Carolina.

As James confessed later to a distinguished correspondent, he came away from college with "a most sublime idea of my own scholarship, and all that sort of thing. . . ."[27] When the ship hove to about July 24, 1843, in the harbor of Charleston— where just a month ago one of the city's papers had quoted Milton again concerning Hugh S. Legaré, and both of the city's papers had draped their issues in black—the new arrival might be excused for feeling that, given half a chance, he could carry on that name and fame. Why, his ship's very title was prophetic. It was the *Gladiator!*

---

[25] "The Late Attorney General of the United States," *ibid.*, June 29, 1843, p. 2, cols. 1–2. W. G. Simms employed the same quotation on the occasion of JML's death. (See introductory quotation, chap. VIII, below.)

[26] "Tribute to Mr. Legare. By Mr. Justice Story," *Globe* (daily edition), June 30, 1843, p. 2, cols. 1–2. The news of subject's death first broke in Washington in *ibid.*, Thursday evening, June 22, 1843, p. 3, cols. 2–3.

[27] JML to Henry Wadsworth Longfellow, Aiken, April, 1850. (Longfellow Papers, Harvard College Library).

III: GETTING STARTED

Some of the family profess to believe that our race was descended of the pirate duke "Rollo" of Normandy, were entitled to the bar *dexter* on the shield and had for crest a boar's head, with the motto, "Le gare," beware the boar.

However that may be, it was for a time so believed & my own proud father would carry his head high among his contemporaries, striking his breast with his palm & exclaiming, "I always knew I had royal blood in my veins." It was infinite amusement to his intimate friends, upon meeting him, to step aside, next the gutter, & uncovering their heads, they would bow humbly, holding their forelocks in the fingers, as I have heard the peasants in old Ireland would do, & give him, "The top of the morning to your Lordship."

Sydney A. Legaré,
"Memories from the Life of a Ne'er do Weal"[1]

In this family reminiscence submitted to all concerned, "proud father" was that suzerain of Slanns Island, Colonel James Legaré—also of Charleston (two residences), of "Sandy Hill" near Rantowles, in proper season of Aiken in the Up-Country, and at all seasons a proper citizen of what has been labeled "one of the most conservative societies in the civilized world." The unsuspected instigator of his euphoria returned to the second of

[1] The original of this undated MS, with quotation from pp. 2–3, is in possession of its author's granddaughter, Mrs. Ernest W. King, Charleston, S.C. (A copy constitutes Ac. no. 2782, Southern Historical Collection, University of North Carolina Library.) John Sydney Algernon Ashe Legaré (1835–1907) spent his mature years as a magistrate at Adams Run, near Slanns Island. A quasi-fictional volume based on the court experiences of this frustrated cavalier, told mostly in Gullah, is Ambrose E. Gonzales' *Laguerre: A Gascon of the Black Border* (Columbia: The State Co., 1924).

these milieux "ambitious of nothing so much as achieving a reputation. . . ."[2]

First it was necessary to come by a job. James obtained a position in the law offices of a crony of the late Hugh Swinton Legaré who was almost as erudite as that kinsman. This was fifty-four-year-old James L. Petigru. A steady benefactor of young aspirants to the Charleston bar—following James as students in his office would come Henry Timrod, the Legaré cousin A. L. Taveau, and Paul H. Hayne—Petigru may have been impressed with the zeal of his new apprentice. If he was, he probably sensed, as a person himself at home in belles lettres (Petigru was specially fond of Spanish literature), that the zeal was directed elsewhither. This young man cared more for reading French novels, composing verse in the manner of Malherbe, or seeing an effusion of his own make the pages of a local magazine than for boning over Blackstone.[3]

The poem, which appeared in *The Rambler* on October 23, 1843, and is James' earliest known item of verse to reach print, was entitled, "My Sister." Fannie Legaré was three years his junior. If we may judge from the testimony of this tribute, James was not only devoted to her but was pleased to strike an attitude of knightly protectiveness:

> I love her arm to lean on mine,
> To guide her steps aright;
> I love her eyes to speak to me
> Affection pure and bright.
> And proud within my heart am I,
> That come what may, the arm
> On which she rests is strong enough
> To shelter her from harm.

[2] Quotations from, respectively, Clement Eaton, *The Mind of the Old South* ([Baton Rouge, 1964]), p. 22, and JML to John C. Calhoun, Sept. 14, 1847 (Calhoun Papers, Clemson College Library, Clemson, S.C.).

[3] As JML observes of Harry Hugre Myddleton, the hero of his story, "Deux Oies, Vertes," *Graham's Magazine*, XXXVIII (April, 1851), 316, 317, 307, respectively. The local magazine JML specified as the *Southern Literary Journal*—an authentic Charleston monthly (1835–1838), for which he himself would have been too young to write.

Perhaps his clerk showed lawyer Petigru the notebooks he was in process of assembling.[4] Covered with hand-printed extracts from the Greek and Latin classics and illustrated with James's own landscape sketches, they must have spread forth lavishly the raw materials of that creative urge simmering in this youth. Probably the prominent barrister was not displeased when his staff member now pushed the formal production of one aspect of that urge. Following in the footsteps of Mary Swinton Legaré, James contributed to the second annual exhibition for the encouragement of the fine arts at Apprentices' Hall in early September, 1843. The show attracted over two hundred paintings, and among the few singled out for special praise by the hanging committee were James Legaré's *Midsummer* and his *Fisherman's Cottage*.[5]

So within the space of a single season J. M. Legaré had got his name publicly bruited in the fields of art and poetry. With the approach of spring he decided it was time to release to the world his first substantial creative effort in fiction. What ensued must rank as a memorable commentary on that most sacrosanct branch of South Carolina traditionalism: genealogy.

About the first week in March, 1844, a servant was hard at work digging a post-hole in the garden of a lot on Anson Street, south of George. Formerly the property of the Legarés, it was now owned by the Mathews family. Abruptly the servant's shovel came on something. (By a quirk of fate James Legaré chanced to be lurking in the vicinity.) What the tool had struck constituted a titillating item for both the Charleston *Courier* and *Mercury* in their issues of March 15.

---

[4] Presumably lost, they are noted by [Laura M. Bragg], "Cotton Furniture," *Bulletin of the Charleston Museum,* XV (Dec., 1919), 77.

[5] Article signed "Lorraine," entitled "A Visit to the Academy of Fine Arts . . . No. 6, Our Native Artists—*Legaré, Jackson, Gilchrist,*" Charleston *Courier,* Sept. 16th, 1843, p. 2, col. 3, and an unsigned "Communications," *ibid.,* Sept. 27, 1843, p. 2, col. 3. On the hanging committee were Charles H. Lanneau and Samuel Henry Dickson. Mary S. Legaré, together with Thomas Sully's daughter, made sketches of the Congregational Church and of Bacon's Bridge on the Ashley River (see [Mrs. Elizabeth

. . . the spade, at about the depth of three feet, struck a hard substance, supposed to be a brick, but which, on being brought up, proved to be a small oblong iron box, in good preservation, divided in the center, and fastened by springs. The date of the box is 1682, shewing it to be 162 years of age. On opening the box a roll of parchment was found, not the least decayed, with the manuscript perfectly complete inside. It proved to be the genealogical tree of the Legare family, (of which the late HUGH S. LEGARE was a descendant), from their origin in the year 912 . . . .[6]

Before you knew it the *Daily Advertiser* in far-off Boston, where Hugh Legaré had breathed his last, picked up the story. So did the Baltimore *Republican,* on April 3. For representative families of the Low Country here was a thought-provoking, perchance momentous, topic for tea-time colloquy!

At this point a gentleman up in Baltimore who preferred to cloak his identity under the initial "P" wrote an angry letter to the *Republican & Daily Argus* there. He begged leave to state "that the said box *was cast in this city* but a short time since, and I have this day seen the pattern from which it was cast . . . ." He didn't know the motivation behind its manufacture, but he did know that the person ordering it had requested the pattern be destroyed. "Belonging myself to the Old Democratic School," P intoned, "I am of course opposed to aristocracy; and any attempt made at this day to rake up

---

A. Poyas], *Our Forefathers; Their Homes and Their Churches* [Charleston: Walker, Evans & Co., 1860], p. 100).

[6] "Discovery of an Interesting Document . . . ," Charleston *Courier,* March 15, 1844, p. 2, col. 3. Colonel Legaré's great-granddaughter, Mrs. Ernest W. King, in a letter from Charleston, March 30, 1942, to CCD states, from family tradition, that JML managed to

be present when it was dug up, & caused much excitement, as being something very old & authentic, he was a wonderful language scholar, etc., but it was discovered that the parchment was not as old as it should be and the joke was on him [*sic!*], & some of the family were furious, but my grandfather, Sydney Legaré, born 1835, & who was also educated in France & Germany, being a graduate of Heidelberg University, took it as a great joke and laughed over it.

claims to nobility, should meet with the condemnation of every true American."[7]

This communication caught the eye of William George Read, a prominent Baltimore lawyer. Read had formerly lived in Charleston, where he was an intimate friend of the city's first Roman Catholic bishop, John England.[8] He also knew Colonel James Legaré slightly, having met him when the Colonel came up to Baltimore in June, 1842, to see his daughter graduate from Saint Joseph's Academy. Promptly Read got off an epistle to an acquaintance in Charleston, Lucius Northrop, confirming all the Baltimore paper proclaimed.

"The person ordering it," Read had ascertained of the box, "said he did not care how old and rough looking it might be, as he only wanted it to put some parchment in. He also requested the pattern to be destroyed which has not been done, and the found box can be identified by it if our suspicions are right. Now all this may have been only a hoax, yet as villainy may be intended, I think it best the family should know the facts."

Northrop went at once to Colonel James Legaré with the news. Furiously the Colonel dashed off a letter to Read in Baltimore. He begged him to spare no expense (which he would cover) to acquire the box pattern and obtain all the particulars on the individual who first commissioned it. The Colonel confessed that the uncovering of the box "was a subject of some gratification to the Legare family" and that this was his first inkling of any skulduggery. "Most of the family," the Colonel pointed out icily, "are those who venerate religious positions, and are not at all identified with worldly distinctions." If need

[7] "P" to the editors, Baltimore *Republican & Daily Argus*, April 3, 1844, p. 2, col. 6.

[8] Peter K. Guilday, *The Life and Times of John England, First Bishop of Charleston (1786–1842)* (New York: America Press, 1927), II, 407. On Sept. 27, 1844, Read was elected to honorary membership in the Calocagathian Society, one of the two literary and debating groups at JML's alma mater, Saint Mary's College.

be, he personally would hasten to Maryland. "I pledge myself
to expose the author . . . of this base machination."[9]

Read replied on April 6. He had taken all needful steps. "I
applied to Mr. Denmead for the pattern of the box; but he
declined selling it, as it has become a matter of such notoriety,
and his own character may possibly be implicated. I have therefore ordered a casting, which will cost a trifle, and shall be sent
to you by the first opportunity. You will then be enabled to
identify the found box by comparison."[10]

That was what happened. Presently Colonel James Legaré
took the painful step of addressing another open letter to a
newspaper for vulgar eyes to peruse. The editors of the *Courier*
gave it prominent space on April 10. He had found upon
investigation, said the Colonel, that the entire business was a
hoax. Family delicacy, therefore, enjoined any further prosec-
tion of the wretched affair.[11]

From that time on, in certain branches of the family, one of
their name rested in infamy under the designation of "Iron-Box
Legaré." A few thought the whole thing was a wonderful joke.
And anyway, on April 13, 1844, the country had a fresh titilla-
tion with which to beguile itself. The episode, which broke in
the columns of a New York newspaper, is well-known today as
"the balloon hoax." Its perpetrator was another Southern man
of letters, Edgar A. Poe.

James Legaré had made a name for himself, but at the
expense of his health. Overwork at Petigru's office brought on
a succession of lung hemorrhages. After trying doggedly to stave
them off, he gave in and abandoned the city for the mountains
of Georgia. En route the valetudinarian acquired a boon that

[9] Read's letter to Northrop and Colonel Legaré's response to Read are
both printed by the Colonel in his lengthy communication to the editors of
the Charleston *Courier,* April 8, 1844, p. 2, cols. 5–6. Northrop was the
soldier Lucius B. Northrop, future Commissary General of the Confederacy.

[10] Will. Geo. Read, Baltimore, April 6, 1844, to James Legaré (three-
part letter cited in n. 19, chap. II, above).

[11] See Charleston *Courier,* April 10, 1844, p. 2, col. 2.

had not come his way at Saint Mary's College: admission to a society. On August 16, 1844, in a meeting convened for the purpose, the Phi Kappa Literary Society of Franklin College at Athens (now the University of Georgia) paid him the compliment of election to honorary membership, the latest name on a shining roster.[12]

It was probably at this time that Legaré got his first look at those paired showpieces, Toccoa and Tallulah falls in Habersham (now Stephens) and Rabun counties in extreme northeast Georgia. Regional writers had been celebrating them in prose and verse for some years; and young Legaré's evocation of their Cherokee-haunted tradition is in the pattern:[13]

> How many of the banished race,
> Those red old warriors of the bow,
> Have slumbered in this shadowy place,
> Have watched Toccoa flow.
> Perchance, where now we sit, they laid
> Their arms, and raised a boastful chaunt,
> While through the gorgeous Autumn shade
> The sunshine shot aslant.

Whether the legend-struck tourist wandered through this picturesque wilderness with a girl—say, Georgiana Maxwell, of Aiken, to whom he dedicated his earliest known elegy, "Mise-

[12] Noted, under the date given, in the "Phi Kappa Minutes—1835–1853," Special Collections Division, University of Georgia Library, Athens. J. Screven was the society's clerk and one Palmer its president, as is noted by E. Merton Coulter in *College Life in the Old South* (2d ed.; Athens: *University of Georgia Press* [1951]), p. 109, who here confuses JML with Hugh Swinton Legaré. Among other honorary members were Rufus Choate of Massachusetts, John Tyler and Judge Beverley Tucker of Virginia, Langdon Cheves and Waddy Thompson of South Carolina, and John A. Quitman of Mississippi.

[13] At this period Robert M. Charlton, Henry Rootes Jackson, and William C. Richards all erupted into print over Toccoa Falls. Tallulah has bestowed its name upon everything from a fire engine to motion picture actress Tallulah Bankhead. See *Time,* Nov. 22, 1948, p. 76; *Life,* March 28, 1949, pp. 36–37; and E. Merton Coulter, "Tallulah Falls, Georgia's Natural Wonder: From Creation to Destruction," *Georgia Historical Quarterly,* XLVII (June, Sept., 1963), 121–57, 249–75. Coulter's exhaustive survey overlooks JML.

rere"—is conjectural.[14] Another girl he knew at this time was John C. Calhoun's niece Martha.[15] Then there was Mary C., of Savannah. James may have visited that city during his Georgia tour, since his tribute to Mary, "Quae Pulchrior," appropriately different in tone from the dirge for Georgiana, is dated August, 1844:

> Thy white glancing shoulders,
> Thy ivory arms—
> What pencil can paint thee,
> What lip chaunt thy charms!
> Superb as a Queen is,
> Yet gentle and kind.
> Where sunny-eyed beauty,
> Thy mate can I find?
> (In *thy* heart's depth, you murmur.)

He definitely visited Savannah some time the following spring, returning to Charleston in the last week of April, 1845, aboard the steam-packet *General Clinch*.

As the result of this explosion of cultural activity, James Legaré was now acquainted with a representative group of Low Country literati. Those transplanted Englishmen, William C. and T. Addison Richards, had accepted his epithalamium (for some unidentified damsel), "All Hail the Bride!" for their local magazine, *Orion*.[16] During 1845 the area's Number One man of

14 JML identifies her in his letter to Simms from Charleston, May 6, 1845, concerning the publication of "the manuscript vol" cited in my text. Her death notice in the Charleston *Mercury*, April 22, 1845, p. 2, col. 5, reads: "DIED at Aiken, on the 18th inst., EMMA GEORGIANA, third daughter of Wm. R. and Anna M. Maxwell, of North Santee, aged 16 years and 7 months."

15 In a postscript to his letter to Calhoun of Sept. 14, 1847, JML says: "Pray remember me, Sir, to your niece (Miss Martha) when you see her, whose pleasant acquaintance I have by no means forgotten." W. Edwin Hemphill, editor of *The Papers of John C. Calhoun*, has by elimination identified this girl as Martha Maria ("Coodie") Colhoun, one of the children of John F. Colhoun by his wife, Martha Maria Davis. Contrary to many of his kinsmen, the Senator preferred to spell his surname with an *a*.

16 A copy of *Georgia Illustrated in a Series of Views . . . by T. Addison Richards . . .* , ed. William C. Richards (Penfield, Geo.: W. & W. C. Richards, 1842) is in JJL Coll.

letters, William Gilmore Simms, printed four of Legaré's verses, including those on "Toccoa" and the tributes to Georgiana Maxwell and Mary C., in his own Charleston periodical, the *Southern and Western Monthly Magazine and Review*. Simms also accepted James's Western tale, "Going to Texas." Captioned as being "from an unpublished novel," this item may already have stirred an interest beyond Carolina. In a letter of September, 1844, to the Philadelphia and New York literary man Rufus W. Griswold—who was completing an anthology to be entitled "American Spirit of the Age"—his Manhattan competitor, Evert A. Duyckinck, suggested that one of the articles might well be solicited from Simms. The topic Duyckinck hoped Simms would discuss pertained to "Legare & the Southern & Western Novelists."[17]

A different type of narrative, the verse legend of the Congaree country and General Marion, "Du Saye," earned an additional compliment for Legaré: Simms included it in his gift miscellany, *The Charleston Book*. This volume, which appeared in November, 1844, in time for the Christmas trade, found twenty-two-year-old James rubbing elbows with a roster of regional talent, most of whom were his seniors.[18] The gift book contained essays or poems—his was second longest of all—by such acquaintances of himself and his father as Joel Poinsett, J. L. Petigru, J. D. B. DeBow, and the late Hugh S. Legaré. Samuel Henry Dickson contributed what would in time become an oft-quoted paean to Carolina, "I Sigh for the Land of the Cypress and Pine." William Henry Timrod (father of a youth five years junior to Legaré with whom he would have much in common as a literary figure) was also represented. So was

[17] E. A. Duyckinck to R. W. Griswold, Sept. 3, 1844 (Griswold Collection, Boston Public Library). (This letter was noted in passing, without identification of JML and with the wrong month, by George E. Mize, "The Contributions of Evert A. Duyckinck to the Cultural Development of Nineteenth Century America" [Ph.D. dissertation, New York University, 1954], p. 59.) Griswold's projected anthology did not see print.

[18] A list of all the contributors to *The Charleston Book* is given in the Charleston *Courier*, Nov. 26, 1844, p. 2, col. 2.

the painter John Blake White,[19] together with two confrères, Charles Fraser and Washington Allston.

Simms had even offered to look over a collection of writings Legaré had gradually produced, in the ultimate hope of finding a publisher. On the envelope of a letter James sent him about the project on May 6, 1845, Simms scribbled: "A young writer of considerable talent." The naturalist John James Audubon (a reader of the elder Legaré's agricultural periodical, the *Southern Cabinet*) agreed to try to get the manuscript printed; and in mid-May, 1845, the young author actually submitted it to Audubon's onetime publishers, Carey & Hart, in Philadelphia.

Yes, things were looking up for James Legaré.

But his lungs were still acting up. And John D. Legaré's financial assets were going down. The result was that some time during the first half of 1846 the entire family forsook Charleston and moved half-way across the state to the little town of Aiken in Barnwell District. From now on, though he did not suspect it, James Legaré's orientation would become almost as much Northern as Southern and, where it was Southern, more Up-Country than Charlestonian.

[19] White contributed an essay on capital punishment (see Paul W. Partridge, Jr., "John Blake White: Southern Romantic Painter and Playwright" [Ph.D. dissertation, University of Pennsylvania, 1951], p. 194).

IV: UP-COUNTRY EXILE

I learned your arrival in Charleston only this afternoon, and let me say how much pleasure it will give me to receive you here as a guest. We live here in most primitive style—pretty much as one would on a maroon; for this place is noted as a resort for health; and residing here for the present with that end in view, we cannot consider it a home.

Legaré to Rufus W. Griswold,
Aiken, S.C., May 31, [1846][1]

The village of Aiken had begun to come into its own as a resort for convalescents following the Panic of 1837. Though it did not appear to, it stood at seven hundred feet above sea level and was the highest point between Charleston and the Savannah River, off to the west. In addition to pine-scented air and the absence of both humidity and mosquitoes, its healing foci were two—the Coker and Calico springs, hedged round with clusters of kalmias, azaleas, and other fragrant shrubs. The main street was shaded picturesquely by Pride of India trees.[2] It was on this thoroughfare near the railroad cross-

---

[1] Quoted, by permission, from the MS in the Griswold Collection, Boston Public Library; published in *Passages from the Correspondence and Other Papers of Rufus W. Griswold*, ed. William M. Griswold (Cambridge, Mass.: W. M. Griswold, 1898), p. 230, where it is conjecturally assigned to the year 1847. The earlier year is more probable, on the basis of Griswold's Charleston sojourn as offered by Joy Bayless, *Rufus Wilmot Griswold: Poe's Literary Executor* (Nashville: Vanderbilt University Press, 1943), pp. 109–13. By the time the prominent Manhattan editor and bon vivant received Legaré's invitation he had already left Charleston.

[2] Paul H. Hayne, "At Aiken," *Appleton's Journal*, VI (Dec. 2, 1871), 623–26. Like JML a member of the Charleston aristocracy, Hayne by the 1850's owned "Copse Hill," sixteen miles west of Augusta, and settled there in 1865.

ing, at 719 (now 241) Laurens Street, a one-story cottage of two rooms, with a yardful of ancient oaks, that in 1846 the Legarés settled down. It was one of the very first dwellings to have been erected in the town.

Sister Fannie was occasionally away from home, and brother Joe presently returned to Charleston for good. This left the parents and James. John D. Legaré was reaching rock bottom financially and in due course declared himself bankrupt. In the spring of 1848 he would accept appointment from the Polk Administration as postmaster of Aiken to help keep the wolf outside the oak-shaded yard.[3]

James meanwhile eked out his own living in three ways: by writing for magazines, by teaching, and by painting. In the New York gift book for 1847, *The Opal,* edited by the painter and auctioneer John Keese, the young Carolinian placed two poems, in company of such compeers as the Messrs Longfellow and Whittier. From June through September of the same year verses by him appeared in each issue of the *Southern Literary Messenger* at Richmond. Two summers later his tale about an aspiring artist, "The New Aria," took second prize for fiction in William C. Richards' *Weekly Gazette* at Athens, Georgia.

Legaré also attempted the rather ambitious scheme of having a school for "finishing" the local girls. After one year, however, he had to abandon this as too time-consuming of his literary and scientific pursuits. He would probably have been astonished to learn that, three-quarters of a century later, a pupil of one of *his* pupils would testify to the value of the tutelage.[4] For two

[3] See, respectively, William Gilmore Simms to James Henry Hammond, Charleston, Oct. 17, 1849, in *The Letters of William Gilmore Simms,* ed. Oliphant et al., II, 563–64, and the Post Office Department "Journal," XX, 130, and XXVII, 55, Industrial Records Branch, National Archives, Washington, D.C. John D. Legaré held his postmastership for the period April 11, 1848–April 7, 1852, when he resigned in favor of JML. For two judgments against him—one by Burges & James for $1,149.56, plus costs, and one in favor of Joseph Walker for $775.66—see Charleston Court of Common Pleas, Journal No. 10, p. 211 (Nov. 7, 1846).

[4] Rev. G. Croft Williams, "James Matthewes Legare and His Poetry" (Columbia, S.C., [*ca.* 1922]), p. 3.

years he offered lessons in drawing to a couple of students, including one of the Ravenel sisters of Aiken. Steadily, if irregularly, for its own sake and for money, Legaré painted. In "The New Aria" the hero inquires rhetorically of the heroine, "What if he were to paint accurately the lovely landscape visible from the foot of the avenue of oaks, beyond the suburbs of the city, where they had so often wandered during their long walks of late?"[5]

The city may well have been Augusta, that "capital" of Middle Georgia, whose spires could be glimpsed across the pine lands, eighteen miles distant from the summit of Chalk Hill outside Aiken. To an Up-Country Carolina girl, visiting Augusta could mean entering, entranced, "this gay bazaar of the South . . . ." To a cosmopolitan Englishman it could mean entering "a queer little rustic city . . . a great broad street 2 miles long—old quaint looking shops—houses with galleries—ware-houses—trees—cows and negroes strolling about the side walks—plank roads—a happy dirty tranquillity generally prevalent." Doctors and shopkeepers, the Englishman observed, were "the society of the place, the latter far more independent and gentlemanlike than our folks—much pleasanter to be with, than the daring go ahead northern people."[6]

It was at the home of one of these shopkeepers, to Augustans well known as the prosperous merchant, John Marsh Adams, with residence on the Sand Hills outside town, that Legaré began lessons in painting for the family children during the summer of 1847. Three or four times already his attempts at resuming the serious intellectual study of his Charleston inter-

[5] JML, "The New Aria: A Tale of Trial and Trust," *Richards' Weekly Gazette,* II (May 26, 1849), 1–2. This and other prize articles were published by Richards in book form the same year. See Commentary, "The Sword and Palette," below.

[6] See, respectively, Mary E. Moragné, *The Neglected Thread: A Journal from the Calhoun Community, 1836–1842,* ed. Delle M. Craven (Columbia: University of South Carolina Press, 1951), p. 59 (February, 1838), and *The Letters and Private Papers of William Makepeace Thackeray,* ed. Gordon N. Ray (Cambridge: Harvard University Press, 1945–46), III, 563, 567 (February, 1856).

lude had been aborted by spasms of lung disease. The present schedule terminated the same way. The first week in September Mrs. Adams advised her husband: "Mr. Lagare [*sic*] is gone and I am glad[;] you have no idea what a trial it has been to me his having been so extremely ill here, and you not at home; however it is all over now and I have done the best I could; if anything was done that should not have been it was error in judgement not in feeling."[7]

If there had in fact been any hard feeling, Legaré did not hold it. His hostess's memory would have mellowed had she chanced to hear him reflect, just a few years later, in a widely read magazine:

> What would become of us in sickness, ladies, deprived of your attendance?—what would become of yourselves, if it did not come natural to you all from the finest lady downward, termagant and gentle alike, to smoothe pillows, decant medicine, and perform numberless offices in no respect agreeable, but with the most exquisite gentleness and devotion.[8]

Moreover Legaré's activities in the Augusta area had at least one positive side. They enlarged his circle of acquaintance to include others of the representative people of the area besides the Adamses. James and his father now approached some of them with a proposal.

The proposal was for a general-information, *Reader's Digest* type of periodical to be issued twice monthly, starting January

[7] [Sarah Susannah Adams], *As I Remember, and Other Reminiscences* (New York and Washington: Neale Publishing Co., 1904), p. 108. An earlier tutor to the Adams girls was Capt. John Rogers Vinton, U.S.A. (1801–1847), a West Pointer stationed at the Augusta Arsenal, 1843–1846. His letters describing the Adams family and the Augusta scene are in the Vinton Papers, Duke University Library.

[8] JML, "Pedro de Padilh," *Graham's Magazine*, XXXVII (Dec., 1850), 375. "The most relentless and insidious foe of humanity in ante-bellum South Carolina was disease," writes Rosser H. Taylor, in *Ante-Bellum South Carolina: A Social and Cultural History,* "James Sprunt Studies in History and Political Science," Vol. XXV (Chapel Hill: University of North Carolina Press, 1942), p. 90.

next, and selling for only $3 a year. Well aware of the high mortality of magazines in the South, the Legarés had nevertheless persuaded themselves that they could launch this one, provided (1) they were paid invariably in advance and (2) they obtained enough subscribers. In August, 1847, they prepared a printed prospectus and began circulating it. The leaflet read as follows:

JOURNAL OF LITERATURE

EUROPEAN AND AMERICAN.

A Work, the Three Leading Designs of Which Will Be:

1st. To place in the hands of the reading public selections from all the principal Reviews, Magazines and Journals of England and the Continent, as well as from those of the United States;

2nd. To accomplish this at ONE-HALF the charge to each subscriber, that is demanded by the Publishers of "LITTELL'S LIVING AGE," a periodical of similar construction; and

3rd. To afford sufficient pecuniary benefit to the undersigned, the Editors of the present work, to induce its permanent continuance.

The first of these ends will be attained by extended foreign and domestic arrangements, by critical discrimination in the selection of articles from the mass of literature under our hands, and by a patience and industry, the best guarantees of which will be our entire embarkation in the enterprise. To the man of science, the journals and published proceedings of scientific societies—to him of letters, criticism and essays from the ablest pens of Europe, (such as the Foreign Quarterly, London Quarterly, Edinburg, Westminster, Reveu [*sic*] des deux Mondes, and many others of less note in Great Britain and on the continent, afford,) in addition to those of our own country—will render the pages of each number acceptable. To ordinary and more numerous readers, selections from Blackwood, the Dublin University, Frazer's, the New Monthly, English Sporting Magazine, Asiatic Journal, Bentley's Miscellany,

Punch, and numerous Magazines both at home and abroad, cannot fail to offer a pleasing (because carefully selected) variety: nor will the articles be curtailed, but if good enough to warrant admission to our columns, will be re-published entire. Finally, for the gratification of those engaged in Agricultural pursuits, extracts of what is most worthy of note, in the pages of a wide connection of foreign and domestic works of that character, will be made by the senior Editor of this production, who for many years occupied the Editorial chair of the "Southern Agriculturist."

In less than a month the Legarés had obtained promises of subscription from seven of the leading personalities in Augusta. They included the lawyer and former attaché to the American Legation at Madrid, Henry Harford Cumming, together with his brother, Colonel William Cumming, notorious duelist and acquaintance of Presidents Monroe and Polk. There was the Hon. William T. Gould, a trustee of the Richmond Academy in Augusta and, as son of the principal of a renowned law school in Litchfield, Connecticut, founder of one in Augusta. (A recent student had been Richard Malcolm Johnston, future author of local-color tales.) There was the Hon. Charles J. Jenkins, onetime Attorney General of Georgia, several times Speaker of its House of Representatives, future governor of the state. There was Judge John P. King, past United States Senator from Georgia, currently president of the Georgia Railroad. And there were the Wildes—Judge John W. Wilde, president of the board of trustees of the Medical College of Georgia at Augusta, and his brother (who would be dead within a few weeks of subscribing to the Legarés' project), Richard Henry Wilde, former United States Congressman, translator of Tasso, biographer of Dante, and composer of that popular lyric, "My Life Is Like the Summer Rose."

Armed with these testimonials, the younger Legaré sallied forth to trap the biggest lion of them all, the absolute political dictator of his home state.

"It is true, Sir," he scribbled round the margin of a hand-copy of the prospectus listing his Georgia subscribers, "that *all* of these gentlemen are well acquainted with me, and four of them are the warmest personal friends I have anywhere, and that I am an utter stranger to you, yet I trust for this reason after all I have narrated, you will not refuse my request."

The request had been proffered *in extenso* in an accompanying letter from Aiken, September 14, 1847. Its addressee was that golden-throated statesman with the sunken eyes and overflowing hair, John Caldwell Calhoun, of "Fort Hill" plantation near Pendleton village—former United States Congressman, Secretary of War, Vice President, Secretary of State (succeeding Hugh S. Legaré), and currently in his second term as Senator from South Carolina. Fortunately for young Legaré the harassed sectionalist was at the moment relishing the quietude of his home acres between sessions of the Congress.

The epistle Calhoun now received may or may not be the first that James Legaré sent winging off to persons of prominence with whom he was unacquainted. But it is typical and, for its creator, became almost a genre. Extensive, grammatically involved, scrupulously penned, here is a literary production employing all the stylistic elements of "manly" appeal, pathos, personality projection, learned allusion, and discreet flattery. With little change the document could be transmuted into an "Essay on Lofty Aspirations," or some similar effusion to be found in all the magazines.

Since Legaré's effusion may in due course be perused in *The Papers of John C. Calhoun,* two extracts will serve here. After touching on his ill health, "thus it happens," James continued, "I cannot but regard the last year as one wasted in my life, since during that period I have awaited (not *idly,* indeed) the fulfilment of promises made by friends, as yet without result. At length I have resolved (comite fortuna, as Steuchus writes on his title page) to do for myself,—and in what manner, the Prospectus enclosed, will, Sir, inform you."

"I have," Legaré went on, *"too much* at stake, from any false ideas of delicacy, to leave that to a hireling which to prove successful should be assumed only by myself, and thus in person I design obtaining subscribers—an end the attainment of which will be materially assisted by the recommendations of those to whom we (Carolinians) are accustomed to look up with respect, or, as to you Sir, with honest pride, trust, and (yes, I for one speak from my heart), affection, thus reversing the bearing of Cicero's nam laudem adolescentis propinqui existimo &c &c.

"Do I then ask too much for a stranger, Sir, when I beg that you will, if you approve of my enterprise, write in your own hand [under] the heading I have referred to, *(with what more it may please you to add)* on the blank page of my subscription book, enclosed,—and first enroll yourself among the subscribers in Carolina?"

Promptly the great man said yes. Regretting his correspondent's poor health, Calhoun terminated his note with the avowal: "We want, above all other things, a Southern literature, from school books up to works of the highest order."

A month later the Senator favored Legaré with a second missive. While this must be presumed lost, the fact of its dispatch may also be presumed to demonstrate the effectiveness of James's postal campaigning. In a trice Calhoun reaped another essay. This one, sent from Aiken on October 26, 1847, introduced an additional element in the Legaré epistolary genre: the anecdote.

"In illustration, dear Sir, of the *real* benefit your name will bestow, I will mention (among many) one amusing little incident. A leading lawyer at ——— (in Carolina) became a few days ago so interested in the enterprise, that he requested me to let him canvass for me, and accordingly together we went to, among the first, the Sheriff of the District. I did not foresee much promise of success in the Sheriff's countenance, and indeed when Mr. ——— had concluded a famous exordium on foreign literature in general and that of Carolina in particular, hesitation was plainly portrayed in the manner of the former gentleman. 'Come' cried Mr ——— in a happy moment —'You were a warm "Nullifier," were you not, eh?' 'Yes to be sure,' returned the Sheriff his countenance lighting up in a moment—'that I *was!*'—'Very well,' returned my friend 'let me read you what Mr Calhoun has written here.' The Sheriff listened with gratified ears, took up his pen on the instant and signed his name, a firm convert to the cause of Southern Literature, while Mr ——— caught my eye and smiled!"

Legaré also introduced the young-love motif:

"As an axiom it may be taken that none are so jealous of our State and it's institutions, as our neighbours the Georgians. Conceive then, dear Sir, the weight of your influence, when a young lady *(very dear to me)* from that State, wrote in reply to my statement of your kindly worded letter, that henceforward she 'would regard Carolina as *her* native state, and Mr Calhoun's politics forever should be her's!!!' "[9]

But 'twas all to no avail. Despite the Legarés' shining roster of supporters, yet another Southern literary organ foundered in a sea of troubles and was heard from no more.

One Saturday at the end of April, 1848, James Legaré called on the rector of Saint Thaddeus' Church in Aiken. This was Rev. J. H. Cornish, who had begun his ministry there only a few months after the Legarés' arrival. He desired to become a candidate for confirmation, Legaré explained, but he had been baptized by a Presbyterian minister. Though he would have preferred baptism by a clergyman of the Episcopal faith, he was reluctant to undergo examination as to the validity of that sacra-

[9] In this letter JML confesses awe of Col. William Cumming, "by reason of his eccentrick habits of retirement"—a quality adumbrating the statement by Cumming's great-nephew that the Colonel "seems to have become something of a recluse in his later years . . . ." (Joseph B. Cumming, Augusta, Ga., March 17, 1953, to CCD.) Throughout this book, in quoting from contemporary sources, errors in spelling or punctuation are noted but rarely, to avoid cluttering the text. JML, for example, customarily writes "it's," when he means "its."

ment because doing so would cast a painful imputation on his parents' belief, and dishonor and offend them.

This scrupulousness must have satisfied Mr. Cornish; for on Thursday, June 29, 1848, Legaré and five others were confirmed at Saint Thaddeus' by the Right Reverend Christopher E. Gadsden, D.D., Bishop of South Carolina.[10] On September 2 James became a communicant.

For the rest of his life he remained a devout one. Even if snow blanketed Aiken—as happened, for example, on New Year's Day, 1854—Legaré (and his then wife) nevertheless made two of the paltry four members of the congregation to show up for services. He was interested in, if not a member of, the Society for the Advancement of Christianity in South Carolina, the church's missionary arm.[11] When, in the spring of 1855, the male members of the parish assembled for the purpose of electing their first local wardens and vestrymen (hitherto the vestry had been composed of Charleston appointees), Legaré was made secretary. At this meeting he was one of the five vestrymen elected and then was designated. chairman of the vestry. On Easter Monday, 1857, he became one of the two wardens of Saint Thaddeus'. Eventually he served as Senior Warden.[12] It is not too surprising to find him at this time dip-

[10] These and subsequent data on JML and the Legaré family *vis à vis* J. H. Cornish are based on excerpts from Cornish's diary in manuscript in the Southern Historical Collection, University of North Carolina Library, as transcribed and forwarded to CCD by R. Conover Bartram (Mrs. Edward T. Bartram), of Aiken. Mrs. Bartram is editing the entire diary, selected portions whereof have been published as "The Diary of John Hamilton Cornish, 1846–1860," in the *South Carolina Historical Magazine*, LXIV (Apr., July, 1963).

[11] Bartram, "Diary of John Hamilton Cornish, 1846–1860," p. 82.

[12] *Ibid.*, (July, 1963), pp. 145, 147, and 152. Among the vestrymen for 1857 was the industrialist William Gregg, Sr., whose wife was a communicant. His home outside Graniteville, "Kalmia," was named for the flower he admired as much as did JML. (See Broadus Mitchell, *William Gregg: Factory Master of the Old South* [Chapel Hill: University of North Carolina Press, 1928], p. 86.) In connection with the Advancement Society Mr. Cornish transcribed *in toto* a letter to JML from Bishop Thomas F. Davis, dated Camden, May 12, 1856 (Bartram, "Diary of John Hamilton Cornish," p. 149).

ping into S. D. Baldwin's *Armageddon: or, the Overthrow of Romanism and Monarchy* . . . . Here is another instance of the generalization, several times advanced by students of Carolina culture, that beneath the Froissart finish there was often to be detected a Puritan undercoating.[13]

Though a steady churchgoer, James was, like his brother Joe, always rather shy (some thought, of an "almost morbidly diffident temperament . . ."). Whereas sister Fannie played the organ at Saint Thaddeus' and worked with the choir,[14] James preferred not to mingle overmuch with congregation or townspeople. Despite this, his dark good looks and intense personality had by 1847 attracted a young Middle Georgia girl who, as Legaré informed John C. Calhoun, speedily became "very dear to me." She was Anne C. Andrews, a daughter of the late John T. Andrews of Augusta, Georgia, and Temperance his wife.

There was a saying in the Low Country of South Carolina that the name of a lady should appear in public print twice only, once when she married and again when she died. So far as the records go, James's mother, Mary D. Mathews Legaré, attained to only fifty per cent of this standard.[15] About his future wife we know a bit more—something of her taste in reading.

[13] Paul W. Partridge, Jr., "John Blake White . . ." (Ph.D. dissertation, University of Pennsylvania, 1951), pp. 209–10. JML autographed *Armageddon* in March, 1856 (see CCD [4], no. 56).

[14] Bartram, "Diary of John Hamilton Cornish," p. 153. The comment on "diffident temperament" is from [Laura M. Bragg], "Cotton Furniture," *Bulletin of the Charleston Museum,* XV (Dec., 1919), 76–77. "Their sister Fannie was engaged to be married, but her sweetheart died while they were engaged, & the story was told to us by an old lady from Aiken (now dead) that he was buried there & that she expected to be buried by his side; I cannot remember who he was; but anyway she died in Charleston, & her brother Joe buried her here" (Mrs. Ernest W. King, Charleston, March 30, 1942, to CCD).

[15] Nearly identical notices in the Augusta, Ga., *Constitutionalist,* March 29, 1865, p. 3, col. 2 (file in the Cincinnati, Ohio, Public Library) and in the Augusta *Daily Chronicle and Sentinel,* same date, p. 3, col. 4 (file in the University of Georgia Library) read: "DIED. Suddenly at Aiken, S.C., on Wednesday, 22nd inst., Mrs. John D. Legare." The "Register of Burials" at Saint Thaddeus' Church reveals that she was buried the next day. In none of his extant writings does JML mention his mother.

Anne Andrews and her Augusta cronies were as a group attracted to Froissart's *Chronicles*. She herself owned and put her signature on copies of Byron's *Childe Harold,* Cowper's *The Task,* Goethe's *Correspondence with a Child* (in translation), Mrs. Jameson's *Characteristics of Women* and her *Sketches of Art, Literature, and Character,* Mary Russell Mitford's *Recollections of a Literary Life,* the Hon. Mrs. Norton's *Poems,* Shakespeare's *Complete Works* in one volume, and the Rev. H. Hastings Weld's *Dictionary of Sacred Quotations.*[16] From which the generalization may be hazarded that Annie would offer no undue intellectual competition to her future husband. Conversely, her bookish proclivity, such as it was, would enable her to sympathize with his vocation.

She evidently did. If the testimony of Legaré's fiction and verse alike may be adduced, he loved her devotedly. Especially did they relish strolls in the woods around Aiken, with one of their favorite haunts—paeaned by James in song and story— being "a seat of branches against one of the trees next the stream . . . cushioned with moss . . . ."[17] The year 1848, wracked with wars in Europe and the aftermath of war in America, was, for two young people in the Carolina Up-Country, another kind of time:

> Oh, happy spring-time of the heart,
> When love is daily food,
> Through which are dangers counted naught,
> And difficulties woo'd!

When James gazed about him, it was not Aiken or Augusta his eyes discerned:

16 All in JJL Coll., they bear Annie's inscriptions dating from "Xmas 1843 Augusta Ga." (Shakespeare) to "June 1860" (Jameson's *Characteristics of Women*). Here, too, are a couple of volumes inscribed by her father. The Froissart, translated by Thomas Johnes, bears in its backmatter these penciled signatures: [Mrs.] *Caroline A. Barry, Annie C. Andrews, Bettie Elliott, Emma Wray, William E. Barbour* [?], *Fanny Legaré, Dick* [?] *Crawford.*

17 JML, "The Lame Girl," *Sartain's Union Magazine of Literature and Art,* IX (Aug., 1851), 106.

In smiling light Arcadia lay
Green sloping in her hills;
Burst from the mossy rocks and grey,
Innumerable rills.

Now and henceforth, when girls' eyes were mentioned in James's poetry, they were apt to be brown. At times his devotion to his future wife impaired his judgment (as when he agreed with Annie that "The Hemlocks" was his finest effort to date).[18]

Legaré's only volume of verse, *Orta-Undis*—which Carey & Hart had presumably rejected, but which William D. Ticknor in Boston consented to bring out—had been distributed by late May. (The title poem means *sprung from water,* or *waves.* Legaré probably refers to Hesiod's account of the Aphrodite Anadyomene, "rising from the sea.") The year 1848 was far from a stellar one in the annals of American belles letters. Nevertheless, the Carolinian's offering had to compete for readership with such other productions as James Russell Lowell's verse satire, *The Biglow Papers,* Stephen C. Foster's *Songs of the Sable Humorists,* William Tappan Thompson's volume of comic letters in the dialect of rural Georgia, *Major Jones's Sketches . . .,* and Edgar Poe's prose poem on the mysteries of Man and the universe, *Eureka.*

Early in January, 1849, Legaré called on Rev. J. H. Cornish of Saint Thaddeus' Church, together with his sister Fannie and Anne. The latter was now formally his "intended." But if the pair had hoped to marry soon, they were frustrated by James's nemesis. As it had at Charleston five years earlier, hemorrhage of the lungs struck again. It kept him house-bound or abed until December.[19] A poem composed during this bleak period reflects the situation succinctly. The fourth stanza reads:

[18] See Commentary, "The Hemlocks," below. Preceding quotations in text are from "The Sword and Palette," verses 133–36 and 193–96, respectively.

[19] J. H. Cornish, MS Diary, ed. Bartram (University of North Carolina Library). (See n. 10, above.)

You and I embarked together
When all Earth was full of speech,
And the kiss of every ripple
Said, "I love thee" to the beach.
Now night broods across the waters,
Far from sight or sound of shore,
And the straining ear is sated
With the labor of the oar.

Its author entitled the poem, "A Husband to a Wife," and John R. Thompson up at Richmond published it in his *Southern Literary Messenger* for January, 1850. In March, Anne and James were married at the home of the bride's mother, Mrs. Temperance Andrews, in Augusta, Georgia. The ceremony was noted in both the Charleston and Augusta papers.[20]

Courtship, and now marriage, had not interfered with the groom's proclivity for seeking out targets of a more professional potential. Without prior warning, September 22nd last, Legaré had launched the following missile toward probably the most prestigious littérateur in all the land—one who was, like himself, a villager but resident in a village for more cosmopolitan than Aiken. This was Henry Wadsworth Longfellow, sixteen years his senior, of Cambridge, Massachusetts.

To address you with the ease of an old acquaintance, rather than the formality of a new, would call for at least courteous excuses, if I did not feel an inescapable reluctance to dissembling in any degree where I owe so largely of gratitude. For your words which I keep safely in my heart, have more times than I can enumerate, imparted new courage and faith, and that chiefest of blessings, peace: you draw your bow so well where you are, that here you may find your arrow leagues away; shot at random but high up towards Heaven, and so by Heaven's providence borne hitherward. Between poets also (I could quote your

[20] The marriage was performed by the Reverend Edward E. Ford, Rector of Saint Paul's Episcopal Church, Augusta (which celebrated its bicentennial in 1950). For documentation see CCD (3), p. 549n. On Oct. 6, 1850, Annie was a communicant at Saint Thaddeus' Church, Aiken.

own opinion for you, that I call myself so rather because of what I purpose than what I have done)[21] there is too much held in common to suffer any great concessions to custom by which others are bound and thus I feel all the inclination not merely to make this the beginning of a friendship, but indeed to avow on my part, one of long standing.

But of such things I must not venture to speak now, because I have no wish to cheat myself out of a pleasure long promised, (but unluckily, scarcely nearer realization now than formerly), that of talking them over with you, one day, in person. Besides I have a service to ask and a proposal to make, which are the real occasion of my writing, and I like better to write the text than the preface of a request, as of a book. With a short life before me—a truth, but scarcely a sad one—I am naturally anxious to crowd into it's [*sic*] compass all I may, that our Lord when He comes may receive another with the talent he had entrusted. No particle of my love and appreciation of what is elegant in literature has fallen from me, but I feel constrained, whatever my pursuits under more favorable circumstances might have been, to bend my mind to graver labours; and if I would leave behind a name worth the mention, to take the most direct if most arduous road to it's attainment. Somewhat guided by these views, and somewhat by former readings, I have engaged in a weighty work—History of the conquest and civil wars of the Pacific Islands—a subject incredibly neglected thus far, and that too when many of the detached Spanish and French chronicles possess all the charm and adventure of romances. My only fear is that my means will fall far short (for as Aristophanes had it, Plutus seldom passes my door even, since I have abandoned all things for a literary life) of the amount necessary to the collection of books and MSS in so many different tongues, and so far to be sought. I am therefore desirous of ascertaining how near home many

---

[21] Possibly a reference to some of the literary and philosophical ruminations of the German baron in chap. 3 of Longfellow's novel, *Hyperion: A Romance* (1839). The preceding allusion is to Longfellow's well-known "The Arrow and the Song," in his *The Belfry of Bruges, and Other Poems* (1846). JML had referred to this poem also in a letter to the brothers Duyckinck, June 11, 1849 (printed in full in CCD [1], pp. 221-22).

may be procured. Were I to visit Boston, could I obtain ready access to the Cambridge Library? (the best and richest I believe in the Union); and is there a copy of the catalogue you can forward to me? If none, you can—if you will be at so much trouble to oblige a hitherto stranger,— ascertain from the original what vols are to be found there worth consulting. I suppose the larger number exist in Spanish (I design soliciting Mr Prescott's[22] good offices in that direction, as he probably possesses copies of many rare Spanish MSS)—a few in French, and others in Dutch. The latter language I have never attempted, but imagined I could quickly master it with the aid of German, until Bishop Elliott wrote me a few days ago, that Lieber[23] assured him he could not read a word of Dutch until he learned English. Thus, in the Bishop's words, I am nearer than I thought even to the former. But no one can tell me better than yourself if this is literally so.

And now to refer to a subject closer my heart, if less grave in its relation. Of all my pet-books none more frequently accompany me in those long luxurious rambles in deep woods you (and Kavanagh!) Mr. Churchill I mean —the beautiful youth with a bee in his bonnet! know so well how to enjoy, as the Waif and Estray; books, like the necklace of real pearls Brantz Mayer[24] detected on the neck of some squallid [*sic*] dame in Mexico, made up of gems, each a poet's fortune, strung together for the sake of convenience possession and transportation.

I think it likely, since the publication of the last, you have collected other poems of rare beauty or worth, per-

[22] William Hickling Prescott (1796–1859) had published his widely read *History of the Conquest of Mexico* in 1843 and that of Peru in 1847. There is no evidence that he and JML ever met, nor has correspondence between them come to light.

[23] Stephen Elliott, Jr. (1806–1866), Protestant Episcopal Bishop of Georgia, son of the botanist and co-founder of the *Southern Review* at Charleston, himself sired novelist Sarah Barnwell Elliott. Francis Lieber (1800–1872), founder of the *Encyclopedia Americana,* was professor of history and political economy at South Carolina College, now the university, at Columbia.

[24] Mayer (1809–1879), Baltimore lawyer and currently president of the Maryland Historical Society, was secretary to the American Legation in Mexico, 1841–1844. Churchill, a young village schoolmaster, is the protagonist of Longfellow's novel, *Kavanagh* (1849).

haps not yet enough to form a vol. I too have been gathering with like intent, but so fastidiously as scarce to possess a dozen pieces. What if we were to unite our treasures, and so suffer them to become household words—to all lovers of true poetry, at once? If it pleases you to do so, you can write both proem and afterpiece, or else allow me to write one. I have jumped resolutely with eyes shut into the midst of this proposal, for I feel sensibly how I solicit no small thing in offering to couple my unknown name with yours before the public; and in consequence, I refrain from forwarding you my collection, until I learn you do not receive the offer itself with equal distaste and disapprobation.

Terminating "with the highest possible esteem, yes, even with deeper feeling," Legaré posted his disquisition.

Longfellow's reply was prompt. Even though the Harvard professor's letter of October 2 was silent as to the Carolinian's closing effrontery, it should have made its recipient glow at its general tenor.

Going to College yesterday, in the rain, I took your letter from the office. It was a friendly visitor on a dull day—doubly welcome, for the opportunity of his visit, and his pleasant words. Let me assure you, I already knew you. I have long possessed and highly prized your volume of Poems, so full of tenderness and "the dew of youth." I am glad to know more of you; and with great alacrity will be of what service I can to you in your new literary undertaking, which certainly has a romantic charm about it.

Our College Catalogue is in several large oaken [?] volumes; and it would be troublesome to send, and very unsatisfactory is it to see only the titles of books. Your best course would be to come at once to Boston. Our October is very pleasant, and November sometimes—not always. Take a room at Mrs. Cleverly's in Beacon St. opposite the Athenaeum, which has a fine library—next door to Mr. Ticknor's, who has another fine library, and within pistol shot of Prescots, who has a third. The College Library is also within your reach, and you would have every facility for carrying on your investigations. What materials there are here for such a work as yours, I know not; but they are probably better than you would find elsewhere.

As for "Estrays in the Forest," I have done with all that kind of work forever, I think. Still, I should like very much to see your collections. I had a call, the other day from Mr. Richards,[25] who spoke very kindly of you. Should you come to Boston, of course you will not fail to let me know your arrival immediately.

There was even an afterthought, from one plagued by facial neuralgia and worry over a sickly wife: "P.S. I am sorry to hear, that your health is so feeble. Would not a change of air benefit you?"

So far as is known, James Legaré never got any closer to Massachusetts than New York City, and then not for two more years. Whether he mailed his post-*Orta-Undis* collection of verse manuscripts to Longfellow for perusal is also unknown. In any event he had one solid preoccupation to tax his flickering energies: the establishment of a household.

Following the Augusta wedding the young couple had elected to settle down at Aiken with the elder Legarés. It was not long before the husband—whose "pecuniary affairs," he had earlier informed the Duyckincks, "at present, by a succession of mishaps, are much straitened"—established a cottage in the yard for himself and his bride. In due course Annie, like Louise, the heroine of James's story, "The New Aria," could contemplate happily a little "house with its three rooms and little porch in front, and the chintz curtains in the windows, chintz covered couch and plain white ceilings. . . ."

Thus happily ensconced, sometime in April, 1850, Legaré got off a second missive to Henry Longfellow which is at once typical of his rather involved epistolary style, revealing of his home situation, and suggestive of the appreciable projection of personality he could attain when not striving for effect.

[25] Presumably either William C. Richards, the Athens, Ga., journalist, or his artist-brother, T. Addison Richards.

LEGARÉ'S HOME IN AIKEN, SOUTH CAROLINA

Then at 719, now 241, Laurens Street

(Lista's Studio of Photography, Aiken, South Carolina)

I received a message at second hand from yourself a few days ago through an eccentric genius whom I once met in upper Georgia—Mr. Scherb.[26] I rather incline to the belief that but a fraction of the original came so far, but there was quite enough, to set aside a doubt which has long possessed me, as to the exact light in which you really regarded my former very audacious proposal! You must know, I left college with a first honor, a most sublime idea of my own scholarship, and all that sort of thing, and have ever since been arriving at a juster understanding of what I *do* know—all of which is very natural, and (I imagine) not a matter for lamentation, since a tree surely loses its flaming blossoms before the fruit appears. However, at intervals, the ancient extravagance returns, and so it chanced I wrote to propose a literary co-editorship which must have amused (and surprised) you as much as it vexed myself, when I regarded the proffer I had made in its true relations. Well, there is one very pleasant incident founded on all this that I did not impress you so unfavorably as I thought to have done—indeed as I thought I *had* done (despite the pleasant tone of your written reply) until our Gallic acquaintance removed the impression. But let us drop the subject altogether now—in point of fact, as "cousin Foenix" says, it is not over and above entertaining. Does Mrs Longfellow bite off her thread (as Mrs Churchill did!) in sewing? My wife, sitting beside me while I write, is doing so, with that indifference to what is termed "making the blood run cold" which might have been "a wise provision of Nature" in primitive times, but certainly not while Sheffield exists! Mentioning Mrs Churchill reminds me of M. Montègut's critical opinion of yourself in the Lit: World of the middle of last January. Since opening a French copy of Lord Byron, I don't think I have been so much amused at anything in the way of French appreciation; especially where M. M cannot understand the fitness of the lecture which the Schoolmaster delivers to his wife, "and the propriety of instructing her in the singular

[26] Emmanuel V. Scherb, a German from Basel, and a poet. He first visited Longfellow in May, 1848, on introduction from a Mr. H., of Savannah. See Samuel Longfellow (ed.), *Life of Henry Wadsworth Longfellow, with Extracts from His Journals and Correspondence* (Boston: Ticknor & Co., 1886), II, 120.

and complex problems of a certain Indian poem" ! ! !²⁷
How one question leads to another—Do we (here at the
South, where the name is unfamiliar) correctly lay the
accent on the *first* syllable of K*a*vanagh? I wonder if it is
cold with you yet, or do you sit with wide-open windows
as I, with a vase full of fresh roses on the table close by. I
wish you could pay us a visit, and at this season above all
others, when in a lonely dell I could show you, from the
brow of the steep descent to the musical stream at it's base,
exten[ds] a dense copse of blossoming calmias and azalias
[*sic*] and the ground under foot thickly sprinkled with blue,
and white, and yellow flowers—"so thick you scarce can
see the grass" as Tennyson has it.²⁸ Or not to go so far (this
warm weather) you would certainly be pleased with the
appearance of our rustic porch—and that for other reasons
than because my bonnie wife would bring you (seated in
state in the rustic chair in the abovementioned porch the
cushion whereof is of openwork vines stuffed with green
(gray) Spanish Moss) a saucerfull of the strawberries
which, being later than usual, are only now becoming
abundant,—and which she has purpled her fingers in pick-
ing. Everything, indeed, about our corner of the house (for
I live at present with my father) is made in rustic fashion
—pretty much as the trees, you know, would construct
bookshelves and flowerholders and such like things, were
they to reverse the fable of Daphne,²⁹ and fail to shake off,
with their bark, the twisted habits of action common to
"Titans of the Wood." I am talking of all these things that
I may more easily introduce a few words I wish to say
directly of myself, that (as I hope earnestly this is the
beginning of a long friendship—and *now* I address not the
poet, but the man your own works show you to be) you
may not be ignorant altogether of the personalities attach-
ing to the "undersigned" (vide Micawber): for thanks to

²⁷ JML quotes accurately from "A French Critic's Opinion of American
Literature and Authors," *Literary World,* VI (Jan. 19, 1850), 51, being a
paraphrase of an essay by Emile Montégut in a recent issue of the *Revue
des Deux Mondes* at Paris. Montégut's opinion of Longfellow, "of Swedish
origin," was low: too bookish, too superficial in both verse and prose,
worst of all too unintellectual.

²⁸ Alfred Tennyson, "The Two Voices" (1833), verse 453.

²⁹ JML had evoked this mythological figure a year earlier in verse 199
of his poem, "The Sword and Palette." See Commentary, below.

Mr Griswold and others, no reader of best things is ignorant of most that concerns you. But let me avoid egotism by brevity—So I am aged twenty six, married (lately), and reside at this place chiefly for the sake of health for health giving this dry pine atmosphere certainly is. As for occupation, authorship is my chief, and from it and a less individual source, my moderate income is derived —Fortune for once showing herself just and wise in giving my cousins of the name, of cotton[,] land and lazy content an equal abundance, but to me only a little fame and wider ambition and more earnest, than ever attaches to soil of any extent in acres. Don't misunderstand me—not vulgar ambition—petty longing for distinction, but one based in the hope and by God's help—design of performing my own portion at least of this life's labor, not because I cannot do it (as some) with the hands, but because it is *better* to do it with the head. With these views I seldom now appear in the magazines, preferring to shun rather than court the popular eye by works (such as that unhappy little Orta Undis—what a name!!) of which I will soon learn to think with regret and even selfcontempt for their weakness. However, despite this, I believe I will be a regular contributor to 'Graham's' during this year—Graham himself having advanced reasons enough to shake my determination not to be so compromised in regard to a work I now have in hand and am earnestly bent on completing forthwith.[30] By the way, he tells me you are exclusively engaged in like capacity. As for the Insular History concerning which I wrote to seek your advice in my former letter, I have laid it aside for the present, my funds (on the closest calculation) proving too little to meet the expenses of a Continental researches. And now, without having said a fraction of the pleasant things I designed talking over,—indeed saying little that has not the Ego written on it's face—I see the end of my paper under my hand, like one who seeing in perspective by the roadside the house at which his friend stops, wishes the way was longer—and wonders their gossiping is so soon ended: for Reason herself would revolt at a *third* page of rambling Ms. Do you (in Boston also!) know anything of Thomas Powell of England, a man cer-

[30] Probably "Pedro de Padilh," which ran in *Graham's Magazine* for August–December, 1850.

tainly of marked genius (what a fine poem his "Edith" is)
but of whom none of my N York correspondents can say
one word of good.[31] I have such reverence for genius that
it troubles me always to hear it's possessor decried—Do you
know any good of this anomaly?

Whether Longfellow did or no, a literary man of less questionable pretensions in due course appeared at the Legaré
cottage. This was the dapper Richmonder, John Reuben
Thompson.

Just Legaré's age and, like him, a onetime law student beguiled into belles lettres, editor Thompson—who had been
wooing the Carolinian's support by complimentary copies of his
Southern Literary Messenger—was making a swing through the
Palmetto State this winter of 1850–1851. In January he spent
a day at Aiken with the (as he found him) "young and gifted
Legaré." His host introduced Thompson to his friends and also
entertained him at a meeting of the literary club, composed of
the younger men of the town. Before a blazing fire they all
puffed on cigars and discussed their writing aspirations.[32] One
may imagine James giving forth with some such opinion as this,
which he had dispatched to another editor the preceding
summer:

> Oh, we authors, with our vanity and butterfly wings not
> to be handled without leaving some of our brightness on

---

[31] An Englishman, Powell (1809–1887) became one of the bohemian
frequenters of Pfaff's Restaurant in New York City. Charles Dickens,
among others, thought him a complete scoundrel. See Wilfred Partington,
"Should a Biographer Tell?" *Atlantic Monthly*, CLXXX (Aug., 1947),
56–63. Concerning Powell, JML had remarked to Evert A. Duyckinck
from Aiken, Feb. 13, 1850: "I admire his genius greatly, and as for the
the matter of his late misfortunes (with my limited information I have no
right to use a harsher term, nor any inclination either), I *never* suffer an
Author and an everday man to be *confounded* together in my estimation
of the first—to *unite* the two is quite another thing. Besides, God knows
only, who of us all is fit to cast the first stone."

[32] Joseph Roddey Miller, "John R. Thompson: His Place in Southern
Life and Literature . . ." (Ph.D. dissertation, University of Virginia,
1930), p. 44. See also *ibid.*, pp. 137–38 and n.

the fingers touching ever so gently; and you critics, whose object, as a class, is to thrust a 'good specimen' through with a great pin and leave the unhappy insect to stiffen in the position in which impaled; is it any wonder such ill will commonly lies between the two, or that Mr Lowell has written a book to turn the tables for once![33] Indeed my idea of a "Critic" is of a personage so awful and blood-thirsty, that I have never been able to regard you as be-longing to the ranks of our implacable enemies, and cannot help thinking the fable of the jackdaw and borrowed plumes for once reversed (for we all see how your dingy, are too scant to conceal your finer feathers), and after all you are one of us in disguise.[34]

It was in one of his cottage's three rooms that Legaré main-tained his school for young ladies. All of the chambers gradually acquired the embellishments of his aptitude, both artistic and mechanical. The sitting-room walls came alive with figures of wild animals, birds, and flowers. Plaques and panels shone from the attentions of his brush:

> Mr. Legare was sitting on his porch one day when he saw two friends on their way home from a hunt. He called to them to come in and let him see what they had killed. As they held up their trophies, a duck, a partridge, and a rabbit, Mr. Legare painted each on the panel of one of his doors and on the walls. The pictures are still there. When Mr. Morgan bought the house he had some of the paintings cut out of the walls to better preserve them.[35]

[33] James Russell Lowell (1819–1891) had published anonymously his verse satire of contemporary men, "A Fable for Critics," in 1848.

[34] JML, Aiken, July 5, 1849, to Evert A. Duyckinck. Following "dingy" JML has unintentionally omitted some such word as "plumes."

[35] Catherine W. Morgan, "Life of James Mathewes Legare," Aiken, S.C., *Standard and Review,* Feb. 15, 1942, p. 5. The parents of Miss Morgan (now Mrs. St. Clair Arbuthnott), the late Mr. and Mrs. Thomas R. Mor-gan, bought the Legaré place and much enlarged it, as it stands today. Three bedroom panels are still in place. For an external view of the house see Dorothy K. MacDowell, "Morgan Home: Second Oldest in Aiken," Aiken *Standard,* Feb. 10, 1970, p. 4.

PANEL PAINTING BY J. M. LEGARÉ IN HIS AIKEN HOME
(Lista's Studio of Photography, Aiken, South Carolina)

As in his other cultural endeavors, Legaré was inclined to be frustrated. "For I suppose it may be in verse as it is in painting—," he advised John R. Thompson, "if I paint a piece which I take a strong aversion to in the end, the family, and callers who chance to see it, say—'how pretty'—and so for the reverse!"[36]

As for sales, perhaps Legaré, like the artist-hero of his story "The New Aria," was saved from despondency at this prospect only by the placid faith of his spouse:

"But you must not imagine you find no purchasers," says she "—that would never do to begin with! I don't fancy you to be either a Raphael or Rembrant [*sic*], but have not your paintings been admired beyond measure by those who are esteemed good judges?"

"Yes, while there was something to be gained by flattery—perhaps."

"Well, we will see who is right. Do you paint and I will read, and only do your best, dear Harry, and I have no thought that we can quite fail."[37]

She was right. Legaré did sell paintings. For two of them he also won prizes. We can see why, on hearing this story about a panel decoration:

> One of his pieces,—a water mellon, with the open slice, showing the seeds, was one he felt more proud of. One day, sitting in the room, and working on it, a bird flew in and tried to peck at the seed. This was also in the days before wire screens. He always said this was the greatest compliment he had ever received.[38]

[36] JML to John R. Thompson, Aiken, Feb. 1, 1850 (printed in full in CCD [1], pp. 226–28).

[37] JML, "The New Aria," *Richards' Weekly Gazette,* II (May 26, 1849), 1.

[38] Mary H. Ravenel, Aiken, S.C., Dec. 20, 1941, to CCD. Miss Ravenel's "eldest sister did some pretty work in oils, under him. We also for many years had a large oil painting of a winter snow scene, with an old mill, and boys out skating. No doubt there may be some homes in South Carolina now, where there may be some of his work." The painting cited may be identical with *A Winter Scene* (see p. 132).

The household had its own bird. This was a mockingbird or thrasher the couple called "Ollie" and had taught to say a few words. It occupied a large cage in the sitting room. As the cage was never barred, Ollie took off in the morning on food forays outdoors and, upon return, would perform his ablutions in the fountain. The fountain was the central feature of the cottage's main room: James went to the trouble to rig up a power device in the adjoining bedroom so that it could flow. There was also a handsome dog, "Lands," who doubtless took the place of the children the couple never had.

Outside, Legaré was equally industrious. Over the years he brought into being a formal flower garden of intricate pattern. There was a rockery, walks bordered by evergreen hedges, even a pair of their favorite rustic seats.[39] They called their place—and one trusts the head of the household was not guilty of this—"Turtle-Dovey."

[39] Williams, "James Matthewes Legaré" (see note 4, above). From Columbia, S.C., Nov. 16, 1948, Professor Williams wrote CCD in part as follows: "My little look at him was taken in 1920, I being then Secretary of Public Welfare for this State. I came across Orta Unda [*sic*], of which I had never heard, and I recognized immediately that it contained pure poetry, original and musical. I found out that Legare spent his latter days in Aiken, my old home. So when I was in that town I looked up an old friend, a Mrs. T. G. Croft, an aged lady who had in young womanhood lived across the street from Legare. She was then a Miss Allison. From her I got the information of the person of Legare that I put into my paper on this subject."

V : THE POET AND HIS VERSE

In a word, then, Legaré was a man who, at a time and amid influences that furthered anything rather than the study of perfection in the matters of art, surrounded by writers of facile and nerveless verse that was constantly and fulsomely praised, set himself a fairly high standard of artistic workmanship and labored with great care and no small success to attain that standard. Hence, while in many of the Carolinian writers of his day it is not hard to find isolated lines or stanzas that are pleasant enough, Legaré succeeded in writing at least a dozen poems which, though not impeccable, may be unhesitatingly praised as wholes. They have a studiously plain charm, a clear, fine melody, a touch of austere beauty. Anthologists of our poetry, North or South, can never afford to overlook them.

Ludwig Lewisohn,
in *Library of Southern Literature,* VII (1909), 3,193

As a glance at Appendix II to the present work will reveal, poems by J. M. Legaré have been anthologized for 91 years (1845–1936) and reprinted for 106 years (1848–1954). Virtually all of the selections have been drawn from the slim volume of 102 pages containing just 30 pieces of verse, *Orta-Undis, and Other Poems,* which William D. Ticknor of Boston released there in February, 1848. Yet before Legaré's other controlling interests—fiction writing and mechanical invention—usurped his time, he published 19 additional poems which the anthologists never saw. The preponderance of these appeared in the narrow cluster of years from 1848 through March, 1850, in February, 1852, and during July and August, 1856. Nevertheless, this tiny total was enough to earn the sickly, sequestered songster an established place among the versifiers of his day.

Several dozen other versifiers were equally established, but today they are forgotten. One reason this fate has not overtaken James Legaré's verse was the care with which he approached its composition. In so doing he had his frustrations. On mailing a complimentary copy of *Orta-Undis* to Thomas Powell, Legaré informed that New York journalist:

> With the exception of scarce three poems I am ashamed of the contents already, although it has been out little more than eighteen months or so. The very lenity with which the critics generally handled it, as not worth analysing, quickly convinced me of the incapacity of the book to obtain a foothold in the world of letters. Poor Poe, I at least had no reason to mingle a weak sense of relief from danger, with my heartfelt regret for his death; for there was no likelihood of his ever pouncing upon my unlucky bit of Latinity. "Leo tacet."
>
> I *think* I have written and published, since the issue of the vol., far better poems than any in it; the two best (perhaps) appearing in a Southern periodical not likely to have fallen under your eyes. And as a counterpiece to the dissatisfaction with which I regard my former trials,—I hope, by God's grace, to live long enough to have a name worth owning: for as I never paint without an inclination to thrust my canvass through with the malstick, when it comes to finishing the painting, from sheer inability to embody what is as clear as day in my brain, so I am nearly as seldom satisfied with the success of my pen.

Given Legaré's piety and general intenseness, it seems not too much to say that he came to poetic composition with an almost reverent commitment. Only three days before sending off his little book to Powell, he had addressed the editor of that same "Southern periodical" he had mentioned in passing. This was John R. Thompson, whose *Southern Literary Messenger* Legaré was anxious to see flourish and now offered to help by an occasional contribution at standard rates. "I only wish," he told Thompson, in a letter from Aiken on November 13, 1849,

I might with justice to myself, write gratuitously in aid of a result of far more political weight than our petty politicians can understand—the refinement of the people by mental contact. Meanwhile, accept the enclosed copy of verses for your next no—like most of my short poems they have no merit but earnestness. I have been critically accused of affectation, but except in a few instances, I think with little justice. For at least one thing is certain, I write only when touched to the soul or moved by some more transient emotion—and all I say is verily out of my heart. I could not avoid smiling the other day, as I told Mr. Clark, at Mr Hueston's (of the Knickerbocker)[1] business expression "I enclose (such a sum) in pay (!) for Thanatokallos"—as if I would have written that poem for any mere "pay" whatever.

Legaré had begun at the local level, with items in the Charleston periodicals, notably Gilmore Simms's *Southern and Western Monthly Magazine and Review.* Branching out regionally, he soon became a featured author in Georgia. On May 12, 1849, his Arthurian "romaunt," "The Sword and Palette," won second prize, earned him ten dollars, and graced the front page of William C. Richards' *Weekly Gazette* at Athens. In November of the same year, in Charles Wheler's competing periodical at Athens, a similar ballad-type effusion—this time from the German—"The Two King's-Children," was spread all over the front page. But these sheets were, Legaré confided to J. R. Thompson, just "petty Georgia papers." He wanted better than this. As it happened, his appearances therein had already earned it for him.

The first two weeks in May, 1848, found poems by the Carolinian in succeeding issues of one of the abler magazines in the country. This was the *Literary World,* put out at New York City by the Duyckinck brothers, Evert Augustus and George Loring, and Legaré at the beginning was content to offer his

---

[1] Samuel Hueston was publisher of *The Knickerbocker Magazine* for the period 1849–1857. The poem JML here offers Thompson was probably "A Husband to a Wife."

verse gratis in order to receive such an accolade.[2] Not until early 1850 could he even afford to subscribe to the periodical, but, as he reminded the brothers before then,

> I have several times sent to the Lit: World gratuitous articles, because in manly characteristics your journal stands foremost in America, and to my view it is better to be read by a few on whose capacity of appreciation an author can count, rather than glanced at by innumerable readers of Graham, Godey, and the like. Indeed my best poems, "Maize in Tassel" and two or three others, appeared first in your columns for the above reason.[3]

In July, 1848, Legaré saw his lengthy "Ornithologoi" ("Bird Voices") heading the entire thirty-third volume of a magazine he tended privately to disparage. This was George Graham's very popular monthly at Philadelphia. The poem faces a large and "high-toned" engraving of a white-robed woman reclining amid foliage and engaged in reading. The illustration is captioned: "Drawn by [William] Croome from a sketch by the Author. Engraved expressly for Graham's Magazine by W. E. Tucker."

That same month what was probably the most prestigious periodical in the land, the Clark brothers' *Knickerbocker* at New York, sent this advisory winging to its subscribers. The subject was the little *Southern Literary Gazette* at Athens, Georgia:

2 JML to the Duyckincks, Aiken, May 8 [1848?]. Excerpted in CCD (1), p. 221. At this date the editor of the *Literary World* was still Charles Fenno Hoffman. Evert Duyckinck did not return to control until September, 1848. See Perry Miller, *The Raven and the Whale: The War of Words and Wits in the Era of Poe and Melville* (New York: Harcourt, Brace & World [1956]), pp. 188–89.

3 JML to the Duyckincks, Aiken, June 11, 1849. Printed in full in CCD (1), pp. 221–22. His high opinion of the *Literary World* has been echoed by modern scholarship. "It was unquestionably the best literary weekly of its time," says John P. Pritchard, *Literary Wise Men of Gotham: Criticism in New York, 1815–1860* ([Baton Rouge:] Louisiana State University Press [1963]), p. 170.

The "Gazette" bids fair to do much toward extending the
literature of the South. We hope often to hear through its
columns from Mr. Legaré and Mr. [Henry Rootes] Jackson. Both these gentlemen are true poets. Their verse is
quite a refreshing exception to the "words, words" which
passed for "poetry" and which were at one time "indi-
genous voluminously" from certain prolific sources in that
region.[4]

If Legaré's denigration to the Duyckincks of the Graham/
Godey sort of women's magazine was anticipatory, he got his
reward. One year later he had, with an assist from Evert
Duyckinck, placed a poem in "The Old Knick" itself. This
piece, Legaré assured the Duyckincks, was "the most thoughtful,
earnest, and good-designing I have yet composed. . . ."[5] It
was his rebuttal to William Cullen Bryant's "Thanatopsis"—
"Thanatokallos" (Legaré's rendering of the Greek for "Beauty
in Death"). Probably he did not know it; but *The Knickerbocker*, fecund though each issue was with all forms of writing,
numbered among its contributors fewer than five per cent who
were Southern.[6]

As the result of this type of press comment, the Aiken author
became well enough known nationally to attract that inverted
form of compliment, satire. In 1851 the New York journalist,
Augustine Duganne, enshrined him along with Thomas M.
Chivers et al. in his *Parnassus in Pillory*.[7] Three years later the
Ursa Major of Southern writers, William Gilmore Simms, was

[4] *The Knickerbocker Magazine,* XXXII (July, 1848), 85.
[5] JML to the Duyckincks, Aiken, June 11, 1849.
[6] According to Herman E. Spivey, *"The Knickerbocker Magazine, 1833–
1865: A Study of Its History, Contents, and Significance"* (Ph.D. dissertation, University of North Carolina, 1936), p. 32.
[7] See [Augustine J. H. Duganne], *Parnassus in Pillory: A Satire. By Mot-
ley Manners, Esq.* (New York: Adriance, Sherman, 1851), p. 79. The passage, slightly altered, appears in Duganne's *Poetical Works: Autograph
Edition* ([Philadelphia?: n.p.], 1865), p. 214. The reference has been
erroneously attributed to Hugh Swinton Legaré by Emma L. Chase and
Lois F. Parks (eds.), *The Complete Works of Thomas Holley Chivers,
Vol. I, The Correspondence . . . 1838–1858* (Providence, R.I.: Brown
University Press, 1957), p. 107.

listing Legaré's name for the Duyckincks as one of those authors they ought not to miss for inclusion in their proposed anthology of American literature.[8]

What kind of verse was James Legaré producing to effect this kind of reaction?

Basically he was a lyrist of the Romantic school, and his main themes were the grandeur of love and the charm of nature. Where he produced narratives, one might treat of a contemporary event ("The Lighthouse"), but three would be evocations of the exotic in time or place ("Du Saye" for the American scene, "The Sword and Palette" for the English, "The Trouvére's Rose" for the French). In an American decade throbbing with verse about Indians—as vestiges of the Lost Tribes of Israel, or what have you—Legaré's two poems adducing the red man, "Toccoa" and "Tallulah," do so only incidentally in developing themes of nature and romance. In a decade charged with political verse and personal satire, Legaré has no single item therein. (At Charleston alone, the year *Orta-Undis* appeared, no less than four poetasters erupted into print in vituperation against Northern malevolence.) In a decade furnishing an appreciable number of poems treating the theme of revolution, there are none by Legaré.[9]

Here is, however, a Romantic poet who has a goodly part of his imagination rooted in classical tradition. The title poem of *Orta-Undis* is entirely in Latin. Three other pieces in the little volume bear Latin titles. Legaré's personal library contained seven titles by Latin authors. Two of his poems carry Greek

---

[8] Simms to Evert A. Duyckinck [Dec., 1854], in *The Letters of William Gilmore Simms,* ed. Oliphant et al. (Columbia: University of South Carolina Press, 1954), III, 337. As of June 7, 1848, Simms had acquired through his New York publisher one copy of *O-U* for 75¢ (see *ibid.,* p. 51).

[9] See John B. Harcourt, "Themes of American Verse, 1840–1849 . . ." (Ph.D. dissertation, Brown University, 1952), pp. 682–83, 227–29, respectively. To the poetasters here cited should be added Robert P. Hall, *Poems* . . . (Charleston: S. Hart, 1848); Dr. John Simons, *Poems* (Charleston: John Russell, 1848); and Augustin L. Taveau, *The Vindication* (Charleston: Walker and Burke, 1848).

titles, and there are several lines from the Greek in "A Woman of Canaan." There are allusions from Latin and Greek history and legend in "Enchantments" and "On the Death of a Kinsman." Into the lilting, adolescent atmosphere of that romance of chivalry, "The Sword and Palette," abruptly rear up the libidinous figures of Daphne and Silenus. The first-personal, very Christian meditations of "Thanatokallos" suddenly invite one's attention to the case of Aria and Caecinna. An authoritative critic has summarized succinctly this aspect of Legaré's corpus:

> Legaré remained strictly within the Southern tradition: a classicist, his title poem is in Latin; an occasional poet, he wrote an excellent and memorable tribute to his kinsman . . .; a lover of nature, he wrote well on that popular and difficult subject. In these poems his romanticism, his indebtedness to Wordsworth, Schiller, and Tennyson, can be found, but playing over this romanticism is the precision of mind natural to a classicist.[10]

But if Legaré's imagination was rooted in the ancient classics, its flowering was distinctly amid the culture of his own time and place. His adaptations from the German—"The Golden Ring" or "Bald Gras Ich," and "The Two King's-Children"—are in essence Romantic ballads. Of the four German titles in his library one is by an eighteenth-century author, Gellert's *Fabeln;* one is Wilhelm Megede's collection of *Gesänge und Lieder;* and the remaining two are Goethe's *Faust* and *Werther* (the last an award volume from Saint Mary's College, where Legaré had won three Premiums in the language). His single Spanish title is the *Fabulas* of the eighteenth-century poet Tomás de Iriarte (who was such a continuing favorite in America that Longfellow swore he had read him a hundred times).[11] Legaré had

---

[10] Edd W. Parks, *Segments of Southern Thought* ([Athens: University of Georgia Press], 1938), p. 94.

[11] See Stanley T. Williams, *The Spanish Influence on American Literature* (New Haven: Yale University Press, 1955), II, 160–61. The author has overlooked JML's appreciable reaction to this influence.

earned two Premiums in Spanish at Saint Mary's, long ago; and among his college mates there had been Manuel Navarrete from Mexico, Mateo Sobrino from Yucatán, and José Fabré from San Jago de Cuba. Though French verse was known to Legaré, its impress is palely pervasive rather than specific, and its sole representative in his library was the *Songs of Béranger,* in translation.

The American section of Legaré's bookcase is remarkable mainly for its meagreness. Yet several American authors were much admired by him, and the shadow of their presence may be detected in his stanzas. The Carolinian's favorite native poets were probably Longfellow, Poe, and Philip Pendleton Cooke in that order. On learning of Poe's death (October 7, 1849, at Baltimore) Legaré, in a letter to John R. Thompson a month later, said flatly:

> . . . his poems rank first among my pet books, those almost-sacred few kept on a small shelf apart from mere library volumes, and (sometimes one, sometimes another) companions of long rambles through the woods. I felt far more grieved at his death than I would at that of many a relative; for I *do* love genius in whatever shape manifested, and best of all in a true poet. Both before and since his death, I have earnestly maintained his cause against such "small people" as have no charity for the failings of great men, forgetting that delicate organization, not less of soul than of body, can seldom support harsh contact uninjured. There is only one glad thought, that God who knows intimately every spring of action and weighs all temptations more justly than any man can,—will surely be more merciful to those whose temptations were greater, by reason of the very greatness of the gifts He bestowed.

The two probably never met. But a trace of Poe's swaying rhythms may perhaps be detected in verses 104–105 of "Ornothologoi," and his hovering presence felt in the raven of verse 66 of that poem and in the epithet in verse 9 of "Enchantments."

Nor did Legaré meet Philip Pendleton Cooke, though he wanted to. He acquired a copy of Cooke's *Froissart Ballads*

(1847) the year of its publication, and when he heard of the Virginian's death at the age of thirty-four, he burst out:

> How keenly I felt (and feel) the death of poor Cooke! I am far from being a nervous temperament, but the sudden intelligence of the death of a man of *genius* always affects me restlessly for a time, and with some instinctive feeling of what kind I cannot tell, I selected *his* "poems" from among my "pet books," and paced the room with it in my hand (it was twilight) until the emotion was passed. Poe's death moved me much in the same way—I *cannot* bring myself to weigh for a moment a man's sad infirmities *against* his genius. What a speechlessly lovely place (or estate) must that Heaven be, where *all* are possessed (only in an inconceivably greater degree) of what we call "genius" here.[12]

Of all Legaré's American library purchases Longfellow was best represented, with seven titles. Over the years he who has been called "the world's leading minor poet" became a kind of mentor, something of friend, to a degree a model. (The two apparently did not meet.) Legaré's "The Lighthouse" can bear comparison with Longfellow's "The Wreck of the Hesperus," while the Carolinian's "The Reaper" is superior to the New Englander's poem treating that general theme. Legaré also owned volumes of verse by Christopher Pearse Cranch, George William Curtis, and Thomas Buchanan Read.

He was amused by Lowell's "A Fable for Critics" and moved by Bryant's "Thanatopsis." He was so moved that he composed his much lengthier "Thanatokallos"—his only known composition in blank verse—in part as a rebuttal of Bryant's "view of death." (Legaré would undoubtedly have been gratified that Paul Hamilton Hayne reprinted "Thanatokallos" entire in the issue of *Russell's Magazine* carrying his obituary.) In offering

---

[12] JML to John R. Thompson, Aiken, Feb. 1, 1850 (printed in full in CCD [1], pp. 226–27). In a Nov. 13, 1849, letter to Thompson, containing the lament for Poe quoted in the text, JML desired to make the acquaintance of Cooke, who died the following Jan. 20 (printed in full in CCD [1], pp. 224–25).

the piece to the Duyckincks in June, 1849, the Aiken poet explained his own view of death as follows:

> To speak frankly, my pecuniary affairs at present, by a succession of mishaps, are much straitened—and yet much as I require even small remittances at the moment, should you not judge the poem worth *any* sum to *yourselves,* pray publish it also gratuitously, for I cannot reconcile myself to seeing a work, short but written out of my soul rather than head, adorning the pages of a lady's magazine, although each line were paid for in gold instead of commoner coin. I offer it to you *first,* and yours it must be, even if my labor (in a pecuniary sense) be lost. One thing is certain—the poem has not been written with a primary view to gain—*then,* you know, I could only have written out of my head, no more: But because I wish to lend my aid to the overthrow of that frightful creed in which we are all reared—unchristian horror of death, or more properly, of dying. And as you will readily discern by the title alone, I desire this to oppose (for I speak only of the *moral,* not of artistical effect and finish) the great poem of Mr. Bryant. How unfortunate it was that so masterly a poet should have taught so sad a doctrine in Thanatopsis—for as Longfellow well says; there is no knowing in whose breast one of these our random arrows may descend—and *that* must have descended into many. The more impressed I am, by repeated perusals, with the nobleness of the poem *as a poem,* the more have I regretted that treating as it does wholly of death, it should so regard the end of all as to render it of all others the last one dying would wish to read and muse over. A grand edifice in Literature—a vast pyramid of granite, with graves of Kings in its heart: a cloudy column like that which led the Israelites by day— but will it turn to a pillar of light for any when night draws on?[13]

This completes the tale of James Legaré's ascertainable cultural comradeship with compatriot poets. If, however, we may

[13] JML to the brothers Duyckinck, Aiken, S.C., June 11, 1849.

extrapolate from the number of books devoted to other poets in his library and from a demonstrable influence upon his fiction, then the literary atmosphere ostensibly most congenial to the Aiken exile was not American but English.

Legaré owned eleven titles in English verse, and all but one were by authors contemporary with himself. Alexander Smith was there, and so was Leigh Hunt (whose "Abou Ben Adhem" may have suggested Legaré's "Ahab-Mahommed"). Both the Brownings were represented; and Elizabeth Barrett in particular —she was a favorite in Charleston at this time[14]—evoked "warm regard" in the Carolinian. He possessed two of her titles, both of them autographed by his wife Annie and himself. Bulwer-Lytton's *The New Timon: A Romance of London* was on Legaré's shelf, as were the *Humorous Poems* of Thomas Hood. Henry Taylor's *Philip van Artevelde* was to Legaré harmless "drudgery," while Martin Tupper was simply "that little divinity of the ladies."[15]

Joe Legaré had presented his brother with the two-volume, 1846, Ticknor & Company edition of Tennyson's *Poems*—a reprint of the famous 1842 English publication—and James also owned the complete *Works* issued by Ticknor & Fields in 1856 (the first title in their popular "blue and gold" pocket editions). By the late 1840's Tennyson had become a favorite with Low Country readers; and the shadow of "Locksley Hall" may hover somewhat over Legaré's "The Lighthouse." Probably the English master's Arthurian legendizing in "Morte d'Arthur" stimulated Legaré's early "All Hail the Bride!" and contributed to

[14] Guy A. Cardwell, Jr., "Charleston Periodicals, 1795–1860: A Study in Literary Influences . . ." (Ph.D. dissertation, University of North Carolina, 1936), p. 119, which is also source for the succeeding statement about Tennyson's popularity.

[15] JML to Thomas Powell, Aiken, Nov. 16, 1849 (printed in full in CCD [1], pp. 218–20). This letter and that of Nov. 13, 1849, to J. R. Thompson contain JML's widest ranging comments on things literary. For his published corpus the largest number of literary allusions is found in the tale "Deux Oies, Vertes," *Graham's Magazine*, XXXVIII (Apr., 1851), 304–23.

the general atmosphere enveloping "the quaint, blackletter, old romance" perused by the heroine in "The Sword and Palette." If this be so, it exemplifies the thesis that, since it was American favor, not British, which first gave Tennyson his popularity, then those American writers and critics who admired him opted, in so doing, for the fashions of their own time rather than those of the Neoclassic period.[16]

Which, from the world's literature, were Legaré's supreme choices, those works he refers to from time to time as his "pet-books"? Taking his phrase literally, conceding that he might have praised certain volumes in order to ingratiate himself with a given correspondent, one finds the following titles to be the Carolinian's favorites:

AMERICAN LITERATURE

Cooke, Philip Pendleton	*Froissart Ballads, and Other Poems* (1847)
Longfellow Henry W. (editor)	*The Waif: a Collection of Poems* (1844)
———— " ————	*The Estray; a Collection of Poems* . . . (1847)
[Mitchell, Donald Grant]	*Reveries of a Bachelor* . . . (1850)
Poe, Edgar Allan	corpus

ENGLISH LITERATURE

Dickens, Charles	*David Copperfield* (1849-1850)
Powell, Thomas (editor)	*The Living Authors of England* (1849)
Thackeray, W. M.	*Vanity Fair* (1847-1848)
———— " ————	*Pendennis* (1848-1850)

But a discussion of "influence," while far from barren, is but a framework and a delineation. Legaré's modest best is such

---

[16] According to John O. Eidson, *Tennyson in America: His Reputation and Influence from 1827 to 1858* (Athens: University of Georgia Press, 1943), p. xi.

precisely because he therein speaks with his individual voice, not that of Ulysses or the Village Blacksmith.

This voice carries a markedly religious tone. As William Gilmore Simms declared, in reviewing *Orta-Undis* for the *Southern Quarterly Review* at Charleston, Legaré's stanzas convey "fine moralities that crown the verse. . . ." This quality, so much out of fashion today, was generally admired in Legaré's own, and the tendency runs all through his production. It extends from such a relatively early piece as "The Book of Nature" to his last known poem, "The Lighthouse." It is the whole point of "Ahab-Mahommed" and "Maize in Tassel." It infiltrates such unlikely subjects as "Ornithologoi." It infests—from today's point of view—some of the finest efforts, such as "Flowers in Ashes." Legaré's awareness of the Godhead is intense and enduring. We should expect such a man to mingle in circles that found pleasure in composing the kind of sermonizing letter somebody mailed him one day from Charleston.[17]

Legaré's voice is also, at times, self-complacent. The tone of "The Rustic Seat," and the attitude of the woman who recites "The Hemlocks"—here is humble gratitude for the bestowal of a poet's love. And the poet's bardic assurance of the immortalizing quality of his lines in "Last Gift" is close to obnoxious.

It is Legaré's terse, true sweetness when treating those authentically immortal themes, love and nature, that constitute his slender yet solid claim to lasting reputation.

Of the former theme, little need be said. The values and nuances of love are spread all through Legaré's verse, for all to see. This love may be regenerative, as in "Janette." It may be protective, as in "A Husband to a Wife." It may be religious, chivalric, connubial, fraternal, or worshipful. But it is never passionate. Simms generalized on the subject well enough when he observed, in 1861: "To many of our readers, it is well known

---

[17] Anon. to JML at Aiken, postmarked Charleston on envelope, date illegible. This fragment was found enclosed in John D. Legaré's copy of *A Dictionary of the Holy Bible* . . . (New York: Harper, 1835), in JJL Coll.

that he was the writer of a volume of very delicate and genuine poetry; sweet, graceful, felicitous and classical—not powerful or passionate—but singularly happy in phrase, and pure and exquisite of fancy."[18] A later South Carolinian generalized as follows:

> Legare wrote sweetly and pleasantly, and he should be more widely known. As he wasn't given to heroics, he has not found a place in our popular collections. But he did produce poetry worthy to be placed beside that of Timrod and Hayne, and far above some of the vapid stuff on which we have long been nourished and told that it was made from wheat grown on the sides of Olympus by the gods, whereas it is an imitation that was concocted when the gods were looking the other way.[19]

As a poet of nature, it is interesting to ascertain through word count the several features of natural life which, on the testimony of his verse, most appealed to J. M. Legaré. Among birds, four share priority in the frequency of their appearance in his stanzas: the owl, mockingbird, crow, and wood dove. Thereafter the field is divided among many species, from linnet through jay to eagle. Verses 154–219 of "Ornithologoi" ("Bird Voices") may be viewed as an explicit condemnation of the thoughtless slaughter of bird life which Legaré had made implicit in an essay for a Georgia magazine at this same period. "Ornithologoi," by far his longest poem, is a not inconsiderable achievement, which should take its rightful place among the very few American poems celebrating birds.[20]

18 [W. G. Simms], "Domestic Resources," Charleston *Mercury*, Nov. 29, 1861, p. 1, col. 3. Mary C. Simms Oliphant and T. C. Duncan Eaves believe that this anonymous article "can safely be ascribed to Simms" (*The Letters of William Gilmore Simms,* IV, 161n.).

19 Rev. G. Croft Williams, "James Matthewes Legare and His Poetry" (typescript in possession of author's family; Columbia, S.C., [*ca.* 1922]), p. 15.

20 For background see Commentary, below. The essay was JML's "The Inside of a Pie," *Wheler's Monthly Magazine* (Athens, Ga.), n.s. I (Sept., 1849), 53–55 (discussed in CCD [3], p. 532).

As for trees, the pine stands topmost in Legaré's favor. Oak and cypress come as poor seconds, followed by the willow. As with most Romantics, the healing and inspirational qualities of nature were very real for Legaré. To one correspondent he put it this way:

> I wish you could have seen as somebody (who was it?) saw in Cornelius Agrippa's black palm-fluid, how *We* (I, 'and one dearer') read your 'Edith,' ensconced in a high-backed rustic seat in the quiet woods, where from a hilltop, our eyes rested on the far blue hills—Does not a far horizon seem always to enlarge your very sense of existence?

To John R. Thompson, on offering him the refusal of "The Hemlocks," Legaré put it this way:

> This poem I design to contain all that is deepest and worthiest in my musings and speculations in those most suggestive of all places, deep silent woods—not silent as some South American woods are from lack of life, but from the absence of all human labors or voices.[21]

Among flowers the rose is Legaré's favorite. The haw blossom is a strong contender. Third place is shared by the yellow jasmine—since 1924 the State flower of South Carolina—and the kalmias, or laurel. (A few minutes' stroll out of Aiken lay Calico Spring, a picturesque dell,[22] and two miles beyond town there was a little settlement, noted for the luxury of its homes, called Kalmia.)

Concerning one of Legaré's specific reactions to flowers the critic and novelist, Ludwig Lewisohn, observed, in 1909:

> In regard to such a poem as "Haw-Blossoms" one may drop at least the careful use of the word 'verse' and say

---

[21] JML to Thomas Powell, Aiken, Nov. 16, 1849, and to John R. Thompson, Aiken, Feb. 1, 1850, respectively. A similar reference to forest stillness occurs in JML's long tale of exploration in central Guatemala, "Suppositious Reviews," *DeBow's Review*, X (Feb., 1851), 162.

[22] See Amory Coffin, M.D., and W. H. Geddings, M.D., *Aiken; or Climatic Cure* (Charleston: Walker, Evans, & Cogswell, 1869), p. 19.

openly that here is poetry—not rich or elaborate or lofty, but unmistakable in its soft undertone of melody, in its accurate and restrained vision.

In 1950 John Gould Fletcher (the first Southern poet to win the Pulitzer Prize), who was projecting an anthology of Southern verse to include poems by Legaré, spoke out just as strongly on another of the Carolinian's reactions to growing things: " 'Maize in Tassel' and 'To Jasmines in December' . . . suggest to my mind that these poems may enlarge my own, as well as possibly others', appreciation of Legaré's very remarkable gift for the apprehension of nature, and for flowers and plants especially."[23]

A quarter-century earlier one who was neither poet nor novelist but Secretary of Public Welfare in South Carolina, G. Croft Williams, had given good general expression to the impact Legaré's verses about nature could exert upon a sensitive nonspecialist:

> Legare like Timrod had a subtle sensing of nature: the odors of the woods, the glint of petals with drops of rain on them, the movements and voicings of small wild creatures—these mingling with the emotional elements of the poet come to us in a new way. Spring is, to us folk of prose, a new creature, radiant and articulate, when met in company with her interpreter. Only a southern wood in spring, after a shower, could be so feminine and wistful as the one caught in this poem on "Haw-Blossoms."

Whether he is writing of love or of nature or of any other subject that captured his fancy, how many pieces of true artistry did James Legaré produce? Perhaps half-a-dozen poems? Ten? Each reader will make his own estimate. The various critics who reviewed *Orta-Undis* upon its appearance found occasion to compare elements in the little book with the work of writers

---

[23] John Gould Fletcher, "Johnswood," Little Rock, Ark., March 29, 1950, to CCD. Fletcher's untimely death six weeks later aborted the anthology project.

ranging in style and period from Herrick and Herbert through Burns to Poe and Longfellow. The various critics who, in modern times, have appraised the same elements remark upon their "modernity" (in such pieces as "To a Lily," "The Reaper," "Flowers in Ashes"). If we number all the critics from the month of the book's appearance until today, with the idea of ascertaining which of the pieces have been the most reprinted or anthologized—and therefore may be presumed to rank, in expert opinion, as the author's best—this is the order in which they come: (1) "To a Lily"; (2) "Haw-Blossoms"; (3) "Ahab-Mahommed"; (4) "Tallulah," "The Reaper," and "On the Death of a Kinsman."

Ticknor & Company printed 500 copies of *Orta-Undis,* to retail at 50¢ each, with a ten per cent commission risked by author, not publisher. The firm despatched 150 copies to John Russell, the Charleston printer and bookseller, another 150 to his competitor at Augusta, Georgia, Charles E. Grenville, and presumably held the remainder for sale in the Boston area. The little volume was duly advertised in such papers as the Boston *Daily Evening Traveller* (along with Longfellow's *Evangeline* and Tennyson's *The Princess*) and in the Savannah *Daily Republican* (along with Dickens' *Dombey and Son* and Emily Brontë's *Wuthering Heights.*) By about the year 1900 the State Historian of South Carolina came upon "at least a hundred" unused copies of *Orta-Undis* in the second-hand bookstore of John O'Mara at 87 Queen Street, Charleston. He and a professor at the university helped themselves.[24] Today, known copies repose in twenty public repositories including the British Museum.[25] Among private individuals who have owned copies

---

[24] Alexander S. Salley, Jr., Columbia, S.C., July 2, 1947, to CCD. The colleague was Yates Snowden (1858–1933), professor of history at the university from 1905 until his death.

[25] Fifteen repositories are listed in CCD (2), p. 427n. To these should be added: (16) Harris Collection, Brown University Library, Providence, R.I.; (17) Maryland Historical Society, Baltimore; (18) Mary Washington College Library, Fredericksburg, Va.; (19) University of Chicago Library; (20) Strozier Library, Florida State University, Tallahassee.

are Francis Bowen, professor of ancient languages at the College of Charleston, and Henry C. Sturges, the Connecticut collector of Americana.

Despite such relatively scanty circulation—and despite Legaré's own denigration of his brain child (see page 59, above) —most of the contemporary critics had smiled on *Orta-Undis*. Between April, 1848, and October, 1849, it received fourteen reviews or brief notices in cities scattered from Boston to New Orleans. Of the lot, only two could be termed downright unfavorable.

Legaré himself sent or presented copies to John C. Calhoun; to his onetime college mate, J. D. B. DeBow, now publishing his *Review* in Louisiana; to the editor of the Charleston *Mercury,* Colonel John E. Carew; to the New York editor and journalist Thomas Powell; to a Mrs. Hall; and to a man named Edwin Richards, who gave it to a girl named Carrie Crumpton, whose copy is now in the New York Public Library. Legaré's epistle of presentation to the scapegrace Powell, a total stranger—purple with praise of Powell's poem, "Edith," and his anthology, *The Living Authors of England,* crammed with literary allusion, lacquered with bonhomie—was a performance at least the peer of his self-introduction to Longfellow.[26]

The concluding sentence of the letter to Powell referred not to poetry but to a prose piece by Thomas Carlyle. The happenstance serves to point up an aspect of Legaré's career which meant considerably more to him than the same aspect did to his fellow poet, Professor Longfellow: the writing of fiction.

Perhaps, from a practical point of view, this was as well. In May, 1849, Ticknor & Company had remitted to their Southern author, as his financial returns from the sales of *Orta-Undis, and Other Poems,* the sum of $23.59.

---

[26] JML to Thomas Powell, Aiken, Nov. 16, 1849. JML assured Powell that the forthcoming publication of the latter's *The Living Authors of America* (New York, 1850), had not motivated his letter. The title in question contains no JML item.

VI: THE POET'S "LEFT HAND"

At the South, *literary* men—especially the *very very few* who dare make *Literature a profession*—, are strangely, and *painfully* isolated. For *years past,* this has been the case, and for years *to come,* I suppose, the same condition of things will prevail.

Every So scholar or *writer* of any note has had reason to complain of it.

If we go back to the time of that *magnificent genius,* and profound scholar, *Hugh S. Legaré*—, (believe me! these words *are not* extravagant!) —, we find that despite *Legaré's practical vim & tact,* which *aided* by his information and native talents, carried him from a high position at the Charleston bar, up to the *Attorney Generalship* of the *U. States*—, —he nevertheless, complained of the *drawback* to advancement, and *local recognition,* which his *literary fame,* in *earlier* life—, prove to be—; and so it was with Gilmore Simms, with Kennedy, with Pendleton Cooke, with Poe, and lastly with our poor friend *Timrod!*

Paul H. Hayne to Moses Coit
Tyler, "Copse Hill," May 16, 1873[1]

It is an interesting question whether James Legaré was better known as poet or as story teller. Verse was more frequently published in the mid-nineteenth century than it is today, and considerably more relished. On the other hand fiction has always attracted a wider readership, and it can also be argued that the impact of a novella, or even a long tale, lingers more deeply in reader memory by virtue of length and time consumption.

However this may be, Legaré began getting his fiction into print—if we exclude the Legaré Genealogy from this category

---

[1] See *A Collection of Hayne Letters,* ed. Daniel M. McKeithan (Austin: University of Texas Press, 1944), pp. 319–20.

—just a little over two years after his maiden appearance in poetry. Through the happenstance of war and conflagration it stayed in print for almost five years after his death. The bulk of it appeared during the years 1848–1851 and 1853–1855. It was published in the same cities across the land that witnessed the advent of his verse (with the addition of New Orleans), and the calibre of the magazines accepting it rose steadily.[2]

Whereas Legaré published forty-nine known pieces of verse, he published only seventeen known pieces of fiction. These range in length from less than a page to two ten-chapter novellas. They are more varied in character than his verse, and may be assigned to the following roughly chronological genres:

1. Western Stories
2. Humor
3. Historical Romance
4. Adventure Romance
5. Domestic Sentimentalism
6. Satire

The influence on Legaré's fiction of at least these authors can be demonstrated: from the United States—Francis Parkman's *The Oregon Trail* (1849), and John L. Stephens' *Incidents of Travel* in Central America and in Yucatán (1841 and 1843, respectively). (Even P. T. Barnum enters the picture.) From England—W. M. Thackeray's *Vanity Fair* and *Pendennis* (1847–1848 and 1848–1850, respectively).[3] Notwithstanding

[2] JML's fiction appeared as follows: 1845, *Southern & Western Magazine & Review,* Charleston; 1848, *Southern Literary Gazette,* Athens, Ga.; 1849, *Richards' Weekly Gazette* and *Wheler's Monthly Magazine,* Athens, Ga.; 1850, *Graham's Monthly Magazine,* Philadelphia, and *Southern Literary Messenger,* Richmond; 1851, *DeBow's Review,* New Orleans, and *Sartain's Union Magazine of Literature and Art,* Philadelphia; 1853, *Putnam's Monthly Magazine* . . . , Philadelphia; 1854, *The Knickerbocker Magazine,* New York City; 1863–64, *Harper's New Monthly Magazine,* New York City.
Detailed analyses of all save "Miss Peck's Friend"—not identified as JML's until 1961—are supplied in CCD (3). They are analyzed from another point of view in CCD (4), pp. 220–30.
[3] See CCD (3), pp. 531–32, 539–40, 541–43 (Barnum), 551–54, and 558–59, respectively. To publicize some recently acquired freaks, "Two

Legaré's proximity to and familiarity with Middle Georgia, his stories exhibit virtually none of the local color which that area had evoked in A. B. Longstreet and William Tappan Thompson and would presently evoke in Richard Malcolm Johnston and Joel Chandler Harris.

Two of Legaré's stories—"The New Aria," in *Richards' Weekly Gazette,* and "The Lame Girl," in *Sartain's Magazine* —won prizes, the latter from among more than four hundred competing manuscripts. (Legaré and Henry William Herbert, or "Frank Forester," appear to have been the only prominent prize winners.) A third, "The Loves of Mary Jones," marked the Carolinian as probably the only Southerner, and definitely the only Southern author of note, to appear in the handsome memorial anthology, *The Knickerbocker Gallery* . . . (New York, 1855), issued as a tribute to Lewis Gaylord Clark, editor of *The Knickerbocker Magazine.* In his acknowledgement from Aiken, December 22, 1854, of a circular appeal issued by George Pope Morris, the Manhattan poet and journalist, Legaré cheerfully consented to donate a piece gratis to the *Gallery,* proceeds from the sales of which, it was hoped, would enable Clark to acquire a Hudson River cottage—as Legaré phrased it, that "proposed substantial token of appreciation. . . ." Among other contributors shone such names as Bryant, Halleck, Holmes, Irving, Longfellow, Lowell, Mitchell ("Ik Marvel"), Taylor, and Willis.

Yet James Legaré's fiction is, by today's standards, third-rate at best. Its seminal curse is verbosity. Because of this, his satire is shallow instead of sharp; his adventure tales are bombastic instead of adventurous; his dialogues become disquisitions. Though Legaré went on record against the fiction peddled by the women's magazines, his own prize stories are prize examples of such fiction. This is not hypocrisy, just inability.

For what we have here, at least in part, is a response to the

---

Remarkable Aztec Children," via a pamphlet in adventure-story mode, Barnum borrowed liberally from Stephens' volumes; and JML borrowed from both sources.

demands of the average reader at the time; and the time's demands were low. Yet here is also, in passing—fragmentarily —a revelation of certain of the ideas and attitudes of a significant Southern author, all too few of whose letters or other personalia have survived as a window thereto. The chief values of James Legaré's fiction, therefore, are autobiographical rather than artistic.

There is only one formal statement of opinion on cultural matters that James M. Legaré is known to have put into print and which can be identified. This was a column anonymously published by the Charleston *Mercury,* one October morning in 1849, under the title, "Magazines of the Day." Its four close-printed paragraphs have two themes: castigation of the scale of values purveyed by the fiction in women's periodicals (unspecified), and praise for *The Knickerbocker Magazine*.

Now, "The Old Knick" had printed Legaré's poem "Thanatokallos" just the month before and would release "Janette" three months later. Its co-editor, Willis Gaylord Clark, had been awarded an honorary Master of Arts degree from Legaré's alma mater, the College of Charleston. Hence it may well be that, in putting forth his column, the Carolinian was following the widespread practice of "puffing" an acquaintance's periodical in exchange for value received or anticipated.[4] We know he did this for the Northern journalist Thomas Powell's anthology, *The Living Authors of America* (New York, 1850)—sending laudatory notices of the volume to Charleston and Augusta newspapers and promising Powell to do likewise in the *Southern Quarterly Review* and *Southern Literary Messenger*—but the critiques are entombed beyond resurrection in the anonyms that fill the journals of the day.

Legaré also entered the lists on behalf of the *Messenger* itself (which published eight of his poems, more than any other

[4] For background see Sidney P. Moss, *Poe's Literary Battles: The Critic in the Context of His Literary Milieu* (Durham: Duke University Press, 1963), pp. 79–81 *et passim*.

magazine). When its editor, John Reuben Thompson, called for help in May, 1850, Legaré was quick in giving it:

> I hasten to reply to your note received only this aft, for I sincerely feel with you in your mixed personal and literary position. Tomorrow I will write to friends in different parts of the country, urging the claims of the Messenger—the only manly literary publication of the South; even De Bow's Review when altered from it's present purely mercantile character (he has written to solicit articles with that view) will be far from competing in point of position. I will also without awaiting your permission, make such *delicate* use of the confidence you repose touching the Messenger's "impaired constitution" in the columns of various papers as, with an earnest desire to produce a reaction in the lethargic perception around, I may judge best suited to bring about that result. Finally, I will hasten my long procrastinated visit to Charleston (the late winter and Spring must bear the reproach of my detention here) with the view of proving by personal applications, the sincerity of my good wishes and hitherto useless promises. . . .
>
> [P. S.] My wife—sitting next me—is as much touched as myself at "the picture" you have lightly sketched, and has just written to a relative in N York to forward you *her* name and subscription May the *best* fortune attend you.[5]

If Legaré was in fact a puffer, he was but a minor combatant gesticulating along the sidelines of a busy battleground situate in the distant centers of Philadelphia and New York. His forehead did not glint with nearly so much sweat of strife as did his fellow Carolinian's, Gilmore Simms.[6] And, to whatever extent the

---

[5] JML to Thompson, Aiken, May 22, 1850. All of the quotation save the postscript is printed in CCD (1), pp. 228-29. See also Joseph Roddey Miller, "John R. Thompson . . ." (Ph.D. dissertation, University of Virginia, 1930), pp. 150, 155. Though Thompson frequently rejected the verse offerings of Augustin Louis Taveau of South Carolina, he did not scruple to request Taveau's financial aid (see Thompson to Taveau, Richmond, May 11, 1850, in the Taveau Papers, Duke University Library).

[6] For Simms's share in the Gotham literary feuds see Perry Miller, *The Raven and the Whale: The War of Words and Wits in the Era of Poe and Melville* (New York: Harcourt Brace & Co. [1956]), *passim*.

Aiken littérateur may have been taking up the joust, the concluding paragraph of "Magazines of the Day" enunciated a
credo that no thoughtful person could decry: a plea in support
of literary standards and in denunciation of provincialism:

> With a clear conscience, too; and more than that, I recom-
> mend the Knickerbocker to the good offices of every one
> who would get his money's worth really and truly twelve
> times in the year. There is but one obstacle in the way with
> many—a disinclination sown and fostered by a few inter-
> ested publishers, to encourage anything Northern to the
> prejudice of similar merchandise at the South. As if such
> a thing existed as *local* literature—local not in point of
> contributors, but of readers—as if merit would not be its
> own best advocate, and without extrinsic and erroneous
> advocacy, extend its circle of usefulness far and farther; for
> instance, cause Southern periodicals to number Northern
> patrons, instead of the reverse as it now stands. Let me say,
> I have no interest in all this, not common to many of my
> readers. I am myself a Southerner, born and bred, with
> rational attachment to my native State, and interest in its
> social developments, equal to that of the most enthusiastic.
> But while we import our sardines and segars, in place of
> patriotically indulging in "Americans," and substituting
> indigenous mudfish for a relish, I see no good reason for
> stinting my intellectual appetite when better food is within
> reach.

Not only that: Legaré wanted to supply some of the food.
He took his fiction, like himself, seriously; and of all the kinds
of fiction which interested him, he was at the moment taking
historical and adventure romance most seriously of all.

These two categories of fiction were intermingled on Legaré's
writing desk with that "weighty work," the "History of the Conquest and Civil Wars of the Pacific Islands," which he had
touched on during his letter to Longfellow of September 22,
1849. A month earlier he had sent a more specific proposal on
the same subject to a crony of his ex-mentor Petigru—one of
the prominent citizens of his native State, James Henry Ham-

mond, whose three-thousand-acre plantation "Silver Bluff" in Aiken District stretched along the Savannah River south of Augusta, Georgia, within striking distance of the town of Aiken.

Hammond had served in Congress from South Carolina and been its Governor in 1842–1844. Now in indolent retirement, he was hospitable and ingratiating, vain and self-pitying. Of ordinary birth, Hammond had married a Charleston heiress of equally humble but far wealthier status. When he sent a genealogist to England to establish his lineage, and the investigator reported that his employer's ancestors had been mere yeomen, Hammond was so vexed he tore up the documents submitted and refused to pay the fee. This former public servant was a gifted public speaker; but "more influential upon the Carolinian mind than what Hammond said, was what he was. He was the baron of his district and one of the great barons of the State."[7]

To the forty-two-year-old planter the twenty-five-year-old Legaré wrote, out of the blue, in August, 1849, requesting help in getting his historical and literary efforts before the public. Hammond, aware of his own deficiencies as a critic, promptly got off a note of inquiry to his friend William Gilmore Simms down at "Woodlands" on the Edisto River in Barnwell District:

> A short time ago I recd a letter from J M Legare from Aiken stating that he had a novel & important proposition to make to me & would meet me either in Augusta or at my house. I of course invited him here. By todays mail I recd the enclosed, which I beg you will read over & return me as *soon* as possible with your advice &c. It may not be in accordance with Mr. L's views that you or any one should see this & I would not trouble you or expose him but that he makes a somewhat extraordinary proposition to a perfect stranger. I never saw him. I don't know who he is. I feel sure he is the author of "Orta Undis" & the

[7] Elizabeth Merritt, *James Henry Hammond, 1807–1864* (Baltimore: [Johns Hopkins University Press], 1923), p. 116. This study should be supplemented by reference to Clement Eaton, "The Hamlet of the Old South," chap. 2 in *The Mind of the Old South* (Baton Rouge, 1964), pp. 21–42. Neither author mentions JML.

"Legare Genealogy," but on this I may be mistaken. The poem shows sprightly parts—the forgery I do not think should exclude him from benefit of clergy, tho much against him. His flattery to me is not very adroit, since it might well offend my *amor propiâ* to suppose I was not as likely to be distinguished for my own merits, as for being his patron. Still I should take pleasure in doing what I could afford to do to promote a man of genius. Is he such? Or is he a sharper as the forgery might imply? Or is he not the forger? Is he really dying as he seems to think?

After these questions about himself do tell me if his novel is likely to realize *any thing* for him & if so how much? And if you could give me some idea of the sum he wants. I have no money to spare & and was never less in the humor to give. This man has not the slightest claim on me. But I have the utmost sympathy for a man of education—especially a man of genius struggling with poverty & with, what is even worse than that, ill-health. I feel it a moral duty to share something with such a man, and a public one to aid in bringing out any literary work calculated to do good & add to the reputation of So/C. I will write indefinitely to him & *decide* on nothing till I hear from you—.[8]

Then Hammond responded to Legaré, inviting him to visit "Silver Bluff." The author prepared to do so, assuring Hammond, in reply, that he would "gladly lay before you all my literary plans, and also relate much that may interest you in connection with the Oykaza MS, when we meet."[9] Presumably this was a source, or draft, of Legaré's "History of the Conquest and Civil Wars of the Pacific Islands." The poem is unidentifiable. Also offered was an adventure romance featuring that ever-popular theme, a lost city, in this instance a metropolis tucked away in the jungles of Guatemala.

---

[8] Hammond, "Silver Bluff" (near Silverton, S.C.), Sept. 2/3 (postscript), 1849, to W. G. Simms (James H. Hammond Papers, Vol. XVI, Library of Congress). At the moment Simms was in Charleston.

[9] JML, Aiken, Sept. 6 [1849], to Hammond. This otherwise unidentified item may have been one of those referred to by W. G. Simms in the last sentence of his belated tribute to JML: ". . . many other of the writings of Mr. LEGARE, still remain in manuscript" (see "Domestic Resources," Charleston *Mercury*, Nov. 29, 1861, p. 1, col. 2).

Meanwhile Simms—whose interest in Spanish America as a locale for fiction was of long standing—had agreed to try and interest a publisher in these materials. When Hammond learned this, he informed the senior author, September 20:

> It is very kind to me & generous to Legare to offer to serve him in getting out his work. You evidently do not fear him & this detracts somewhat from your generosity, though not from your kindness. You need not fear him. I have the work & have read it. You were right. He has fancy but no imagination or genius—What a curse to have the one & not the others. I hardly know what to say of the novel. It is a strange story & very ingenious. The style is simple & clear, in imitation of De Foe, but wholly wanting in his verve & without any trace of his tender touches & profound reflection. True to what I fear are his instincts it is a regular *imposture*. A bona fide narrative of pretended discoveries in So America, without the least hint any where that it is not true, & with the greatest painstaking to pass it off for actual fact. He has found the people who built the marvellous structures described by [John Lloyd] Stephens living in similar ones in an inaccessible valley. He describes their abodes with minuteness, but furnishes no new details—their manners & customs which are sufficiently absurd, & dwells wearisomely upon their birds & brooks, & flowers & animals & children. There is very little narrated in which a *man* would take an interest. Even his hair-breadth 'scapes are evidently *contrived* & do not alarm him nor the reader; & the bloody rites of one set, & the mild & childish customs of the other—for there are two nations in one valley—are equally dull.
>
> . . . Still I am not indisposed to help him if I can with his History. His clear style & care in details might tell in that, though there will be nothing profound or brilliant. I speak to you of course in the strictest confidence about this matter. Perhaps I should not do it at all. But Legaré imposed no secrecy. But don't mention it for my sake . . . . Money is *scarce* with me . . . ."[10]

Three weeks later Hammond further informed Simms:

[10] Hammond, "Silver Bluff," Sept. 20, 1849, to Simms.

I returned Legare's MSS. & condemned it. He was greatly hurt & I equally so to have had any thing to do with it. But I told him I would do as much for him as I ever intended to do under any circumstances but I did not say what [,] for I have not seen him & do not know how to service him. As to setting up for a Maecenas that I am not able to do. I would cheerfully advance him a hundred dollars a year or the equivalent for two or three years while writing his History, but I fear so small an offer would wound him as much as the censure of his present work. But I can't do more—[11]

Whereupon Hammond received this opinion from Simms of both the Legarés, mailed from Charleston on October 17:

When you consulted me anent Legaré, I was studious to say nothing that might disparage his claims. But now, I may mention that I think lightly alike of father & son. The former, Burges[12] claims to have been deceived by. B. says that he got his endorsement a week or so before his declared bankruptcy and when his condition was fully known to himself. The son (B. tells me) is keeping school at Augusta, & he has no reason to suppose him more an invalid than usual. He is vain & ambitious, & is the author of an article in the Mercury a few days ago, disparaging all the Northern Magazines but the Knickerbocker, the Editor of which he knows I denounced in print as a liar &c. The fact is that every petty poetaster of Charleston looks upon me as an enemy. Yet scarcely a Southron has ever received a kind word in the South, unless from my pen; and even Legaré is indebted to me for a genial notice in the present issue of the Review.[13]

In the face of such an assessment from his friend, Hammond sent word to Legaré that he could not sponsor him with his fiction but that he would stand him $200 to travel up to Cam-

11 Hammond, "Silver Bluff," Oct. 12, 1849, to Simms.
12 James S. Burges, publisher of the *Southern Quarterly Review* at Charleston.
13 Simms, Charleston, Oct. 17, 1849, to Hammond. See Oliphant et al. (eds.), *The Letters of William Gilmore Simms,* II, 563–64.

bridge, Massachusetts, the following summer and search for materials at the library there (meaning Harvard College's) in furtherance of his history project. To Simms the planter confided: "Unless the work is really worth something, when done, I will not aid in foisting it on the world. Pliny said there was no book but had *some* good in it. But I think it a sin to publish one that has not a great deal of good in it—tho' I have been guilty of publications of little value myself—but I charged them on no one. Legaré's ambition is awful. You must excuse his puff of the Knickerbocker—*he did it for bread.*"[14]

And here the matter rested.

The adventure romance about a lost city, under a non-title of "Supposititious Reviews," ended up in *DeBow's Review*. The "Oykaza MS"—if this was in fact Legaré's treatment of the "Spanish *(Insular)* History of conquests," as he elsewhere described it for the benefit of John R. Thompson— was laid aside for the nonce. It was doubtless never completed, and probably made one among the "many other . . . writings of Mr. LEGARE" which William Gilmore Simms would take cognizance of when composing the Aiken author's obituary.

Elsewhere, however, Legaré's projects were not so aborted. During the latter half of 1850 *Graham's Magazine* ran his historical romance "Pedro de Padilh," which was a direct offshoot in fiction of his basic idea for the Insular History (with the locale shifted from the Pacific to the Azores). Well before its appearance, moreover, the same Philadelphia publisher had dug down into his backlog and come up complacently with some Western stories the Carolinian had sent him long ago. The result thereof was this special item in the June, 1850, issue of *Graham's*:

> J. M. Legare.—The sketches of Mr. Legare, "Life on the Prairies of the Farthest West," which appeared in the April and May numbers, of Graham, were written for us some two years since, and are no evidence of the maturity

[14] Hammond, "Silver Bluff," Oct. 28, 1849, to Simms.

of style, since acquired by this elegant writer—ably as they were written. We hope soon to lay before our readers a series of articles from his pen, which place Mr. Legare in the front rank of the contributors to Graham. South Carolina, with three able writers, Legare, Simms, and Godman, is ably represented in "Graham."[15]

These pieces were almost the earliest of Legaré's three published attempts at Western stories. Although he himself probably never got close to the banks of the Mississippi, let alone crossed it, his first fiction to see print—if we exclude the Legaré Genealogy—had also been a Western tale (drawn from an unpublished novel), "Going to Texas," published in "Simms's Magazine" at Charleston in December, 1845.

The two sketches George Rex Graham was now lauding read even more disjointedly than their predecessor. The best that can be said for all three is that they display a commendable effort on the part of the author to work up his background. Legaré introduces a variety of frontier material, ranging from a buffalo hunt to types of food, writes rather persuasively of the Missouri and Teton rivers and of various Indian tribes, and shows a marked awareness of the French settlers in the region. But the over-all result is poor.

Its creator knew this and was horrified at what he regarded as Graham's exploitation of his name. He wrote to Philadelphia in complaint. The publisher replied with an apology and an offer to pay any amount requested. "I declined"—Legaré rehearsed the affair for Longfellow on June 9, 1851—"he persisted, and I again positively declined to receive anything, judging the MS I was ashamed to see in print, not worth remuneration."

The episode nevertheless consolidated an epistolary acquaintanceship. When Legaré learned that Graham was suffering from

[15] "Editor's Table," *Graham's Magazine,* XXXVI (June, 1850), 418. On the now-forgotten Stewart Adair Godman (1822–1853) of South Carolina, see CCD (3), p. 530n. The "series of articles" is probably "Pedro de Padilh."

a chest inflammation, he even invited him down to Aiken to convalesce. On the publisher's presently proposing that he become a regular contributor, James closed with the deal.

At the back of his November, 1850, issue George R. Graham placed a full-page advertisement. In very large type he proclaimed his "Plans for 1851." Among other items he was proud to announce that he had lined up no less than eight exclusive contributors. James M. Legaré was one of them. Some of the others were Longfellow, Lowell, Bryant, newspaperwoman "Grace Greenwood," and critic Edwin Percy Whipple. And in the March, 1851, issue the editor asserted complacently:

> Graham, at least, thinks he has a class of young writers now, who ask no odds in fair encounter: Lowell, Read, Legare, Godman, Whipple, Fields . . . form a galaxy unequalled in ability, we will venture to say, by any corps of writers engaged for any other magazine in the world.[16]

"Considering what had passed," Legaré explained to another *Graham's* contributor, Henry Longfellow, on June 9, 1851, "a slight sense of delicacy caused me to refrain from requiring any definite terms beforehand, but I began contributing with the understanding that the first payment should be considered a gauge for the rest, and I had no reason to complain, for my first story extending through some months although very far from well written—and indeed only written because a confounded idea possessed my head which I must needs first write out—was liberally and promptly paid for by a cheque for $200.00 Now painful as the conclusion is, it has been gradually forced upon me that this cheque was the initial[17] of a deliberate swindle on the part of Mr Graham, founded on my lack of business experience, distance from himself, and presumed in-

[16] *Graham's Magazine*, XXXVIII (March, 1851), 280. The authors were, respectively, James Russell Lowell, Thomas Buchanan Read, JML, S. A. Godman, Edwin Percy Whipple, and James T. Fields.

[17] Following this word JML has inadvertently omitted some such noun as "step." The story was probably the historial romance, "Pedro de Padilh."

ability to better myself when wronged. For with all faith in his honor, and having a couple of lesser literary engagements which partially defrayed my current expenses, I suffered Ms after MS to be printed without mention of the pecuniary inconvenience his (supposed) carelessness subjected me to; on the contrary, at his suggestion I allowed those engagements to drop and devoted my time entirely, I may say, to his service. For which services—and with my pen alone to depend on for an income— for six months work I have received nothing."

About March the author had sent a hint up to Philadelphia. Silence. To all subsequent queries from Aiken, more silence. Finally Legaré computed that he had written six hundred dollars' worth of stories for *Graham's Magazine* (which published more of his prose than any other periodical) without receiving a cent in return. Out of frustration he appealed to the widely published occupant of "Craigie House," on Brattle Street in far-off Cambridge:

> . . . if from your position at the head of our profession in America, and experience as an author, you will counsel me what can best be done in this case: for although in a Court of Law no doubt I have abundant proof in Mr Graham's letters and in the publication of MS, to obtain a verdict, I fear the sum would be dearly purchased in the end by a violation of Christ's law; and I cannot of course truthfully threaten an appeal I have no wish to make.

Longfellow promptly sent suggestions which led Legaré to engage a lawyer in Philadelphia. The attorney was instructed to collect, but forbidden to carry the case into court. By late summer the suit was under way, but the episode left a sour taste in the mouth of the complainant. As he elucidated its effect to Longfellow, busy with his classes at Harvard:

> I should have said before, that I have felt this loss more than I should otherwise have done, because it sadly interferes with a settled purpose. It is so much the custom at the

South to fill literary posts, such as college Professorships, with New England men, that one born to the soil has slight chance of preferment until eminence of some sort has already been gained: and thus I have looked of late to letters and literary industry alone for the accumulation of such moderate means as may place me beyond *immediate* need, and so, free to write in what manner and concerning whom and what I will. There is a wide waste field here— and Mr. Simms our only novelist of much note, rather cheats us, I fear, with delusive fancies and dreams of questionable chivalry, than tells us straightly what we are and what we might be.[18]

By the spring of 1852 Graham would have succumbed to the wiles of the Philadelphia lawyer and paid up. Legaré nevertheless was constrained to inform Longfellow: "You express interest in my progress— I wish then you would forget all I have yet written — If I can help myself, I will never be a magazinist. I am too labored a writer. I write under too many disadvantages—and with too much unavoidable want of finish, when writing for a magazine—to help looking back on my printed writings with very chided vanity."[19]

It would be several years, notwithstanding, before the Aiken author ceased feeding the maw of the magazines. At this point, indeed, he was fairly embarked upon sending them what stands today as his most significant fiction, his satire. It is comprised of six tales, including Legaré's two lengthiest efforts. All but the earliest of them were very probably written during the decade of the 1850's. They appeared in print as follows:

| 1850 July | "Story of the Hà-Hà" | *Southern Literary Messenger* |
| 1851 April | "Deux Oies, Vertes" | *Graham's Monthly Magazine* |

18 JML to Longfellow, Aiken, June 9, 1851.
19 JML to Longfellow, Aiken, July 18, 1851. The letter was to advise of "the basket of peaches and nectarines which leave Charleston *tomorrow* in the 'Southerner' for you."

1853 May– July	"Miss Peck's Friend: A Novel in Ten Chapters"	*Putnam's Monthly Magazine* . . .
1854 Oct.– Nov.	"Fleur de Sillery"	*The Knickerbocker Magazine*
1855	"The Loves of Mary Jones"	*The Knickerbocker Gallery* . . . (New York, 1855)
1863 Nov.– 1864 Jan.	"Cap-and-Bells: A Novel in Ten Chapters"	*Harper's New Monthly Magazine*

Legaré's reason for composing them was probably as much to give vent to his opinions as to earn money. The fact that he chose to express his opinions through the medium of social satire provides a panorama of what one isolated but perceptive American writer found distasteful in the American scene. His target locales—where they can be identified, for locale, here, was not stressed—were, in chronological order, Charleston and the Carolina Low Country; Newport, Rhode Island; rural New York State; and Saratoga Springs, New York. The targets were those standing ones of the satirist from Lucilius' day to Thackeray's: social snobbery or frivolity in general, and the human types who practiced them.

Along the way the Carolinian found occasion—very, very occasionally, via Thackerayan asides to the reader[20]—to reveal his explicit opinions on the current state of literary practice. A triad of opinion emerges: (1) on the historical novel; (2) on plots; and (3) on the heroines of what are today classified as stories of the Sentimental School.

Concerning the historical novel Legaré pleaded for greater realism. "I cannot persuade myself," he declares, during one of his own efforts in the genre,

[20] "I like," he says, "to gossip confidentially now and then about matters which indirectly affect my characters . . . " ("Pedro de Padilh," *Graham's Magazine*, XXXVII [Sept., 1850], 145).

. . . that what is called human nature has undergone much alteration in the exchange of an iron for a broadcloth suit, and it is very certain people ate, drank and slept in those remote times much as we now do, although your stilted romancers seldom recognize the fact, and make their heroines as unlike tangible women . . . as their heroes are exemplars of the mendacious gifts of their biographers. In the matter of speech, through which we mainly receive impressions of fictitious personages, it is extraordinary what fustian is palmed on a credulous posterity, as the veritable domestic talk of nobles, knights and folks of lesser condition. There is no comedy, high or low, in the conceptions of many of these authors. . . . Every body struts around in buskins and speaks tragedy, nothing less; and as to the fooleries enacted by pages, grooms, and servitors of all kinds, there is no end to them. . . .[21]

Now, on every one of these scores Legaré had, during the course of the novella just quoted, offered counterwriting. But the novella fails. Not from lack of theory: from lack of talent to apply the theory effectively.

Concerning the plots in contemporary fiction, Legaré deplored their triteness:

Always the same scenery of brick and mortar; always the same actors whom you remember,—like indifferent acquaintances,—by their dress; always the same cockney atmosphere of smoke and cheese. And if the tale strays into the country, the house is, ten to one, a suburban one with a green gate and brass knockers; or it is only a family party from the city, out summering. So the reader must needs live over again in his magazine, the petty details of his everyday life, with scarcely ever a breath of fresh, wholesome air from the woods as Nature planted them; he must be content to stick in his holiday buttonhole, a dahlia in place of a bunch of violets.[22]

Here Legaré at least practiced his preachment to the extent of

[21] *Ibid.*, XXXVII (Aug., 1850), 92.
[22] JML, "The Lame Girl," *Sartain's Union Magazine* . . . , IX (Aug., 1851), 106.

locating his stories at rural watering places and villages. But his people, again owing to deficient artistry, are always "the same actors." This is especially true of his heroines.

"A milk-and-water heroine," said Legaré firmly, "always melancholy, and shedding a profusion of tears to evince sensibility, is the reasonable abhorrence of every sensible reader."[23] On two later occasions he reiterated his declaration of war against the Ideal Girl of the women's magazines. In "The Loves of Mary Jones" he reminds his readers: "After all, it has not been said that Miss Mary Jones was perfect, but only that [the hero] Elkhart believed her so." And in his novella, "Cap-and-Bells," he declares: "But our heroine was not perfect, as perfection goes, or she might have been chosen earlier to play the part of heroine, and the moral as well as consistency of this history no doubt impaired."[24]

The author's fire was leveled, too, against the mamas of the Ideal Girls. These mamas, such as Mary's in "The Loves of Mary Jones," are usually middle class and unhappy about it. Since, however, their husbands have made fortunes in vulgar trade (Charleston factors, Manhattan ironmongers), the mamas compensate by packing their girls off to élite institutions like "Madame Mère de Treubleu's famous school," where they are taught how to comport themselves in high-life. Too often the result is that the damsels acquire only a headful of "folly in fallow minds" (as Legaré had phrased it in "Magazines of the Day"). Worse, they may turn into "selfish, scheming, willful" coquettes like Lizzie Dodge of "Deux Oies, Vertes." It is bad enough that such ninnies are apt to elope with Old World noblemen—like Sir Desining Sneke, Bart., in "The Lame Girl" —who are apt to desert them if a fortune is not forthcoming. They are also apt to degenerate: in "Cap-and-Bells" that "wandering sultana," the Countess von Kreeper (*née* Janey Joy, a

[23] JML, "Pedro de Padilh," *Graham's Magazine*, XXXVII (Dec., 1850), 376.
[24] JML, "Cap-and-Bells," *Harper's Magazine*, XXVIII (Dec., 1863), 40.

spoiled and scapegrace Manhattan heiress), becomes an opium addict and displays "with the air of an empress, the scars on her arms."

This was what could happen if mamas propelled their girls into "advantageous" unions.

Legaré was, of course, waging war against a formidable and perduring American proclivity. As recently as 1965 the president of the McCall Corporation has gone on record with the statement: "Editorially, royalty can't fail. Minor royalty or major royalty, the American public has an insatiable curiosity about it. Kings and queens, crowned or uncrowned; princesses and consorts; dukes and footmen; palace chefs and court gardeners; they can't fail, not on an editorial page."[25]

From his secluded sphere of observation the best Legaré could do was to berate Mary Jones's mama for almost inducing her daughter to wed a New York patroon, Clarence van Trump (son and grandson of Generals), instead of the struggling young sculptor, Tom Elkhart, who really and truly loves Mary: "If the poor child had fallen into the snare," our author inquires indignantly,

> . . . who would have been to blame? Not you, of course, most excellent and moral Mrs. Jones; nor would it have been the fault of her education, of course. We Americans are intolerant of an hereditary nobility, but consent to worship any pretender. We brag of our republicanism, and cringe to self-assumed superiority. In what was this son of a patroon better than the son of a potter? and in how much and how immeasurably inferior? Observe, gentle reader, the present writer is far from believing all men equal; but let superiority be purchased by something more than lawful dollars or the counterfeit coin of assurance.

As the attaché to the French Legation, Fleur de Sillery, sums up the general situation (in the tale of that title): "Do you

25 Herbert R. Mayes, "Notes on Creative Editing," *The Writer,* LXXVIII (Feb., 1965), 19.

know it is not a bad school to study diplomacy in, that of the ball-room? Your belles represent so many blank treaties of amity and alliance, fairly transcribed and full of lies, . . . only waiting for the signature of the high contracting parties to be laid upon the shelf. . . ."[26]

In comparison with his treatment of the mamas and girls, Legaré's handling of the male types frequenting the ball rooms and spas of Vanity Fair is mild. Among them are naval officers —such as Captain Rudder and Lieutenant Felty, in "Cap-and-Bells"—who do too much maneuvering on the dance floor instead of at sea.[27] Or low-born fellows—like Prunelle and R. de la Rue Slipper, from "Fleur de Sillery" and "Cap-and-Bells," respectively—who, themselves simple tailors, visit the springs masquerading as fashionable beaux. Or mere fops, such as "Big Joe" Lamkin, of "Deux Oies, Vertes." Too often the author's satire directed against such as these is, instead of stinging, insouciant. A patina of blandness vitiates the vividness. The only eye-catching thing about them is their names (doubtless drawn from Augustan drama). All this is the more regrettable in that Legaré is undoubtedly writing from at least a small amount of first-hand knowledge.

"Fleur de Sillery", for example, is set at the Ocean House, Newport, and the Ocean House was a resort long favored by the Carolina quality. "Cap-and-Bells" is laid at Saratoga Springs, which Legaré also peoples with Carolina characters. Among these are a rising young statesman, Edward Pawley, of Saint Jude's Parish, and his political rival, Clarendon Gossimer, who is at Saratoga fortune-hunting. Whether Legaré himself ever visited the New York spa is unknown, but he must have observed similar types as a youngster at his father's establishment at Grey Sulphur Springs in Giles County, Virginia. There is little doubt that he is reporting from first-hand knowledge

---

[26] JML, "Fleur de Sillery," *The Knickerbocker Magazine*, XLIV (Nov., 1854), 497.

[27] As Secretary of the Navy in 1838 the novelist James K. Paulding had complained of just such dereliction (see CCD [3], p. 553n).

when he spins the same sort of story, with the same kind of cast, in his other ten-chapter novella, "Miss Peck's Friend."[28]

The locale of "Miss Peck's Friend" is one of the holdings of the prominent Rutridge family, "The Oaks," in the parish of Saint Jude's Santee outside Charleston. The hero is Edward Rutridge, Jr., a handsome and brainy young fellow who is running for the parish seat in the next legislature, "the influence of the family name being not yet worn threadbare." The chief episode is a sort of *fête champêtre* staged by the Rutridges at "The Oaks"—the high point of which the hero defines for Major Peck, father of the titular character, as not a joust "but what was formerly called a carrousel, and nobody is expected to do more than carry off on his lance point, a ring suspended overhead." After the carrousel there is a ball and repast on the lawn, the delicacies spread out upon maroons,[29] *i.e.,* picnic tables specially prepared by the senior Rutridge's carpenters. The plot of "Miss Peck's Friend" is less a plot than a panorama, one of contrasts between authentic aristocracy and nouveaux-riches.

Amy Peck's father is an ex-grocer who has amassed a great deal of money through his merchandizing efficiency. He has now purchased the estate of "Cornhill" and set up as a "Major" in the Fox-Brush Dragoons, though he doesn't even know how to ride. His wife is a pleasant nonentity. Their blonde, bashful Amelia is placed as a *pensionnaire* at The Priory, Goslington,

[28] It may have been this unsigned piece to which W. G. Simms referred in a postscript of a letter to JML's father, John D. Legaré, Charleston, July 24, 1859: "Please give me the titles of all his *longer* writings, in prose & verse, & especially those which were given to the press. If I mistake not, he was the author of one work in prose which was anonymously published." (See *The Letters of William Gilmore Simms,* ed. Oliphant, Odell, and Eaves, IV, 161–62.)

[29] "Miss Peck's Friend," *Putnam's Magazine,* II (July, 1853), 53. The second earliest usage of this rare word occurred in South Carolina in 1785, according to Mitford M. Mathews (ed.), *A Dictionary of Americanisms on Historical Principles,* one-volume edition (Chicago: University of Chicago Press [1956]), p. 1,030.

an exclusive girl's school conducted by Madame Mère de Treubleu.

The second male lead is C. Augustus Twitty, "that worshipper of native aristocracy." Twitty is a steady contributor of "letters from 'Our Country Correspondent' published in the Transcript, recounting VIATOR's visit to St. Jude Estates, whose proprietor's names he always printed out in capitals, and spoke of as 'My friend so-and-so'. . . ."[30] None of these characters is handled harshly by their creator. Legaré reserves his more barbed comments for certain of the Rutridges, the type of family whom C. Augustus Twitty just adored to visit.

Hero Ned's father, Colonel Edward Rutridge, Sr., is at home at "Cypress Hall," which impresses Madame Mère as equal to "a German principality in extent." The Colonel's advice to his son, when the youth finishes college and returns to the Hall, is that "first or none, should be the motto of every Rutridge, Ned."[31] To inferiors, however, he is condescension itself, since he always remembers that "a Rutridge, sir, may talk to whom he pleases, by George! and the man, sir, whoever he be, becomes lifted to my social level pending that interview. . . ." (Never mind that the Colonel has a black-sheep brother who drinks too much.) His daughters, Harriet and Hetty, endorse this attitude. But their brother is a republican gentleman.

"Has my sister Hetty," Ned inquires smilingly of Madame Mère, "been climbing the genealogical tree?" And the author permits the hero of "Miss Peck's Friend" to lecture his other

30 Compare similar locales noted by JML's father, John D. Legaré, "Account of an Agricultural Excursion Undertaken by the Editor, in the Spring of 1843," *Southern Agriculturist*, V (July–Oct., Dec., 1832), 354, 410, 469, 519, and 635ff. This fluently written narrative describes in detail the prominent planter families J. D. Legaré met during his jaunt 'round the Low Country in the Charleston area.

31 Perhaps speaking autobiographically of Saint Mary's College, Baltimore, JML says that Ned, while at college, "had indulged a taste for miscellaneous reading, at the expense of his class honors, and lost the Valedictory, although twice as well informed as the man who got it" (see "Miss Peck's Friend," *Putnam's*, I [May, 1853], 543).

sister as follows: "You are a deuced deal too haughty a girl, in my notion, Hatty. I'd like to know what sort of people your great-grandfathers were before the Revolution. Why, the Governor himself was only a ploughboy, as Cincinnatus was before him!"[32]

When Harriet sneers at Major's Peck's pretensions to lineage, Edward asks, "Do you suppose, Harriet, every white gloved hand you touched at the St. Cecilia's last February claimed kindred with our hidalgos?—Pshaw! . . . you, Hatty, imagine me a thorough leveller and demagogue, because I don't turn my back on the gratuitous courtesies of an amiable old gentleman, who made his money by sugar and salt instead of rice and cotton. . . ."

It is clear that the author who, as poet, could paean the "Stout Huguenots of yore," in "Quae Carior?," as prose writer could not forget that genealogical tree he himself had pruned so gleefully whilst in college, or that the father who had sent him there once ran a store similar to Major Peck's.

To sound out the possibilities of getting into book form a work that was probably "Miss Peck's Friend," Legaré made his first known trip to New York City. He arrived at the beginning of September, 1851. Prior to departure from Aiken he had been corresponding not only with Longfellow but also with Rufus W. Griswold; and after he reached Gotham, he presently received a letter from the reverend gentleman. "I learned, only yesterday," the Carolinian wrote Griswold in acknowledgment, "your sickness, at Stringer & Townsend's[33]—and as the pleasure of

---

[32] *Ibid.*, I (June, 1853), 623. The reference here is probably to John Rutledge (1739–1800), who served as Governor of South Carolina for the period 1779–1782. In "Deux Oies, Vertes," JML also plays on such prominent Low Country surnames as Huger and Middleton, members of both of which families were known to him (see CCD [3], p. 551n).

[33] It is JML's reference to this firm, in a note dated only "N York, Thursday morng:," which constrains assigning it to this time, since Griswold was editing the *International Magazine* for Stringer & Townsend during the period July 1, 1850–April 1, 1852. He resided at the New York

your acquaintance was one of the chiefest I promised myself in this City, I will of course ignore all ceremony and call upon you today somewhere between twelve and two."

The ailing Griswold was at the moment editing the *International Magazine,* a pot-pourri in imitation of *Littell's* along lines corresponding to Legaré's abortive *Journal of Literature,* from five years back. Presumably the two now met for the first time. (It would be interesting to know what the visitor thought of Griswold's "execution," just a year ago, of the works and character of perhaps his favorite American author, Edgar A. Poe.) It may also have been during this trip that the Carolinian paid a visit to Evert Duyckinck at that publisher's offices.

Legaré also maintained contact with Longfellow. "Your last note," he informed the Cambridge professor on September 7, "reached me in Aiken, but I reply to it somewhat more in your neighborhood. It is rather late in season to visit N York, but I have found a difficulty—common enough I suppose to all authors when the surprising complacence with which most of us begin, has given place to more earnestness and better ambition—that of reducing a MS vol to a shape less likely to affect the writer with selfcontempt and contrition, upon it's appearance in print; and after all, it is with only a third of this book completed, that I propose waiting on a publisher."

At once he got back from the sociable Brahmin an invitation to pay him a visit in Cambridge. Regretfully Legaré had to refuse, September 20: "They tell too terrible stories here of the atmosphere of seafogs which envelopes Boston and it's vicinity at this season!" Perhaps "next summer (D V) . . . if accompanied as I hope by Mrs. Legaré whom the necessary brevity of this business visit Northward, caused to remain at home."

On October 1 the visitor set out for Carolina. He had probably not succeeded in finding a publisher for his manuscript. Down in Richmond, John R. Thompson thought he knew why.

Hotel. See Joy Bayless, *Rufus Wilmot Griswold* . . . (Nashville: Vanderbilt University Press, 1943), pp. 205 and 143, respectively.

Because, Thompson put it to Griswold in a letter of December 2, 1851, "the 'Scarlet Letter' hailing from Charleston would have lined portmanteaus. Why can't Legaré find a publisher? Depend upon it, if another De Foe should emerge from the pine-barrens of Carolina, with a Robinson Crusoe under his arm, he would find an Edmund Curll in every book shop of Northern publication houses. Legaré is not De Foe, to be sure, but if he lived in New England it would be different."[34]

Whether true or not, his failure merely stirred Legaré to a wider net-casting. He resolved to seek an outlet across the Atlantic. Accordingly he dispatched the following epistle, out of the blue, to William Edmondstoune Aytoun. This Scots poet, whose popular *Lays of the Scottish Cavaliers* had appeared in the same year as Legaré's *Orta-Undis,* was professor of belles lettres at the University of Edinburgh, and contributed so frequently to *Blackwood's Magazine* that Legaré addressed him as its editor.[35] From "Aiken. S. carolina U.S. March 23 '52," he wrote:

As it is likely the names of few American magazinists cross the ocean, it may be mentioned in manner of an introduction, that I have been a paid contributor of some two or three years standing to the Knickerbocker, Literary Messenger, Graham's, and one or two other leading magazines. The past year however, has been occupied almost exclusively in the composition of a work of more worth and purpose than any preceding it; and little or no hope remaining of an International Copyright law during the present session at Washington, I wish to take what slight advantage an American author may, of the common cause existing between equally wronged parties on either side the Atlantic.

[34] Quoted from *Passages from the Correspondence . . . of Rufus W. Griswold,* ed. William M. Griswold (Cambridge, Mass.: W. M. Griswold, 1898), by Jay B. Hubbell, *The South in American Literature, 1607–1900* ([Durham, N.C.]: Duke University Press, 1954), pp. 341–42.

[35] As did most other people, including W. M. Thackeray. The editors were in fact Alexander and Robert Blackwood. See Mark A. Weinstein, *William Edmondstoune Aytoun and the Spasmodic Controversy* (New Haven and London: Yale University Press, 1968), pp. 37–38.

It is probably known to you, Sir, that—other things being equal—books *pre*published in Great Britain command thrice the sale here they might otherwise hope to do, and that the nearest approach to the advantages of foreign copyright, is to be found in the sale of MS to a trans-Atlantic Journal, and subsequent protection of the book at home. It will consequently give me much pleasure to arrange with your publishers at their usual rates per page, for the first appearance in "Blackwood" of the novel referred to above; and a sufficient portion of the MS will be forwarded to your address, should your reply prove favorable, and the terms you offer not fall short of the pay of the Magazines I have quoted: of course such terms will only be binding in the event of the MS proving satisfactory on inspection.

Of the novel—probably a thick one vol novel—allow me to say merely, that it treats of men and manners in a portion of America more closely united in interests to England than any other, through (the cotton culture and!) little recognized identity of mental education and habits of life; that the chief portraits are of living personages of more or less political and wide repute; and that you will find in the book none of those Yankeisms which some travellers would have one believe characterize all ranks in the U. States.

Au reste—it is scarcely worth mentioning, that as my best effort, I wish this work to rely upon it's own merits, and to appear with no acknowledged authorship; indeed my name could serve it no good purpose in England. And that it is conservative in principle—a claim in itself upon the good will of ancient 'Maga.'

Apparently the good will of "Maga" bestirred itself. On May 19 Legaré quizzed his more experienced Northern mentor, Henry Longfellow, as follows:

Can you tell me what is the standard of reckoning employed by English publishers—that is, whether the page designated as at so many pounds or shillings, may mean a page of print or of MS?

The truth is, I have lately received an offer from an English Editor of some note,—his rates of paying contributors being (he writes) 10£ per sixteen pages. If this means MS pages, why the rates are pretty much the same as Grahams (who, apropos of this *did* pay me at length) i.e. about eight dollars the Magazine page. But if on the other hand, the published sheet is meant—the pay is absolutely less than that of the second and third rate American Magas and newspapers. The MS I have offered I have spared neither time nor labour in producing, and should be sorry to find it obtaining less return *there,* than the hurried and silly articles I formerly sent to Graham's, to say nothing of still worse articles to lesser Journals.

Whether the rates were too low for Legaré, or some other difficulty arose, he did not appear, acknowledged or otherwise,[36] in *Blackwood's* august pages. "Miss Peck's Friend" ran in *Putnam's Magazine* at New York during the summer of 1853.

James had not abandoned his hopes of appearing in a British periodical, and had made contact with *Fraser's Magazine* in London. Concurrently he set his sights on the most prestigious American outlet of them all, *Harper's New Monthly Magazine.* With another novella, "Cap-and-Bells," now complete, Legaré journeyed to New York in the summer of 1853. There at the firm's huge nine-building complex along Cliff and Pearl streets, he sounded out Fletcher Harper. He may then have returned briefly to Carolina, or remained in Manhattan. The first week in October found him querying Harper on the latter's reaction to their talk. From his lodgings at 7, London Terrace, on West 23rd Street, Legaré had this to say, October 6:

You may recollect that some weeks since, during a conversation in your Office, you proposed to receive an article from my pen for *the* Magazine. It is not impossible that in a gentlemanly spirit of kindly regard for the supposed

[36] His name does not appear in the "List of Contributors" to *Blackwood's,* in the Department of Manuscripts, National Library of Scotland (J. S. Ritchie, Edinburgh, Sept. 18, 1962, to CCD).

vanity of a comparatively young author, you may have expressed a wish which, in the abundance of your resources, you may not care to realize, whatever the merit of the article offered may be. If however, you are still disposed to accept a MS in three numbers—about the length of my last story in "Putnam's"—it will give me much pleasure to submit it for the judgement of your Editor.[37] To be candid, this tale was not designed for American publication at all, but for Fraser's Magazine with whom I made sometime since an *optional* arrangement; and is the first of a brief series of similar tales illustrative of American society, in the end to compose a volume. Each of these stories, I have fully resolved to write up to a set standard independent of any considerations of time and labor; which I can the more readily do, as I am not dependant on my pen for maintenance.

In this connection I may be pardoned for believing the tale worthy your attention; indeed it has been re-written I cannot say how many times, cleared of superfluities and condensed, and has been in hand nearly three years, short as it is. Why I prefer offering it to your Magazine rather than Fraser's, scarcely needs an explanation. The princely amount of your pay, and the consideration of nearly two hundred thousand readers!, all counted, are selfapparent reasons.

Should you accept the Story, there are three favors I would beg;—that the authorship remain anonymous; that the first number of the three, appear in the first number of the Magazine for the New year; and that I may receive notice of the *definite* acceptance of the MS, prior to my leaving town—which will be in the course of three weeks —in order that if necessary I may otherwise dispose of it. If you will oblige me with a line to that effect I will leave the MS at your Office at an early day—the first that I go so low downtown.

I hope before leaving the city, to have the pleasure of forming the acquaintance of your son (should he return

[37] Fletcher Harper was himself the effective editor of the magazine but leaned heavily on the decisions of his chief reader, the journalist Henry J. Raymond, recent founder of the *New York Times* (1851). See Eugene Exman, *The Brothers Harper* . . . (New York: Harper & Row [1965]), p. 306 *et passim.*

from Europe soon enough)[38] and perhaps of persuading
him to visit Aiken where I cannot but believe he will be
materially benefitted in health and where I may hope to
aid in rendering his stay pleasant.

Two days later, October 8, 1853, Harper sent Legaré an
encouraging note. The Carolinian stopped by the firm's offices,
where he deposited a part of his story for perusal. Then he beat
a retreat to the balmier climate of Aiken.

In due course he mailed the remainder of "Cap-and-Bells" to
Fletcher Harper. On December 10, through the carelessness of
a day laborer, fire destroyed the entire Harper establishment.
When the news reached him at Aiken, Legaré got off a note of
inquiry as to the fate of his manuscript. Since he did not trouble
to write it until February 16, 1854, he had presumably taken
care to copy out a duplicate of his story:

> Somewhere about the time of your great calamity I sent
> you on the remainder of the MS, the first part of which I
> had placed in your hands while myself in N York. I under-
> stood you at that time to say, that the tale was acceptable
> and would be received if the second part were as good. I
> think your editor has found or will find the second portion
> *better* than the first. At all events I should be glad to learn
> whether it may be considered on file. Although I am not
> dependant on my pen for an income, the careful labor of
> some months at least, is worth a thought and inquiry; and
> independent of the higher pay of your Maga, it would be
> more agreeable to have this my most carefully finished tale
> published in a Magazine of so much larger circulation than
> Putnam's or the Knick! If your editor's decision be favor-
> able, I would also like to learn whether the *first* part of the
> MS were destroyed in the fire or accidentally saved by an
> *alibi*, for instance; in order that I may if necessary supply
> the deficiency.

[38] Either Fletcher, Jr. (1828–1890), or Joseph Wesley Harper (1827–
1886) (*ibid.*, p. 352).

Whatever the nature of Harper's reply, Legaré's novella had in fact survived the conflagration. "Cap-and-Bells" was duly published in *Harper's Magazine*. It is only a pity, for the sake of its author's self-esteem, that publication did not occur till four-and-a-half years after his death.

VII : NATIONAL POLITICS
AND PERSONAL SECURITY

The Messenger must not, most of all at this political crisis, by its fall offer another proof of the shortsighted stolidity of our people. I am fairly sick of the everlasting rant for rights about me, and arrogant neglect of what is nearest and highest!

JML to John R. Thompson,
Aiken, S.C., May 22, 1850

On March 4, 1850, James Legaré's onetime subscriber to the abortive *Journal of Literature,* John C. Calhoun, now fatally ill, sat stonily in the Senate as his "Speech on the Slavery Question," opposing Henry Clay's compromising resolutions on the extension of slavery into the territories lately acquired from Mexico, and urging equal prerogatives for the Southern states, was read for him by Senator Mason of Virginia. On March 7 Daniel Webster of Massachusetts had risen in rebuttal and delivered what became one of the better-known speeches in American oratorical annals. Across Carolina many a voice now rose clamoring for secession from Webster's fondly vaunted Union.

Upon a subject which is traditionally regarded as being close to synonymous with "Southern"—politics—at least one Southern author, James M. Legaré, had very little to say in print. He had not much more to say in private letters. His interests and his abilities lay elsewhere. It is therefore difficult to generalize with finality as to how Legaré stood on one of the most consuming passions of his day, slavery and secession, or, indeed, as to what his precise political affiliation was. Yet just five weeks before the

Webster–Calhoun confrontation he had given a rather clear indication, again to John R. Thompson, of his point of view concerning this tremendous question. In offering the Richmonder his poem "The Hemlocks," Legaré confessed that

> this poem, I am rather ashamed to say, I designed for an NYork magazine [probably *The Knickerbocker*], because it (the poem) is the best, to the prejudice of a Monthly of equal worth and possessing all the claims upon one's better feelings, which well sustained Southern excellence must, in these jealous days, exert even upon one who like myself regards with bitter hostility the firing of our common homestead's roof by demagogues and stump orators at North or South—for there are enough, and more than enough, of such at both. Heaven help us—(not we of the South—for we will be rather the best off,—but *All* of us as a great People, the first and most powerful on the globe)—in case of a Disunion![1]

The tone of these two expressions of opinion on slavery and secession is typical of the tone of all but one of Legaré's very few utterances on the subject. This tone suggests an attitude of balance and the long view. Some of the forces shaping such moderation may have begun early.

Hugh S. Legaré, educated partly in Belgium, had returned to America with an intersectional view of his nation's destiny. He had been flatly opposed to the Nullification movement of 1832 and, had he lived long enough, would probably have shared the subsequent attitude of his friend J. L. Petigru. That Charleston lawyer, James Legaré's onetime mentor, became, as the War between the States edged nearer, notorious throughout the South as the Union Man of South Carolina—a turncoat who "withstood his People [i.e., other Southerners] for his Country."[2]

[1] JML to John R. Thompson, Aiken, Feb. 1, 1850. Printed in full in CCD (1), pp. 226–28. Chapter tag printed in *ibid.*, p. 229.
[2] Latter quotation from his epitaph (by his daughter Caroline), which was published in full, shortly before emplacement of the monument at Saint Michael's Church, by the *Charleston Daily Courier*, March 19, 1868, p. 2, col. 3. It has been reprinted as "Petigru's Famous Epitaph . . . ," Richmond, Va., *Times-Dispatch*, Sept. 3, 1962, p. 8.

Possibly because of his association with two such open minds, the younger Legaré's recorded opinions on sectionalism and slavery have a moderate tone. In his fiction there are only three of them, and two occur incidentally.[3]

The first crops up, of all places, during Legaré's historical romance laid in the Azores, "Pedro de Padilh." Written about 1849, published in *Graham's Magazine* during the latter half of 1850, this narrative of derring-do between the forces of Philip II of Spain and Catherine de Medici at one point gives its author occasion to deplore the brutality inherent in all warfare (as, adds Legaré, the pacifist Elihu Burritt was also trying to show). The author then inserts, undoubtedly alluding to his native state, a castigation of "those military young men who are suffered by their employers to sport moustachios in their shops and counting-houses, and whose chief motive for advocating, in strong language, a dissolution of the Union, is supposed to lie in the admirable opportunity to be afforded of winning undying laurels in civil warfare. . . ."[4]

Legaré's second public comment on politics also emerges incidentally during the course of an historical romance. This was "Ninety Days," a novella laid at Charleston during its siege in the Revolutionary War. As Major John Harden, father of the heroine, prepares to strap on his ponderous sword and sally forth to face the Redcoats, the author injects the following observation:

> Such a blade the major used as I found too heavy to flourish when a boy; it had done its duty in the elder times

[3] In contrast to the estimate that during the decade 1850–1860 no fewer than twenty-six pro-slavery novels were written by Southerners or Southern sympathizers, of which sixteen appeared in 1852–1854 as direct rebuttals to *Uncle Tom's Cabin* (see Thomas D. Jarrett, "William Grayson's 'The Hireling and the Slave': A Study of Ideas, Form, Reception, and Editions" [Ph.D. dissertation, University of Chicago, 1947], pp. 56–57).

[4] JML, "Pedro de Padilh," *Graham's Magazine,* XXXVII (Oct., 1850), 234. JML affirms that people feel the real shock of warfare only when they lose dear ones, as did "more than one acquaintance of mine, now wearing premature widow's-weeds, in the late Mexican war."

and was reposing among the antiquated china on a back shelf of our seldom disturbed pantry. There it was I discovered the veteran rusted in its worm-eaten leathern sheath, and laid childish hands upon it; I think its touch stirred up some martial associations of my ancestry at the first, but after a while I took to hacking wood with it, and in the end it was thrown aside and lost doubtless in some rubbish heap. After all, it only went a little before its time; for you know, brothers, from Maine to New Mexico we are throwing away our Revolutionary swords which we once drew together, and are forging others with less holy design.[5]

"Ninety Days" ran in *Graham's Magazine* for January–February, 1851. Six months later, in apprising Longfellow of that same George Graham's knavery and referring to the latest manuscript story the publisher had failed either to return or acknowledge, Legaré observed:

> I can suppose but one cause for it's suppression: If Mr Graham has it in view to court Southern subscriptions by employment of Southern writers, it is possible my last unhappy Story may have appeared ill suited to his purpose.[6] There was more truth than flattery in it's pages, wholesome truth which by God's grace I will write to the last. If more of it had been told hitherto by those whose proper business it was—if the mental indifference and sloth almost characterising this section of the Union, had been long since written unsparingly against; and erroneous views and traits of fanciful Southern life not portrayed by our sectional novelists—this my native State would not now be proving itself a modern La Mancha and at the mercy of a handful of political demagogues.

Among those demagogues was an individual Legaré went quite out of his way to slam. The slam—his third published commentary on things political—occurs during the course of "Cap-and-Bells. A Novel in Ten Chapters." Laid at Saratoga

---

[5] JML, "Ninety Days," *Graham's Magazine*, XXXVIII (Jan., 1851), 57.
[6] Possibly "Fleur de Sillery," which finally ran in *The Knickerbocker* in late 1854—JML's only known prose contribution to "The Old Knick." For commentary see CCD (3), pp. 555–56.

Springs, New York, written about 1853, this novella is one of its author's two longest pieces of fiction, both of which are satirical surveys of American society in the manner of Thackeray. The individual slammed is ex-Senator, ex-Congressman "Robert Gossimer Gossimer" of South Carolina (who does not figure directly in the plot). We are told that the Senator used up his own and his wife's patrimonies, was always in debt, had a fine town residence but a large estate in the red, owned shares in a bank, but you never learned which bank, etc.

> He signed himself in full in tavern registers and at the foot of party squibs, although, politically speaking, his reputation might have been then represented by a cipher. Indeed, the distinguished gentleman had overshot his mark in the memorable campaign of '51, and had carried his inflammatory oratory to such a pitch that he fell into disrepute when civil war ceased to be meditated, and common sense and commerce joined hands with patriotism for the maintenance of peace. He had been trying ever since to regain his footing; but the past convulsion had brought to the surface other men, and better, perhaps; and, speechify as he would, the people declined on the whole to restore their former champion his arms. He persevered, however, and attended all political meetings and dinners in his parish; returning home from the latter sittings, when protracted, looking much like himself—he usually went to such places looking very *unlike,* with hair roughed back, in ostentatious likeness of a GREAT MAN who had been his contemporary, and wearing an honest face.[7]

Matching all this against ascertained biography, the odds are that "Robert Gossimer Gossimer" is ex-Senator, ex-Congressman Robert Barnwell Rhett, whom many people disliked for personal as well as political reasons. (In 1851 the Beaufort planter, William Elliott, was referring to Rhett as "this bellowing mooncalf. . . .") One of the Fire-Eaters, Rhett was Mr. Secession,

[7] JML, "Cap-and-Bells," *Harper's Magazine,* XXVII (Nov., 1863), 783. The "great man" was probably John C. Calhoun, who had died March 30, 1850, and to whose Senate seat Rhett had succeeded the following December.

glorified, to South Carolinians. If it was for this reason that Legaré lambasted him, then the lambasting proved unanticipatedly ironic: its appearance in print was in a Northern periodical and in the month of November, 1863, when the Confederacy for which Rhett had yearned was entering some of its darkest days.

It was also in 1853 that James Legaré gave voice to his fullest private utterance on the subject of slavery, quixotically enough to a Northerner. It occurred in a letter to Henry Longfellow, upon Legaré's learning that the English novelist, William Makepeace Thackeray—he had arrived in America in November, 1852, for a lecture tour—was contemplating a Southern jaunt. Longfellow, who attended two of the lectures and presently dined with the novelist at James Russell Lowell's, had apparently written something about the famous man's passing near the Aiken area and perhaps meeting with Legaré. In commenting on the proposal Legaré responded, January 15, 1853:

> It will give me sincere pleasure to receive Mr Thackeray as a guest here sometime during his journey South—but how to do so without your friendly aid, I'm sure I do not know; for our countrymen are so notorious now for their lionizing propensities, that foreigners of any distinction at all, are, or ought to be, always on their guard. If I were to write directly to Mr Thackeray, very likely he would suppose the invitation to proceed from one of these sort of people, and return a polite refusal. If you would (with or without mention of this odd enough request on my part,— as you please) offer Mr Thackeray a note of introduction to myself, that would remove all difficulty, and believe me will be an attention I will gratefully remember.
>
> I *do* wish to speak to Mr T, at leisure, if only for a few days or a few hours. Apart from the earnest sympathy I feel in all he had done and said,—I had almost said; and on second thoughts why shouldn't I?—affection with which we invariably mention his name in our family,—apart from all this I wish to say to him in person, a few words which may have their weight, being *true* words, even from me. If this masterly mind, in it's wonderful knowledge of

character and what goes to make up character, should return to England (as did one before him) befooled in regard to a vile but hopelessly necessary American institution, by recitals of individual atrocities here and there, but gathered into bulk, which I and all of us here shudder to recognize as true—*individually* true and *far between*—no less than you do there; if he were to do this, without seeing with his own eyes and weighing it all in the judgement I so highly respect—I do not know how sad and pained I may be. You know I am but a young man—on the eve of thirty; too young to write with authority on so grave a text —yet. But I have been and am gradually contracting my circle of study to this one centre, and would lay aside other composition but for the necessity of providing an income. Well, one of these days I will write of this Slavery[,] as all who have yet written seem too prejudiced or feeble. God knows and will I pray remedy the evil already done our Country—I mean our whole country—by falsehoods of commission and omission from both North and South; and how great a necessity exists for the plain truth and all of it to be told for once. Have I bored you with this harangue? Pray forgive the digression and let us go back to the purpose of this note.

Longfellow's answer, March 15, 1853, advised that Thackeray had left Boston ere Legaré's letter arrived and that since he knew him so slightly anyway, the Cambridge author had decided to abandon the matter.

"How is your health this winter?" the master of "Craigie House" inquired, "and are you coming northward in the course of the year? How much I should like to see you. Ah! would that the North and South knew each other better! My heart has a southern side to it, as I am sure yours has a northern. We would speak of Slavery I am sure, *sans peur et sans reproche!*" Firmly, though never flamboyantly, anti-slavery, Longfellow had offered his *Poems on Slavery* (1842) to the cause of abolition, and only three weeks prior to writing Legaré had entertained the Stowes at dinner.

As things turned out, Thackeray did not reach the Southerner's area at this time. On his second American tour, in 1855–
1856, he did indeed pass through Augusta, Georgia, but whether
Legaré met him then is unknown. In any event it is most unlikely that the Carolinian ever put on paper his own conception
of that "vile but hopelessly necessary American institution."

Meanwhile his "necessity of providing an income"—as he had
reminded Longfellow, in passing—had been met for the nonce.
During the first week in April, 1852, John D. Legaré had
resigned his appointment as Postmaster of Aiken and was presently named one of the South Carolina commissioners to super-
vise the State's contributions to the New York World's Fair, to be
staged at the Crystal Palace in 1853–1854.[8] Before stepping
down, the elder Legaré contrived to get the vacant post turned
over to his son (this was during the closing months of the Fill-
more Administration). James retained the appointment, which
was probably no sinecure, for a little over a year, until July 22,
1853, when the new Pierce Administration ejected him. Though
he had been "in" only one fourth as long as his father, the ten-
ure nevertheless brought him a total salary of $277.93.[9]

Although Legaré, for reasons best known to himself, saw fit to
advise Fletcher Harper in February, 1854—during their negotiations for the novella "Cap-and-Bells"—that he was "not dependant on my pen for an income," the tapping of income sources
rarely ceased to be of concern to him. One of these he had had
at the back of his mind since at least the spring of 1851. Circumstances now constrained him to test its feasibility. On July 3,
1854, he despatched an appeal on the subject to his New England counselor, Henry Longfellow:

[8] See the Charleston *Courier,* June 28, 1853, p. 2, col. 3. Other commissioners included Col. Wade Hampton, R. F. W. Allston, the future
governor, and Stewart Adair Godman.

[9] JML was removed from his interim appointment in favor of one Bethel
T. Rogers (see Post Office Department "Journal," XXXI, 67, and the
biennial *Official Register of the United States* [Washington: Department
of State, 1853], p. 272; Industrial Records Branch, National Archives,
Washington).

Prof: Scherb has informed me that the lately vacated Professorship of Belles Lettres in the University of Georgia (at Athens), will be filled at the next meeting of the Trustees, on or about the first of August approaching; and has strongly urged upon me to become a candidate. To do so with success, as there are several other applicants, it is very essential that I should produce the best testimonial to my literary ability; and I presume the fact of my whole life thus far having been employed in literary studies and occupations, should have it's influence. It cannot fail to be of great service to me under these circumstances, should the opinion you may entertain of the literary *promise* apparent in what I have hitherto written, allow you to address a recommendation on my behalf to the Board of Trustees; although the anonymous publication of my later writings in Putnam's and elsewhere, may preclude so just an estimate as I might prefer. Should I obtain this Professorship, I may anticipate a more worthy as well as more successful literary career than while, as at present, constrained to write with less regard for my inclination and any end in view, than to the saleable nature of the article produced. It is for this reason, a matter of the greatest concern to me that I should be successful in this application; and I have every reason to feel confidence in the result of a recommendation from yourself whose fame belongs to no one section of our Country. Let me only beg further, that should your friendship not fail me at this juncture, you will enclose such recommendations as your kindness may suggest, in a *sealed envelope,* that I may forward it *unopened* to the Board; for on account of the freedom it allows the writer, such testimony must greatly outweigh any other, besides being more agreeable to the applicant forwarding the same.

Whether Longfellow got off the recommendation is unknown. As it happened, he himself had long since come to detest teaching and on April 19 had, to his vast relief, delivered his final lecture at Harvard.

In any event, and despite Legaré's rejoicing in honorary membership in a University of Georgia society, the professorship went at last to Georgia-born Richard Malcolm Johnston, one year his senior and the future author of *Georgia Sketches.* . . . To salve the wound came the appearance this same year, 1854, of a little item that would serve indirectly to boost James's name to the head of a list once more.

The item was a defense of slavery and a slap at Mrs. Stowe, published by John Russell at Charleston. It was noteworthy not for its arguments—they were already commonplace—but its form. It was written in heroic couplets. This was the Beaufort lawyer William J. Grayson's plantation-oriented *The Hireling and the Slave* (dedicated to Legaré's onetime mentor, Petigru). In reviewing a second edition of this effusion, John R. Thompson's *Southern Literary Messenger* proclaimed that its appearance only added to the standing refutation of the North's claim that belles lettres could not flourish coequally with slavery. Why, said the *Messenger,* "the more intemperate of the Anti-Slavery writers have affected to sneer at the South as intellectually sterile, in the face of Legare, Wilde, Pinkney, Poe, Tucker, Simms, Meek, the Cookes, Miss Hawes—indeed of a host of the most popular and successful essayists, novelists and poets that the country has produced."[10]

To be placed at the head of such a "host" must have gratified Legaré. As it happened, however, his interest in belles lettres was, by this summer of 1856, almost as outdated as Grayson's choice of verse forms. Conversely his advocacy of Grayson's thesis—that slavery was a beneficial institution—would seem to be waxing. This may be inferred if we take literally the implication of his statements to an old acquaintance, James H. Hammond (with whom no lasting bitterness had lingered from their mésalliance of seven years back). The planter was now in the United States Senate from South Carolina, and Legaré was attempting to snare his interest in subsidizing certain projects.

[10] "Editor's Table," *Southern Literary Messenger,* XXIII (Aug., 1856), 155.

Hammond, who would resign grandiloquently from his Senate seat upon the election of Abraham Lincoln to the Presidency, gave voice at Washington on March 4, 1858, to what became the most celebrated shibboleth of Dixie. Replying to a speech by Senator Seward of New York, the Carolinian remarked that, in his opinion, cotton was king. He had not originated the phrase, but it kindled the national fancy to the extent that its utterance is today the only reason his name is recalled.

It was about this speech that James Legaré, addressing Hammond from Aiken, March 22, 1858, on another subject, thought it well to declare:

"You may be sure, dear Sir, that all of your friends both here and down the country 'hurra'd bravely' when you ran that grand tilt the other day, against Northern Fanaticism and Humbug. Everybody asked Everybody—'Have you read Gov Hammond's Speech?' Well, give us who know you personally, the credit of not having been in the least surprised, however much we were pleased while reading."

Here is the only ostensibly "unbalanced" statement James Legaré is known to have expressed on the subject of politics. It is well to recall that the statement was expressed in a communication to an important figure whose aid the writer was hoping to attract. For at least six years his mind had been increasingly preoccupied by a new and different field of endeavor. It had now become his major concern. With any luck, it might bring him that personal security he and Annie had so rarely known.

VIII: ARTIST TO INVENTOR NEAR ALLIED

The Government of the late United States recognized the originality and uses of his discoveries, and we believe that he secured patent rights for all his inventions, that were perfected. From our South Carolina Institute he obtained the honor of a gold medal. Here his career was stopped by death, and we are reminded of the touching lament of MILTON in Lycidas. On the very verge of fame, and possibly fortune, and the great eminence in sight—

> "Came the blind Fury with th'abhorred shears,
> And slit the thin spun life."

But his works remain, and we have full faith that the gradually advancing future will crown his name with an enduring reputation, while others will succeed in applying his discoveries and inventions to the advantages and necessities of his country. It appears to us that this is the very time when some of these may be made available to the people of the Confederate States.

[W. Gilmore Simms],
"Domestic Resources," Charleston *Mercury*, Nov. 29, 1861

Legaré's interest in mechanical invention first stirred itself about 1847, a year or so after the family had settled at Aiken. He explained to James H. Hammond, in a letter written in the spring of 1859:

> About twelve years ago my attention was first accidentally directed to mechanical invention, and after some years of vague and useless experiment—for the most part given to a search after Perpetual Motion, that Syren of inventors, from whose fascinations even practical George

Stephenson did not escape for many a year—I at length
settled down upon a conclusion which I have not since
abandoned, viz: of making the principle of the hydrostatic
paradox, a *motive,* rather than as now employed, a *passive,*
power. In endeavoring to realize this idea the past ten years
of my life have been consumed. In it's pursuit I have sunk
all I had or could earn from time to time (for mechanical
experiments are especially expensive) by painting, or by
writing for the magazines, or by drawing lessons, for two
years, to a couple of pupils: one year I even tried a class
of "finishing" young ladies, but these last occupied more
time than I could spare, and had to be relinquished. By
such like shifts I contrived to work along without getting
irretrieveably into debt, confiding my secret and purpose to
no one, and bearing the misery of repeated failures as best
I could. Some of these failures are dreadful to look back
to; as when after a long series of successful experiments
backed by a no less promising series of figures, the results
of many months of thought and study, by a single final
calculation or by the unlooked-for result of some final ex-
periment, I would find the invention I had thought on the
point of being perfected, only a heap of mental rubbish,
and myself bankrupt in purse and, as it seemed to me, in
mind.[1]

Legaré had, about 1852, set up a shop or laboratory adjacent
to his cottage on his parents' Laurens Street property. There he
was, in due course, sought out by various inquirers. Among these
may have come in person another onetime sponsor with whom
bitterness had arisen, William Gilmore Simms. Simms, too, with
the years had chosen to forget their estrangement, and was
pleased eventually to assert in the public prints: "To those who
visited him in his modest workshop at Aiken, his applications of

[1] JML to James Henry Hammond, Aiken, May 15, 1859. Less well
acquainted with Hammond than was JML, John D. Legaré also wrote
him (from Aiken, Feb. 5, Feb. 22, 1858) requesting a set of the twelve-
volume Congressional compilation, *The Exploration and Survey for the
Pacific Rail Road.* (James H. Hammond Papers, Vol. XXII, Library of
Congress.)

ordinary material to works of ingenuity and art, were a source of
continued surprise."[2]

As often happens, some of the applications were a surprise to
the inventor. Legaré's *magnum opus,* toward which his mind
and energy increasingly swung, was a scheme for perfecting an
air-powered engine that would not only undersell the steam
variety but present less danger in operation. During the endless
experiments aimed at this goal he beguiled himself from repeated
failure by dabbling in related fields. As a result, he came up with
three quite different inventions. Two of these earned him United
States patents and in turn steered his inquiries onto two more
devices.

In their approximate order of discovery the Carolinian's principal inventions were: (1) "a PLASTIC FIBRE of great variety
of application, best known as Plastic-Cotton, though cotton,"
Legaré cautioned Senator Hammond, "is only one of it's resources"; (2) an ivory-frame composition, developed as a substitute for the glue-and-whiting compound conventionally utilized
by frame makers; (3) encaustic tiles, in color, for use on floors
and other areas; (4) a light, cushionless easy-chair for reading;
(5) a cheap, non-water-soluble glazier's putty.

The plastic fibre, to which Legaré gave the label of "lignine"
—that is, lignin, a substance related physiologically to cellulose
and constituting the essential part of woody tissue—cost him
seven years' labor. Perfecting the ivory-frame composition required six.[3] He stumbled onto the nature of the putty while
doing his frame research. The idea for the tiles came as he was
experimenting in the manufacture of artificial stone from the
Chalk Hill area around Aiken, amid those same vistas he had

2 [Simms], "Domestic Resources," Charleston *Mercury,* Nov. 29, 1861,
p. 1, col. 2.

3 JML gives these estimates in a letter dated Charleston, Nov. 21, 1857,
correcting the editors of the *Daily Courier* for a statement in their issue of
that day that his inventions on exhibit at the Industrial Institute Fair were
confined to plastic-cotton items. There was a variety, JML pointed out,
each one "a totally distinct product of years of research . . ." (*Courier,*
Nov. 24, 1857, p. 2, col. 3).

admired during his strolls with Anne and which still lured him occasionally to his easel, stool, and malstick. Of the lot it was the plastic fibre that excited widest interest. Simms has described it clearly:

PLASTIC COTTON

By this invention, he solidified the common cotton fibre, by certain chemical agents, which constituted the secret of his discovery. This material, thus prepared, is, at first, so plastic, that it may be moulded by the hand, or by a lathe, or in a frame, and worked into any shape. When dried, the substance became durable and hard, and wore a fine lustrous polish, like a metal. According to the preparations of the materials used, the Plastic Cotton was adapted to various uses. It took the impression of the die. It might be wrought into figures, statues, for exposure in garden grounds, in the open air, or into the most beautiful statuettes for library and parlor—for chimney and table ornament, for decoration of walls, and cornices and ceiling, for furniture, picture frames, and, in brief, every kind of household ornamental work.[4]

The little Laurens Street household served as Legaré's test-stand. The bedroom fireplace was graced with a cotton-fiber mantel and supporting festoonery featuring a human face with a tiny baby for a nose (still to be viewed). Legaré also decorated a pair of wood console tables. A set of shelves, probably a curio cabinet, bore at the top plastic embellishments of a knight's casque and helmet, with vizor open; in the centre was a figure of Petrarch, beneath whom knelt two cowled monks flanking a

---

[4] [Simms], "Domestic Resources," Charleston *Mercury*, Nov. 29, 1861, p. 1, col. 2. JML's invention is not to be confused with products of today's "plastics" industry, which is essentially a modern development (though initially explored in the early 1830's in Europe by French and Swedish chemists). Plastics are resins in their molded form, and all natural products, such as cotton, are excluded from the definition. The modern industry results from an integration of many and unrelated fields of knowledge, including biology, optics, physics, and ancillary disciplines. See Edward L. Kropa, "Plastics," *Encyclopaedia Britannica* (23 vols., Chicago and elsewhere: Encyclopaedia Britannica, Inc., 1969), XVIII, 1–12.

PLASTIC-COTTON FURNITURE BY J. M. LEGARÉ
From among the items designed and fabricated by Legaré,
now at the Charleston Museum, Charleston, South Carolina.

monochrome of Westminster Abbey. The largest item, fashioned entirely of the lignine, was a screen seven feet high in the shape of an oak tree, its leaves intertwined with grape vines. Almost one hundred years later this creation caught the fancy of the features editor of a Charleston paper, who published a large cut of the screen, with the caption, "Plastics: New?"[5]

Sideboards, what-nots, vases, and other items either decorated with or made of the plastic fibre emerged over the years. Some of these Legaré presented to friends; occasionally he instructed Aiken girls in their manufacture.[6] One of the last designs to stir his whim was—as a witness at first doubtful of its success admitted—"a wreath of flowers in *relievo;* but we confess also that the single specimen was conclusive."[7]

Though it is not known whether Legaré tried his hand at sculpting, neither is it surprising, in view of the dexterity just described, that sculptors and their work occasionally stirred him to comment. In his gossipy letter of 1849 to the New York journalist Thomas Powell, the Carolinian had declared: "After all, it is more consistent to write, as Mr Greenough does (did), 'faciebat' than 'fecit' on one's work." In his novella, "Miss Peck's Friend," of 1853, Legaré calls his heroine "a little brunette angel . . . oh ye [Hiram] Powers!" The hero of his tale, "The Loves of Mary Jones," in *The Knickerbocker Gallery* . . . (1855), is a sculptor, and of his chef d'oeuvre in marble his creator has something extraneous to say. Journeying to and from New York, Legaré undoubtedly passed through Washington City. There, at the East Front of the Capitol, he could view the

[5] Charleston *Evening Post,* July 10, 1953 (B-1). One assumes that this is the same screen as described by Catherine Morgan of Aiken, "Life of James Mathewes Legare," Aiken, S. C., *Standard and Review,* Feb. 13, 1942. All four pieces are in storage at the Charleston Museum, presented in 1919 by Emma Susan Gilchrist, of Charleston, to whom JML's brother Joe had given them. (See [Laura M. Bragg], "Cotton Furniture," *Bulletin of the Charleston Museum,* XV [Dec., 1919], 76–77.)

[6] Such as an aunt of Mary H. Ravenel, of Aiken (see Catherine Morgan, "Life of James Mathewes Legare").

[7] According to "Gossyp," Charleston *Daily Courier,* June 9, 1858 (see n. 28, below).

"Discovery Group" by the Italian sculptor Luigi Persico, erected in 1844. What Legaré saw he did not like, and accordingly an aside to the readers of his story advises them:

> But let us all hope, for our hero's sake, that *this* great work may not resemble the wonderful pantomime in marble of COLUMBUS perpetually performing on the steps of the national Capitol, which does so much credit to the taste of the committee who accepted it, and is so much more laughable than any pantomime that was ever acted before.[8]

Shaping either marble or "plastic cotton" required the instinct of an artist. Legaré's lignine, moreover, was capable of adaptations impossible to stone, as Gilmore Simms informed readers of the Charleston *Mercury:*

> . . . his discovery went a great deal further, and by other modifications of his preparation, he extended its employment into the utilitarian. He applied it to the roofing of houses, as a substitute for shingles, tin or slate. He claimed its superiority over all—insisting that his roof of plastic cotton was impervious to water, and incombustible under fire. We have accounts, from private individuals, of numerous experiments which they have seen, in which this material effectually resisted both these elements. Of course it requires to be laid on in proper condition, and by a capable hand. All material requires skillful use, and it is sometimes the case that a failure is reported in an experiment, where the primary conditions of the artist or discoverer have not been complied with.[9]

[8] JML had good company in his opinion. On March 18, 1837, James Kirke Paulding had advised President Van Buren against the employment of Persico because the artist's work was so inferior (Van Buren Papers, Vol. XXVI, Manuscript Room, Library of Congress). On Dec. 23, 1834, J. F. Cooper had expressed a similar sentiment to William Cullen Bryant and William Leggett, editors of the New York *Evening Post* (see James F. Beard [ed.], *The Letters and Journals of James Fenimore Cooper* [Cambridge: Harvard University Press, 1960—], III, 80 and n.).

[9] [Simms], "Domestic Resources," Charleston *Mercury,* Nov. 29, 1861, p. 1, col. 2. Curiously, JML's invention is not carried in M. D. Leggett (comp.), *Subject-Matter Index of Patents for Inventions Issued by the United States Patent Office from 1790 to 1873, inclusive* (3 vols., Washington: Government Printing Office, 1874), II, 1,078, where, of six other

During the summer of 1856 a more than casually curious visitor entered the Aiken cottage. This was William M. Lawton, banker, cotton factor, and president of the Industrial Institute at Charleston. Founded in 1849 by the engineer and Citadel professor, General Abbott H. Brisbane, the Institute Fair each autumn had become a commercial attraction luring exhibitors and inventors from all over South Carolina and adjoining states. Lawton was so struck by Legaré's handiwork he urged him to set examples before the public. In mid-November, accordingly, the inventor journeyed down to Charleston and the Fair Hall on Meeting Street.[10]

He brought with him the reading chair; an engraver's portfolio described as "modeled in wood, Emperor Hadrian, style of the Renaissance"; and what was listed as an Illustrative Library Screen (doubtless the one discussed above). "They are," said the Charleston *Courier* during its coverage of the exhibition, "now occupying a conspicuous position, and eliciting general admiration."[11] Legaré also consented to serve as judge in Department #2, Letter B (agricultural and mechanical machines and inventions), together with the Charlestonians William Middleton, William Seabrook, and Grange Simons.[12]

By the time the Fair ended he had captured the highest award in Department #11 (household furniture). The premium judges—John May, Frederick Richards, and Charles Kerrison—decreed as follows: "J. M. Legare, for an invention by which Cotton is made useful in the construction of fancy furniture, pictures, frames, &c. The Board consider this invention as worthy of great praise for its cheapness, durability and appropriateness. It has stood the test of several years of usage as furniture, is nearly incombustible, and becomes very hard by time. They award a gold medal."[13]

"plastic" listings, the earliest, by a Massachusetts inventor, was not patented until 1860.

[10] See the Charleston *Courier*, Nov. 20, 1856, p. 1, col. 1.

[11] *Ibid.*, Nov. 22, 1856, p. 1, col. 2.

[12] *Ibid.*, Nov. 27, 1856, p. 2, col. 2.

[13] *Ibid.*, Dec. 5, 1856, p. 1, col. 3.

In another section of the Fair another of Legaré's talents was being recognized. This was the painting exhibition. It attracted many artists, professional or amateur, including such well-known Charlestonians as John B. White, Richard Yeadon, Charles Fraser, and Mrs. Samuel Gilman (past editor of the *Southern Rosebud* and wife of the minister who wrote the college song "Fair Harvard"). Legaré had submitted four entries. One of these, a landscape he entitled *A Winter Scene,* was commended by the *Courier:* "The drawing is quite artistical, and the general finish of an order which, with a longer study of color, may be considered eminently high." Of a genre piece the paper declared: *"Kids in the Cornfield,* a rural scene, . . . is regarded by practiced eyes as exquisite in conception and well delineated."[14]

Legaré's two other entries were a second landscape, *Spring,* and an historical painting, *Perry's Expedition to Japan.* (Here we wonder if Legaré had toiled as long over its creation as did the hero of his story "The New Aria"? Like Washington Allston on *Belshazzar's Feast,* artist Harry struggled almost four years on his enormous canvas *The Story of Aria and Paetus Caecinna, of Padua.*)[15] The awards committee was made up of James Rose, Barnwell Heyward, T. C. Hutchinson, Dr. Elias Horlbeck, and Nathan R. Middleton (who next year would become president of Legaré's alma mater, the College of Charleston). For *Spring* and *Perry's Expedition to Japan* the judges awarded the Aiken artist a premium.[16]

By the late 1850's the bookstore of John Russell on King Street had become something of a Charleston institution. While

[14] "Walk around the Gallery of Paintings," *ibid.,* Nov. 26, 1856, p. 1, col. 2. All of JML's paintings have disappeared.

[15] The theme for this painting JML could have found in Pliny, Martial, or Tacitus. Benjamin West had exhibited his canvas *Paetus and Arria* at London in 1773, and François A. Vincent had done likewise at Paris in 1785. (See Bernard Denver, "Benjamin West and the Revolution in Painting," *Antiques,* LXXI [April, 1957], 348–49, and *The Autobiography of John Trumbull,* ed. Theodore Sizer [New Haven: Yale University Press, 1953], p. 111.)

[16] Charleston *Courier,* Dec. 5, 1856, p. 1, col. 3.

swains nuzzled their damozels among the rare editions in a
murky corner, the intelligentsia foregathered at the rear of the
shop and, in armchairs round the stove, exchanged good talk.
The first issue of *Russell's Magazine* would appear in April,
1857, with the twenty-six-year-old Charlestonian Paul H. Hayne
as editor; and Russell would persuade the politician, poet, and
lawyer William J. Grayson to write the leader for it.[17] James
Legaré's onetime legal mentor J. L. Petigru was also an occasional browser at the store. Petigru's Sunday-night dinners for
visiting celebrities such as Thackeray or Sir Charles Lyell—
whose presence in America had been noted by Legaré in "Cap-
and-Bells"—were famous.[18] Did our artist-inventor find a seat at
this prominent citizen's board? Perhaps. Yet these days Legaré's
inclinations were less cultural than scientific. His reading, these
days, while it might include Tennyson's *Poetical Works* or
George W. Curtis' *Prue and I,* also included Appleton's *Dictionary of Machines, Mechanics, Enginework, and Engineering*
and James Napier's *Manual of Electrometallurgy.*[19]

By now Legaré had gotten his frame composition, claim for
the invention of which he held under caveat, tested by a manufacturing firm in New York. A contract for its production was
about to be signed, "which . . . would have placed me in pos-

[17] See Paul H. Hayne, "Ante-Bellum Charleston," *Southern Bivouac,*
n.s. I (Nov., 1885), 327–36. John Russell's personally annotated set of his
Magazine (1857–1860), in the New York Public Library, does not reveal
JML's name as an anonymous contributor. That Hayne had met JML is
almost certain, since the lead article in "Editor's Table," *Russell's Magazine,* July, 1859, noticing JML's death, is very probably by editor Hayne.
When Longfellow was assembling titles for his anthology *Poems of Places*
and desired an item on Tallulah Falls, Hayne responded by mailing him
from "Copse Hill" in May, 1878, a volume of verse by Mrs. Margaret
Preston of Virginia and "also, a little book by *James Legaré* of S.C. a
nephew [sic] of the illustrious Hugh S. Legaré, who died in 1843, you may
remember . . ." (see *A Collection of Hayne Letters,* ed. D. M. McKeithan
[Austin: University of Texas Press, 1944], p. 158).

[18] According to Joseph Blyth Allston, in his review of Grayson's *James
Louis Petigru: A Biographical Sketch* (New York: Harper & Brothers,
1866), in the Baltimore, Md., *New Eclectic Magazine,* VII (Nov., 1870),
615.

[19] See, respectively, nos. 36, 3, 55, and 59 in CCD (4).

session of a small fortune (for me)" as he informed James H.
Hammond. Suddenly, in August, the Panic of 1857 exploded.
This put a stop to all negotiations. Then Legaré fell ill once
more and could do nothing about reviving them. He recovered
somewhat and with the approach of fall again made the journey down to Charleston and the Industrial Institute Fair.

This time an entire section was given over to his exhibits.
Situated at the southeast corner of the main hall, near the door
leading to the rear stairway, a large table was covered with
specimens, models, and patterns of the plastic-fiber, ivory-frame,
putty, and tile devices.[20] In its issue for Wednesday, November
25, 1857, the *Daily Courier* allotted the major space of its
front-page article on the Fair to "the varied and wonderful
inventions presented by JAMES M. LEGARÉ, Esq., of Aiken. . . ."

The cotton adaptation received most attention. Reminding its
readers that the samples shown last year had not at the time
been rendered fully waterproof for roofing purposes, the *Courier*
now disclosed:

> Specimens are exhibited this year, however, of cotton pre-
> pared to resist all weathers, and in two or more stages of
> preparation, the finished roofing being considered quite
> fire-proof, and the unfinished sufficiently so to resist every
> thing short of direct conflagration. All refuse cotton of mills
> and plantations is thus made useful, and the whole cost of
> laying it in, exclusive of labor and lumber, amounts to but
> $2 @ $4 per square, depending on the number of *layers*
> employed.
>   It must be remembered that this falls short of the cost of
> common shingles. Mr. L's close labor in his laboratory and
> a temporary break down in health have caused some delay
> in having the plastic cotton roofing employed to any extent,
> as he rightly judged that a novelty should be first worked
> under the inventor's eye; but we understand that two or
> more houses in this city and several elsewhere are awaiting
> his earliest leisure to inspect the laying on of the new
> material; among the latter a new hotel in Aiken, and the

[20] Charleston *Courier,* Nov. 21, 1857, p. 2, col. 3.

new Methodist Church in the same place. Mr. L. has also entered, we believe, into arrangements for testing its application to car tops—the extreme toughness of this fibrous covering being a great recommendation. At all events, the inventor proposes to test its advantages on the largest scale this current year, and under his own superintendence . . . .

Turning to the ivory-frame composition, the *Courier* declared:

The consumption of this material throughout the Union is immense, amounting perhaps to many hundred thousands in value yearly; for not only is it applied to frame making generally, but to the manufacture of ornate furniture, and interior decorations of houses, ships, &c. This invention of Mr. L.'s has been tested by manufacturers in New York, who have, in every case, pronounced it superior to the compositions now in use, apart from the great advantage of costing but one-fourth the price of the old. We understand that an eminent firm are ready to enter into a highly satisfactory arrangement with Mr. L. as soon as matters can be adjusted.

We are free to say that it was while conducting the above investigation, and with no such purpose in view, Mr. L. obtained what is called in the catalogue "pound putty," probably because its wholesale value is stated at one cent per pound, while but a fraction of a pound of the ordinary glazier's putty can be produced at that cost; at all events, a distinguishing nomenclature is all that is needed. That it works smoothly, is not dissolved by water, and the like, may be sufficiently seen by the specimens exhibited; and its cheapness, we suppose, will especially recommend it in cases where great quantities of putty are used, as, for example, in the beds for steam boilers, or certain kinds of stone laying.

Coming lastly to the inlaid tiles, the *Courier* thought they might well constitute the most significant of all Legaré's inventions. Prevented by his health from personally overseeing the construction of proper castings in metal and earthenware, Legaré had brought with him "only models in colored plaster, and two or three rough casts by himself . . ., together with a section of street pavement in miniature. This section, however, is enough to show what a revolution is likely to be effected in the unsightly *trottoirs* of this and other cities; the peculiar form of the tile and mode of its laying, affording extraordinary advantage in solidity and wear, not less than in beauty, over our uneven brick sidewalks."[21] As Simms, somewhat later, enlarged on the uses of this invention:

> The encaustic tile which we use, and which mostly, or wholly, comes from Europe, has colors superficially laid on, and only upon the surface. But the process of Mr. LEGARE permeates the whole tile with the coloring ingredient, showing the figures equally on both sides. He made of it a beautiful mosaic, suitable for floors, for the sides of chimneys, after the old style of the time of Queen ANNE and the first GEORGES, when pictures from the Bible were silent teachers of the young, above the hearthstone.[22]

When the Fair wound up, Legaré found that he had earned these awards: for his glazier's putty, a diploma; for his tiles, plastic-cotton roofing, and ivory-frame composition, each a silver medal.[23] The year was climaxed for him a few weeks later. On December 29, 1857, the United States Patent Office granted him patent no. 18,980: *Improvement in Preparing Plastic Cotton for Moulding Purposes.*[24] Despite the head of the household's poor health, this new year must have been a hopeful one for the little family at 719 Laurens Street, Aiken.

[21] *Ibid.*

[22] [Simms], "Domestic Resources," Charleston *Mercury,* Nov. 29, 1861, p. 1, col. 2.

[23] Charleston *Courier,* Dec. 23, 1857, p. 4, cols. 1–2.

[24] For annotation and excerpts from this and the ivory-frame patent descriptions, see CCD (1), pp. 229–30n. JML's original Specifications, with supporting documents, for both inventions are case-filed in the records of the United States Patent Office, Record Group no. 241, The National Archives. In the plastic-cotton file he advises the Commissioner of Patents, in a letter dated Aiken, March 27, 1857, that he is forwarding by Adams Express "also a model and drawings of an improvement on the mode of hanging window shades."

From there Legaré addressed Senator James H. Hammond on March 22, 1858:

> You knew so much of my early endeavors to find out what I really was intended for in the economy of Nature, that I fancy you will not be displeased to learn from time to time my progress in the direction in which *alone*, I find I can bring all my energies to bear. The inclosed printed description[25] will give some idea of the first of my inventions, now rapidly getting into use, and likely to push from competition all materials now used for roofing purposes, if not for walls. I have another invention of much value, but of less *general* adaptation also completed. . . .

This last was the ivory-frame composition. On June 15, 1858, the Patent Office issued Legaré patent no. 20,569 on the idea: *Improvement in Ivory Frame Composition.* When the good news trickled down to Aiken, the inventor must have found it tonic indeed. He needed such. At the end of April he was, in the opinion of Rev. J. H. Cornish, "lying still in a critical state," though the pastor noted that the patient's hemorrhaging had ceased temporarily. When the minister paid a Sunday visit on May 30, he could only have been touched at what ensued: the wasted man "made me a Present of the Right to use his plaster cotton & Lignin—."[26]

[25] Doubtless a companion leaflet to the single-sheet printed description of the plastic-cotton patent carried as item no. 39,274 in the Charleston Museum. This offprint from the U. S. Patent Office *Annual Report,* 1857, is signed by JML, with witnesses T. D. Mathews and I. (*sic*) D. Legaré, the latter obviously JML's father, John D. Legaré, the former probably Mrs. John D. Legaré's brother (see n. 3, chap. i, above). An additional witness was the Aiken physician Amory Coffin.

[26] J. H. Cornish, entry for May 30, 1858, MS Diary, ed. Bartram (University of North Carolina Library; see n. 10, chap. iv, above). JML may have made a similar gesture to young Emma Gilchrist, a family friend. "He gave the Patent to my Sister, and told her to destroy," writes Mrs. Leger H. Mitchell, of Charleston, S.C., Feb. 20, 1942, to CCD. JML's is the only "ivory-frame composition" listed as such in M. D. Leggett (comp.), *Subject-Matter Index of Patents for Inventions . . . , op. cit.,* II, 792. Witnesses to the original Specification had been John D. Legaré and JML's wife Anne.

Presently, however, Legaré rallied somewhat. On June 16, 1858, he penned an appeal to Senator Hammond once again:

> Your, as usual, friendly note reached me some time back, —but since then I have scarcely been able to attend to the more pressing business connected with my principal Patent. Over work perhaps, and over anxiety brought on the field my old enemy of eight or ten years ago—I mean, hemorrhage of the lungs.
>
> However, I am endeavoring to make arrangements for transfering a large portion of the conduct of the Patent to other parties, by which in a money view I will be a loser in the end no doubt, but a gainer at present in health.
>
> I inclose you a supplement to our Circular, indicating the true purpose and value of the invention; though these are more fully stated in an article which I cut from the "Charleston Courier" a few days since. The writer very justly seems to regard the use of P-C for mere roofing purposes as of second rate consequence. *I* look upon it as third rate even, in comparison with the other two applications of the invention. This article although treating of the uses of cotton generally, contains so much information relative to *Plastic cotton,* that I also inclose it to you; and I believe it will be really of much service to my cause, if you will be so kind as to have it reprinted in a Washington paper. I do not know one of the Washington editors, or I would not trouble you on the subject. One thing more in the way of a favor; if the Patent Office Report for 1857 (last years) be ready for distribution, will you send me a copy, if you please, before leaving Washington?
>
> I have the vols for 1856. I hope when you return home you may find time to ride over to Aiken, and let me show you some of the results of my works since ~~I retreated~~ my abandonment of literature!

On November 24, 1858, Legaré had this to say to Hammond:

> I wish that I could have had an opportunity for talking with you on many subjects before your return to Washington; but I am sorry to say that I am, as I have been all the year past, a confirmed invalid. Indeed I have not had

the health and energy enough even to push the sales of my Patent, which have been consequently just as planters in different parts of the country have chanced to hear of the invention. However, I hope shortly now to have an able associate in the Patent Right who will be able to manage matters rightly, in spite of the not over scrupulous opposition manifested by some mechanics I have had to deal with already. I think no one can see good specimens of the work in this plastic material, without acknowledging it's immense future benefit and value, especially in the South.

The "able associate" was R. H. Gardiner, a prominent Episcopal layman of Augusta, Georgia.[27] The writer in the Charleston *Daily Courier* of the preceding June, to whom Legaré had called Senator Hammond's attention, was prophesying that builders and roofers would never welcome his cheap substitute because it would infallibly have the effect of destroying their current market.[28] In a subsequent epistle to Hammond the inventor laid emphasis on this very quality. After revealing that "two instances of it's failure having come to my knowledge (although neither were attributable to the invention—as, for instance, in the case of *unburned* Gypsum being used)," Legaré continued:

I have stopped the sale of Personal Rights, wishing neither to risk my own reputation nor that of this valuable invention on the carelessness of those using it. *It should be offered for sale only in a manufactured state ready for use,* and I have a sketch of the simple machinery required for

[27] Mrs. Bryan Cumming, writing from Augusta, Ga., Nov. 10, 1949, to CCD, states that Gardiner, in conjunction with his wife, the former Sarah Fenwick Jones of Savannah, and her sister, Mary Gibbons Jones, paid for the erection of the Episcopal Church of the Atonement at Augusta in 1850. The architect was Edward Gardiner of Philadelphia.

[28] See "Gossyp," on "New Uses of Cotton," Charleston *Daily Courier,* June 9, 1858, p. 1, cols. 4–5; reprinted in *DeBow's Review,* XXV (Aug., 1858), 215–16. Yet in late Feb., 1860—nine months after JML's death— one Samuel J. Felder wrote from Orangeburg, S. C., to John D. Legaré requesting some of his late son's fireproof roofing material (A. S. Salley, "James Mathewes Legaré," Charleston *Sunday News and Courier,* Nov. 1, 1903).

the purpose. Abundant proof can be shown of it's strength, durability, and beauty in this shape, and a house built of *slabs* of Lignine would resemble one constructed of solid blocks of freestone or granite. A factory for these slabs and roofing-plates, if established at Mount Pleasant, opposite Charleston, where land is cheap, and landing and shipment easy, would yield from 50 to 100 percent on cost of crude materials and labor. As soon as I can get my Engine off my mind and temporarily off my hands, I intend to get together a Company for the above purpose, even if obliged to get the stock takers in NYork. Mr Gardiner proposed to have a large building of his own put up in a prominent place in Augusta, *entirely* of Plastic Fibre, walls, roof and all, and then to organize a Company there; but it is too far from the coast, and the plan will never be carried out, if the factory opposite Charleston be started first. There will be nothing whatever to compete with this material when once manufactured; and this is the positive opinion of two or three practical men who have had small faith in it's *general* use by means of printed instructions.[29]

Here was optimism! But here, too, was a plaguing winter for James Legaré. The hemorrhages seemed never to leave him for long. On December 9, 1858, his minister, Mr. Cornish, saw that he was "very low." The repeated set-backs from his experiments on his air-engine, coupled with the tubercular wracking of his body, had left Legaré a legacy of depression which neither travel nor anything else appeared able to lift.

The invalid accordingly submitted to facial blood-letting. This had the effect of clearing his spirits. He began to get about again. And a greater surcease than surgery buoyed him up. After all the years of trial and failure, he now *knew* he had per-fected his engine! All he needed to make his ten-year-old dream come true was that will-o'-the-wisp, capital. Where to turn? Once again he chose to address his long-time confidant, James H. Hammond. Once again, that is, the solitary struggler found

[29] JML to James Henry Hammond, Aiken, S. C., May 15, 1859.

his future hinging on the good will of some distant figure accessible only through the chancy medium of the government mails.

"I hope," Legaré wrote the Senator from Aiken on May 15, 1859, "you will give the contents of this letter your earnest consideration and will hear me out before prejudging my cause: I will be as brief as may be, consistently with a clear statement of facts."

First he rehearsed the saga of his shattering pursuit of the dream, with all this had cost him in money and emotion. Then he descended to particulars:

Mr Ericsson[30] has succeeded in making an air-engine remarkably economical in burning fuel, but the cost of his engines is very great, and they cannot be applied to heavy machinery. I thought even this purpose one which it were best to keep locked in my own breast until success should justify the labor I gave to it's realization; but I did not anticipate that a result so much greater than I had hoped, would crown that labor. My Engine—as it now stands complete in all it's working drawings and minor details— embodies no new principle, (just as Watt's first low-pressure engine did not) and is consequently as clear in it's working capacity, to an intelligent eye, as if in actual operation. In *mechanical* inventions some new principle or theory is sometimes involved, and in *chemical* inventions nearly always; and of course in such cases everything depends on the establishment of *the principle* and on this rack it was that my earlier endeavors were wrecked invariably. This engine is simply an embodiment of well recognized principles and of powers of which tables exist; and where these have failed, I have taken the precaution to fortify my position by reference by letter, to two of the best scientific authorities I know of in Charleston and NYork. I can find room for few words of description here. As it's name implies, viz: DUAL AIR ENGINE, it's motive power is derived not from one source, but from *two*,—that is, from steam and hot air con-jointly, in the proportion of one of the

[30] The Swedish-born engineer John Ericsson (1803–1889), best known in American history for construction of the iron-clad, the *Monitor*, in 1862.

former to twelve of the latter; and by this and by other arrangements of a mechanical kind, but one *lb.* of coal is consumed where six are required per horsepower in the usual steam engine: explosions, even in careless hands is impracticable; and it's power exceeds that of a steam engine of like capacity of furnace and boiler, about ten times. I do not ask credence for these extraordinary claims, on the strength of my own conviction and assertions; the drawings and calculations are simple and easily comprehended and speak for themselves. As yet they have been shown to no one but an intimate friend (R. H. Gardiner) who drove over a few days since, from Augusta, to examine the papers; he has undertaken, at his own suggestion, to ascertain at once the best engine building company, in Philadelphia or NYork, with whom an arrangement may be made in accordance with my views. These views are to sell a share in the Patent to such manufacturing Firm, part of the amount payable in cash, the rest on successful completion of the first engine; the Company to have the whole business management in their hands—in short to act the part which Bolton and his Company did for Watt and his low-pressure engine; my own *practical* ability for carrying out the work, being, I fear, no greater than that of Watt himself. Before, however, any arrangement can be effected or even definitely proposed, it is requisite that the Right to the Invention should be properly secured; and having collected all available information, I find that unless I can take out the Patents for the three most saleable European countries (england, France, and Belgium) simultaneously with that for this country, the invention will be at the mercy of any unscrupulous person who may meanwhile patent it in his own name abroad; such fraudulent patenting by adventurers on the lookout, being not uncommon, unfortunately. To purchase these Foreign Patents is now beyond my means. Thus far I have "lived" at no cost to myself, my cottage being adjacent to my Father's house, and his wish being that we should always meet at meals. I have also dressed with a close economy which only "slop-shops" could supply, and have denied myself still more in the purchase of books: everything, in short, has been sacrificed to the exigencies of my work and to the endeavor to avoid being hampered by petty debts. But during the last two years I have not been able to maintain my position. I have many small debts to pay, which because they *are* small, it distressed me beyond measure not to be able to meet, and no doubt the anxiety they cause is exaggerated by the unnerved condition following on long illness; to me, however, their distress is none the less real for that, and not less a drag upon my recovery. The Patents named above, including the American, together with those debts which call for payment and now cause me so much inquietude, —can be covered by the sum of $1,200—a terrible amount for me to contemplate now, although apportioned among these past years of work as a yearly excess, it would appear small. As I have said, everything has been devoured meanwhile by the one steadfast purpose of my life, and I have been able to set aside nothing; my whole property besides the Patents I will presently name, consisting in my small house and it's adjacent work room or laboratory (as the case may be) together with the rather curious furniture and contents of the former.

Then Legaré detailed for Hammond the three incidental discoveries to which his air-engine research had led. These were the ivory-frame composition, the plastic cotton, and the easy chair. He concluded his *résumés* with the furniture item:

The third and last of these inventions, is a light, cushion-less easy reading-chair which the German who has been recently making some furniture for you, has just contracted to manufacture (in his own name), paying me 20 percent on all sales: he expects to find very ready and extensive sales. Thus you may observe that these inventions have all been supplemental to the chief result for which I strove; and that the last and least of these inventions is the only one regarding which any arrangement has been made, and that *this* has not yet had time to pay.

Now Legaré came to the appeal on which his future seemed to hinge:

I have said that $1200 would meet the cost of the American and Foreign Patents, and relieve my mind of these cares which hinder my recovery. Strictly speaking, however, only half of this sum may be required, as the second half will not be called for until the 1st or middle of August, and meanwhile the sale of the Frame Composition Patent may be effected, or a transfer made of a portion of the Engine patent; it is only in the event of both the above named arrangements being tardy, that the other $600 would be needed.

I earnestly hope, Sir, that you can and will afford me this so very essential help. I cannot make the contents of this letter those of a circular, or even repeat them to a second person. I have long balanced in mind my absence of all claim upon yourself, against the certainty that in your fine intelligence I should be sure to find understanding and appreciation of the work I have been allowed to bring to a successful end. If I were to ask such aid now even in the moment of success, from the two or three of my own name and blood who are considered excessively wealthy,[31] they would give as to a beggar if they gave at all, and would see no reason for having anything better than the engine that now takes their cotton to market; had they lived in Watt's or Stephenson's times, they would have recognized no necessity for improvement in Newcomen's engine, or in the tram-way coal carts of later date: it would be therefore as useless as humiliating to claim before their tribunal, advantages for my Engine over those now in use, as great as those eminent inventors obtained over the motive powers of their day. Do not, I beg of you, consider me vainglorious in writing thus: I do not think I have much of the vanity and small ambition left in me, towards which you had occasion to show me so much kindly forbearance more than once in earlier life. I only say what I really believe; I scarcely think at all of myself in this matter; why should I, when the very simplicity of the idea shows how little it is really the result of these many years of search and labor,

[31] According to the Slave Schedule, U. S. Census for 1860, South Carolina, the following Legarés owned one hundred or more Negroes: (1) estate of Dr. Thomas Legaré (1795–1855), of "Light House Point," James Island—158 slaves; (2) Mrs. Lydia Ball (Bryan) Legaré, widow of James C. W. Legaré (d. 1850), of "Mullet Hall" and Charleston—110; (3) Solomon Legaré (1797–1878), of same—230; (4) Col. James Legaré (1805–1883), of Saint Paul's Parish, Colleton District—304. (Data courtesy of Prof. Chalmers G. Davidson, Department of History, Davidson College, N.C.)

and how readily it might have occurred—or rather, *been suggested*—to any other thinking mind. If I have mentioned my life and health perhaps too often in the context, it is only because their preservation for a time at least, appears to me intimately connected with the completion of the Engine which may require change while in the Builder's hands.

To bring this long letter to a close, will you consent to examine my drawings and specifications at as early a day as your own convenience will allow, either here in Aiken (which will be much the best plan, if you will please me by being my guest)—or if you prefer, in Augusta where I can arrange to be for a day or two without suffering physical inconvenience. I am by no means strong enough to ride even in a carriage to your residence, at present, nor will be for a long while to come, I fear. If you find that my representations are strictly true, and will consent to supply the amount needed, it can be secured to you by mortgage or by partial transfer of any one of the four inventions named, *two* of which are under *full Patent*: the same to be redeemed out of the first made Patent-Sale before mentioned. As I have shown, I have only this security to offer. I hope you will not undervalue it. I do not ask in my own name, but in that of the Invention and of its benefits to others, that you will not refuse my request. It is a petition which I cannot prefer [proffer] *twice,* even with the alternative of my work's dying with me.

This eleven-page epistle, by far the lengthiest of any Legaré letter extant, he penned in his customarily neat script, with careful margins on spotless paper. He wrote it less intricately, and therefore more effectively, than was usual with him. What answer, if any, James H. Hamond returned will never be known.

Exactly two weeks later, on Monday, May 30, Rev. J. H. Cornish made one of the many methodical entries in his journal. This one read: "James Mathews Legare, Sen. Warden of St. Thaddaeus Church, Aiken departed this life at 10 P.M."[32] He was thirty-five and a half years old.

[32] "The Diary of John Hamilton Cornish," ed. R. Conover Bartram, *South Carolina Historical Magazine,* LXIV (July, 1963), 153. Further entries in the MS original indicate that Mr. and Mrs. John D. Legaré,

The splendid dual-air engine, which churned his mind and emotions at every charging stroke—where is it now? Surely it could, had events concurred, have lifted his name to renown across the nation in one sudden, pulsating break-through. Instead it has fallen to the lot of the other part of his nature, a part which he himself had latterly rejected to earn at last for that name—working obscurely, persistently across the long slope of the years—a certain humble degree of eminence which even his engulfing ambition might have been constrained to settle for. A few score lines of lovely poetry penned, now and then, in privacy and in peace, on the flimsiest of warrantors for fame, cheap note paper. . . .

They buried him the next day, Tuesday, May 31, 1859, at 6 P.M., in an unmarked grave, close to the brick wall, in the southwest corner of Saint Thaddeus' churchyard, Aiken, near

---

JML's siblings Joe and Fannie, and his wife Annie were in attendance. Same source reveals that John D. Legaré's death, March 9, 1860, was from cancer of the eye; he was buried in Saint Thaddeus' churchyard near JML. Also interred there are JML's mother and his wife, Anne. Of Anne's demise, Jan. 18, 1862, we learn, in Cornish's words:

"Friday, January 17, 1862. Called on Mrs. and Miss Legare, Mrs Anna Legare, who got a bone stuck in her throat yesterday. I, with the assistance of a servant, carried her in my arms into the Cars for Augusta. A wet drizzling misty day. She is very much prostrated and swollen by what she has already suffered.

"Saturday, January 18, 1862. . . . A servant came to me this evening with the sad news of the death of Mrs. Anna M. Legare. One of my very best friends. Two days ago she was in usual health. Dining, she ate a bird, a delicacy which perhaps some friend had sent her, a piece of bone slipped into her throat and stuck. She put on her bonnet and walked over to Dr. Coffin's. There she had the help of Drs. Coffin and Steener and in Augusta of Dr. Duger, and now tomorrow morning she's to be brought a corpse to be laid by the side of her husband, James Matthews Legare." Quoted from Cornish's diary in R. Conover Bartram, *Biography of a Church: Prelude to the Future. The History of St. Thaddaeus, Aiken, South Carolina,* Supplement ([Aiken, S.C.: for the author], 1967), p. 71.

Recounting substantially the same facts in less detail is Mary H. Ravenel, Aiken, S. C., Dec. 20, 1941, to CCD.

JML's brother, Joseph John (1828–1901), and his sister, Frances Doughty Legaré (1826–1897), are buried in the same plot in Magnolia Cemetery, Charleston, S.C.

THE POET'S GRAVE AT AIKEN, SOUTH CAROLINA
In the graveyard of Saint Thaddeus' Episcopal Church
(Lista's Studio of Photography, Aiken, South Carolina)

the Greenville Street entrance. The grave remained unmarked until February, 1942.

In that year the librarian at Aiken High School—who in 1921 had inaugurated the Legaré Literary Society among the boys and girls of her English course—found that the nickels and dimes of each succeeding senior class had accumulated sufficiently to pay for a modest stone. It was put up, thereby sustaining a tenuous but venerable tradition that has seen a Literary Society in honor of Hugh Swinton Legaré founded at Spartanburg in 1874, a Library Association commemorating Sidney Lanier at Tryon, North Carolina, in 1891, and similar memorial stones arduously effected by little cultural groups at Baltimore to Edgar Allan Poe in 1875, at Nashville to Father Abram J. Ryan in 1886, at Augusta to Richard Henry Wilde in 1896, at Columbia to Henry Timrod in 1897, and at Baltimore to Edward Coote Pinkney in 1941.

Earlier the same day somebody—could it have been anyone but Annie?—took down from his book shelf Volume I of a set of Elizabeth Barrett Browning's *Poems*.[33] She and James, as was their custom, had once put their names to the title pages of both volumes of the set. The person opened this volume to page 284, where began the poem "Catarina to Camoens." Alongside verses 15–16 the person wrote the words (in emotion, getting the day wrong), "Aiken—May 31st 1859 Monday morning." The verses were:

> Blessed eyes mine eyes have been,
> If the sweetest, HIS have seen!

[33] This was the set published at Boston and New York by C. S. and J. H. Francis, 1850 (see CCD [4], no. 28). Also in Vol. I, pp. 278–79, the last twenty-three verses of "A Rhapsody of Life's Progress," beginning, "I am strong in the spirit," are sidelined with a pencil and "J. M. L." initialed beside them. (JJL Coll.)

THE COLLECTED POEMS OF
JAMES M. LEGARÉ

NOTE

In this, the first collected edition of JML's verse, the arrangement of pieces is chronological by publication. Though every effort has been made to uncover first printings, it is probable that those of some of the poems still await discovery. Where more than one version exists (other than reprints after JML's death), the text of the later is given, as presumably having had the benefit of the author's final handling.

At the close of pieces first published or reprinted in *O-U,* JML appended a year date. These have been retained. To pieces published elsewhere than in *O-U,* he normally appended his signature. This has been deleted.

Full references for the critical opinions cited under the Commentary to each poem are listed in Appendix IV.

JML's accentual marks, capitalizations, underlinings, punctuation, and stanzaic patterns have been retained throughout. A few obvious typographical errors have been silently corrected, and the styling of quotation marks has been made consistent (double marks before single marks, even when JML or his publisher and editors followed the reverse pattern).

MY SISTER

Ach! mir ist so wohl bei dir,
Will dich lieben fuer und fuer!
Leopold, Count V. Stolberg

The bright eyed girl I left, hath changed
To one of statelier mould;
Yet is her heart the same, nor hath
My love to her grown cold.
A day I long have looked unto   5
With thirsting heart, is this;
*Quis pudor desiderio,
Tam cari capitis!

The blood that flushes in her cheek
Flows in my every vein;   10
The good old blood of ancient times
Without reproach or stain.
Yet loth am I to think that they
Who held our name before,
From that bright land whence they came,   15
More rare a jewel bore.

Though she is fair as one in ten,
Though round a darker lot
Her smiles would cast a light, I ween
For these I love her not;   20

* Quis desiderio sit pudor aut modus / Tam cari capitis?—Horat. [JML's note].

151

But for the soul, that taper-like
Burns quietly within,
And for the kindliness of heart
And purity from sin.

I love her arm to lean on mine,   25
To guide her steps aright;
I love her eyes to speak to me
Affection pure and bright.
And proud within my heart am I,
That come what may, the arm   30
On which she rests is strong enough
To shelter her from harm.

She tells me all her little joys,
Her troubles and her fears;
I smile with her, I calm her grief,   35
I kiss away her tears.
And thus we journey, hand in hand,
Along this path of ours,
The thorns we crush beneath our feet,
Our bosoms hold the flowers.   40

ALL HAIL THE BRIDE!

To Mrs. B ———.

Hail to the bride whose robe of snow,
Floats purely down in graceful flow;
Whose throbbing heart and roseate cheek,
The maiden's timid fondness speak:
Within whose eye the happy tear   5
Half tells her hope, half paints her fear.
    All hail to her whom chains of flowers,
    Will fetter to her lord's control;
    The idol of my boyhood's hours,
    Once goddess of my soul!   10

Of lofty mind, of gentle mien,
More fair than Royal Arthur's queen,
When Launcelot of the lake became
The warder of his sovereign's fame;
What wonder I should kneel before   15
A shrine so bright, a flame so pure!
    All hail to her whom chains of flowers, etc.

I loved, yet worshipped unconfest,
The image glowing in my breast;
For brighter, lance nor knight hath broke,   20
Nor herald's tongue or trumpet spoke;
In those thrice happy days of old,
When love was purchased not with gold.
    All hail to her whom chains of flowers, etc.

If god-born Phaeton strove in vain,   25
The coursers of the Sun to rein;
If Jeärus his wing betrays,
Fast melting in the noon-tide blaze;
Why should I grieve that I am left,
Who aimed as high, of hope bereft!   30
    Thrice happy be the bride whom flowers, etc.

Thy fetters Love, are iron-strong
In youth, though flower-wreathed along;
But unkind words or glances sear
The leaf, and leave the iron bare.   35
Let HIM so kind a warder be,
The captive's self may dream her free:
    This captive of to-night, whom flowers,
    Will fetter to her lord's control;
    The idol of my boyhood's hours,   40
    Once goddess of my soul!

January 24.

DU SAYE

A Legend of the Congaree

PART FIRST.

Fades in the west, the latest flush
Of summer's gorgeous eve;
With ceaseless moan, of Congaree
The dusky waters heave:
For one unknown the nightly bird   5
Commenceth now to grieve.

And twilight deepens to a night
In every forest glade,
Save one, wherein the soldiers' care
A blazing heap has made,   10
And in the circle of its light
Their toil-worn limbs are laid.

Their arms propped round the rugged trunks,
Or glitter from the ground:
Their steeds the scanty herbage crop,   15
Within the tether's bound:
Nor watch without the camp is there,
Nor wary sentry's round.

Some feed the flame, or seeking bring
Snapt twigs of sun-dried pine: 20
Tend well the haunch of buck, whereon
At once to sup and dine.
Or lazily, half blanket-wrapt,

155

With nodding brows recline.

While others sing wild songs, and pass   25
The cup from hand to hand;
Recount how none of rebel breed
Fierce Tarleton's arm withstand;
And boast of bloody laurels won
From outlawed Marion's band.   30

And here and there, in dizzy flight
The merry sparkles dart:
To mirthful life on every side
Old forest's echoes start.
One only, sad, with drooping head,   35
Sits from the rest apart.

As weeping days in budding May,
More lovely in their tears,
Is she who, warm and soft as they,
A captive's fetters wears.   40
A simple tale of love is hers,
And on my subject bears.

Of gentle blood; her sire's sire,
A Refugee from France,
Had in the noble Condé's cause   45
Unfailing couched his lance.
His son now, sword in hand, beheld
St. George's flag advance.

One came; brave, generous, fair of form,
Strong armed to aid the weak;
They loved, bright Laura, brave Du Saye.   50
Love learneth soon to speak!
Why need I say she blushing gave
The hand none else might seek?

The day is set, the friends are met,   55

The priest in surplice stands;
The oaths are said, the prayers are read,
He joins their willing hands.
Lo! through the open portals swarm
The ruthless tory bands!   60

Unarmed, beset, with frantic rage,
These struggle toward the door;
Borne in their midst, the bride. Their blood
Streams redly down the floor
In vain; across their faltering path,   65
The others furious pour.

Fast ebbs their strength—back, back they reel
The dripping blades before.
Oh, for a rank of Rebel steel!
One volley—all is o'er: 70
Fast bleeds Du Saye at Laura's side;
He fell,—she knew no more.

And now comes one with breathless haste,
And looks that fear denote.
"The Swamp-fox scents our trail," he cries,   75
"Fly!—man with speed the boat."
While yet he speaks, sounds from afar
A bugle's lengthen'd note.

Unconscious all, with lagging gait,
The rescuing squadron nears;   80
On flight intent the others throng
The wide piazza's stairs;
They gain the water's verge, their chief
The lifeless Laura bears.

But keen-eyed Marion marked the crew,   85
And bid his men divide.
With fierce Horry in hot pursuit,
A score of troopers ride;

Too late they win the beach; the bark
Shoots swiftly down the tide.   90

                    *   *   *

Broad shines the blaze; with noisy mirth
Old forest rings around.
And all save grief is loud of tongue
Within the covert's bound.
Nor watch without the camp is there,   95
Nor wary sentry's round.

                    PART SECOND.

Beyond the forest's giant growth
Soft smiles the morning sky;
Deep in the shade, the embers round,
The slumbering warriors lie: 100
Chafes in its bank the stream, as if
Its comrade old to fly.

And forest leaf, and soldier's cloak,
And bank of russet hue;
And stately bough of cypress grey   105
The wave that seems to woo;
All sleep beneath the mantle fresh
Of summer's night-shed dew.

Up darts a startled bird with wheel
Of wing, and warning note: 110
Beneath the nest-hung branch soft glides
A lightly rocking boat;
Close to the shore, the oar-man's grasp
Essays the skiff to float.

And steppeth to the beach Du Saye,   115
Whom Marion's troop had found,
Stretched in his hall, and with rude skill
His recent wound had bound:

But love is aye the surest leech,
Revenge, the staunchest hound.   120

A fox-skin cap, and huntsman's frock
Of grey, the other wore;
A hunter stout, whose swarthy cheek
The Indian's knife-scar bore:
With care he scanned the turf, as one   125
Well skilled in forest lore.

"Hard by this swamp (he said) last eve
Their oozy footpath lay:
Not far from here their camp. —Yet long
Is Marion's toilsome way.   130
Thy heart is stout, thy arm is strong,.
What need of longer stay!"

"Now," cried Du Saye, and led the way,
"Thou well hast spoke my mind."
Old forest's dusky mazes through   135
With noiseless step they wind.
They mark—they skirt the camp; apart
The heart-sick maid they find.

Lightly the captive sleeps,—she wakes,
Du Saye kneels by her side: 140
"Arise," he whispered soft, "and fly
With me, my own sweet bride."
His stalwart arm supports her form,
Back to the grove they glide.

Lo! from the ground a sleeper springs—   145
Loud to each comrade calls:
Ere well the words are said, beneath
The hunter's knife he falls.
Huzza! thou gallant Eagle, who
The Lion's lair despoils!   150

As arméd men where Jason sowed,

Sprang up, so at the blow,
They wake—they shout—they arm in haste;
Fast in pursuit they go!
What may avail the Eagle, when   155
The woodsman bends his bow!

Yet, blade to blade, and foot to foot,
They sell their pathway dear:
On either hand the matted vines
Their stubborn bulwarks rear: 160
Behind, the river lifts his voice
Inviting still more near.

And foot to foot, and blade to blade,
The river's verge they gain,
As sudden from the swoll'n cloud   165
Down bursts the furious rain;
The straitened stream of baffled men
Outpoureth from the lane.

The few behold the many now
Exulting round them wheel,   170
Straight to the bark, a gap they seek
To open with their steel;
But faint from loss of blood and toil,
With failing steps they reel.

Well had the night-dew served their cause   175
In drowning out the spark
Which slumbered, powder-cased, within
The rifle's chamber dark;
For hostile steel and flint in vain
Their latent light impart.

And now a blow the hunter stout   180
Hath dashed upon his knee;
His weeping bride pressed to his side,
His back against a tree,

Fierce stands Du Saye, at bay: a rock
Against a stormy sea! 185

The hunter falls. No hope survives
In Laura's bosom now;
Her arm around her lover cast,
Her hot lips press his brow.
Faint not in heart, brave partizan; 190
Who would not die as thou!

He feels the kiss: a hundred lives
Throb in each bursting vein;
He lifts—he bears—the river's marge
His flying footsteps stain; 195
Aghast the Riders shrink, or brave
The love-nerved arm in vain.

Close to the bank, the fragile skiff
That dances on the tide,
With last convulsive bound he wins; 200
The straightened cords divide!
Far out upon the water's breast
With meteor's speed they glide.

The gunwale dips—the boat drinks deep,
The currents chafe and roar, 205
Above their fair devoted heads
Ere yet the waters pour,
They see their kinsmen gallantly
Come spurring to the shore.

Crash—crash, the shrubs are trampled down, 210
The boughs are bent aside;
Forth from the dreary forest's frown
A rank of horsemen ride.
Tall, dauntless, dark, his restless steed,
Each trooper sits astride. 215

Their chief commands; the horsemen wheel,

At once in circle wide,
Around the foe: on either hand
The rapid waters glide;
Nor space is there for flight, nor yet   220
Dark coppice where to hide.

But Marion, in whose manly breast
All kindly virtues were,
Would fain the lives within his grasp
And wasteful bloodshed spare;   225
When from their line a bullet-shot
Close hisseth past his ear.

With unmoved eye the chieftain glanced
Along his circling band;
Impatient paws the steed beneath   230
Each trooper's swarthy hand.
He spoke; like tempest-breath they sweep
Athwart the narrow strand!

And all is rage, revenge, and fear,
And shout and answering groan;   235
Down trampling hoof, and flash and shout,
And shot at random thrown:
Till to the river's blood-tracked beach
The remnant faint is borne.

Some cry for quarter, and receive   240
The mercy which they gave;
Or, struggling with the stream awhile,
But find a slower grave.
A few are Britons, and these die
As soldiers trained and brave.   245

The skirmish past, two troopers swim
Near to the shore their steeds,
And launch the fatal bark that lies
Embedded in the reeds;

Nor bride nor groom of yester morn   250
The other's pressure heeds.

Apart from where the charge had been,
They lay them gently down;
Above their heads the cypress dark,
Sun-lit, unbends his frown: 255
Dew weeps the stilly morn afar;
The river's plaintive sound.

The soft young cheek, the silken curl
That on the bosom lies;
The chill, damp brow of him who was   260
To her life's dearest prize;
The chieftain looks upon, and tears
Stand in the soldier's eyes.

*QUAE PULCHRIOR?

I woo thee, thou bright One,
With soul and with song.
Thy praise from my bosom
Flows fervid and strong.
I'll teach thee the love   5
That Eurydice knew,
When the passionate hand
Of her Orpheus drew
Sweet words from his lyre.

I seek not, (as Danae   10
Jove conquered of old,)
To dazzle thy vision
With showers of gold.
No jewels I bring thee,
No titled renown.   15
But the lover has hope,
And the poet a crown
For the queen of his bosom.

The blue veinéd temples
Thy soft tresses bind;   20
Thy knowledge, thy genius,
Thy carcanet mind;
Thy gentlest of voices
Thy sunshiny smile,

* To Miss Mary C. . . , of Savannah, Geo. [JML's note].

164

Thy silken lashed eye-lids,
Thy lips without guile,
If e'er such were created.

Thy white glancing shoulders,
Thy ivory arms—
What pencil can paint thee,
What lip chaunt thy charms!
Superb as a Queen is,
Yet gentle and kind.
Where sunny-eyed beauty,
Thy mate can I find?
(In *thy* heart's depth, you murmur.)

Thy soul as a lake is,
Deep, waveless, and pure.
Thy heart as an ocean
That meeteth no shore.
Thou, child of Minerva,
A Venus doth stand.
What gift shall I bring thee
To kiss the white hand
Lying passive in mine?

Thou knowest,—no longer,
With lance lain in rest,
The chosen one doeth
His charmer's behest.
No longer, tall nodding,
His love-lifted plume,
Floats fleet as a meteor
Through battle and gloom,
In the front of the tempest.

Lo, spacious and wide
Are the lists of the world,
Though corslet be rusted,

25

30

35

40

45

50

55

And battle-flag furled:
As matchless the glances
Of beauty—as proud   60
The chaplet—the voice
Of the clarion as loud,
As at Bayard's command.

We earn not these laurels
Through rage and turmoil: 65
No blood-stain the wreath
Of the scholar doth soil:
No tear of the anguished
Can blister that leaf
Whose winning hath cost not   70
One doting heart grief,
Through the breadth of the land.

Oh, far, far more radiant
Olympia's crown,
Than Rome's haughty purple   75
Or Sylla's renown.
Thou—beautiful, glorious;
I—loveless and plain:
What can I—what must I,
Thy love to obtain,   80
With a hope that is dearer?

I steer on an ocean
Broad, stormy and wild,
With heart of a giant,
With arm of a child.   85
My heaven's vast blackness
Doth hold but one star.
I worship—I woo thee,
Bright maid, from afar.
Saidest thou,—"come then nearer"?   90

August, 1844.

QUAE CARIOR?

BEHOLD, nor lands nor gold have I,
Yet great my riches are:
My treasure stands without a guard,
My door without a bar.
Ye who would wealthy live and die,   5
Go seek a love like this:
QUIS PUDOR DESIDERIO
TAM CARI CAPITIS?*

The eyes, the locks, the lips, the smile,
Not these my love retain.   10
A Venus trusting in her charms
Assails my breast in vain.
The soul serene that taper-like
Burns quietly within;
The gentle kindliness of heart   15
And purity from sin.

The blood that flushes in her cheek
Flows in my every vein:
The good old blood of ancient times
Without reproach or stain!   20
Right loth am I to own our Sires,
Stout Huguenots of yore,
From Anjou, Maine, or Languedoc,

* *"Quis desiderio sit pudor aut modus / Tam cari capitis?"*—HORAT.
[JML's note].

So bright a jewel bore.

I love her arm to lean on mine   25
To guide her steps aright;
I love her eyes to speak to me
Affection pure and bright.
And proud within my heart am I
That, come what may, the arm   30
On which she rests is strong enough
To shelter her from harm.

She tells me all her little joys,
Her troubles, and her fears;
I smile with her, I share her grief,   35
I kiss away her tears.
And thus we journey hand in hand
Along this path of ours:
THE THORNS WE CRUSH BENEATH OUR FEET,
OUR BOSOMS HOLD THE FLOWERS.   40

1844.

GEORGIANA

A MOTHER sits beside her child
With lips God only knows when smiled,
And eyes with watching weary,
Her bosom grieving, throbbing, aching,
As one from hideous dreams awaking,   5
Throughout that darkness dreary.

She hears the night-bird from the wood
Mourn in his sable feather hood,
She hears her own heart beating.
The dull watch ticking 'gainst the wall,   10
The leaves that rustle as they fall
Across the window fleeting.

The shadows waving to and fro,
Across the bedclothes noiseless go,
Across the face of DEATH.   15
The bloodless cheeks their life regain,
And part the pallid lips again,
Yet part without a breath.

The golden locks, the waveless breast,
The silken lashes soft that rest   20
Upon the marble face:
All that *was* pure, beloved, and bright,
All that *is* chill and clothed in night,
Sleeps in the shroud's embrace.

Not swiftly spent, but day by day   25
This mother noted pass away
The life with anguish sore.
A sea retreating wave by wave,
That ebbing left to view the grave
Deep yawning in the shore.   30

Oh Niobé, who thus dost mourn
A daughter from thy bosom torn,
Oh plaining heart, be dumb.
TU QUI CUNCTA SCIS ET VALES,
QUI NOS PASCIS HIC MORTALES,   35
JESU DA SOLATIUM.

1845.

TOCCOA

TOCCOA, in Cherokee, *the beautiful,* is a very different spot from TALLULAH, *the terrible.* To see the former, in your mind's eye, imagine a sheer precipice of gray and rugged rock, one hundred and eighty six feet high, with a little quiet lake at its base, surrounded by sloping masses of granite and tall shadowy trees. From the overhanging lips of this cliff, aloft, between your upturned eyes and the sky, comes a softly-flowing stream: This making a soft joyous leap at first, breaks into a shower of heavy spray, and scatters its drops more and more widely and minute, until, in little more than a drizzling mist, it saturates the smooth mosscovered stone, lying immediately beneath. All the way up the sides too, of this precipice, cling, wherever space is afforded, little tufts of moss, and delicate freshly-green vines and creepers, *trickling* through the black fissures in the granite.

There is no stunning noise of boisterous falling waters, but only a dripping, pattering, plashing in the margin of the little lake; a murmuring sound above all others grateful during the noontide heat of a summer's day. There comes also a soft cool breeze, constantly from the foot of the precipice, caused by the falling shower, and this ripples the placid surface of the pool, and stirs the leaves around and overhead ever so gently. After all, Tallulah is a place to be admired, Toccoa to be loved.

TOCCOA

CAN I forget that happiest day,
That happiest day of all the year,
When on the sloping rock I lay,
Toccoa dripping near?
The lifted wonder of thy eyes   5
The marvel of thy soul expressed.
Aloft I saw serenest skies,
Below, thy heaving breast.

On wings of mist, in robes of spray
Long trailed, and flowing wide and white,   10
Adown the mountain steep and gray
We saw Toccoa glide.
Her garments sweeping through the vale,
Began the whispering leaves to wake,
And wafted like a tiny sail   15
A leaf across the lake.

The murmur of the falling shower
Which did the solitude increase,
We heard; the cool and happy hour
Filled our young hearts with peace.   20
Thou satest with a maiden grace,
Thou sawest the rugged rocks and hoary,
As with a half-uplifted face
Thou listenedst to my story.

How many of the banished race,   25
Those old red warriors of the bow,
Have slumbered in this shadowy place,
Have watched Toccoa flow.
Perchance, where now we sit, they laid
Their arms, and raised a boastful chaunt,   30
While through the gorgeous Autumn shade
The sunshine shot aslant.

One night, a hideous howling night,
The black boughs swaying overhead,—
Three painted *Braves* across the height   35
A false PE-RO-KAH* led.
Bright were her glances, bright her smiles,
Wonderous her waving length of hair,
(Ye who descend through slippery wiles,
A maiden's eyes beware!)   40

What saw these swarthy Cherokees
In the deep darkness on the brink?
They saw a red fire through the trees,
Through the tossed branches wave and wink;
They saw pale faces white and dreaming,   45
Clutched their keen knives, and held their breath,
—All this was but a cheating seeming,
For them, not for the phantom's death.

Spoke then the temptress—(maid, or devil,)
"Let the pale sleepers sleep no more!"   50
Whoop!—three good bounds on solid rock,
Then empty blackness for a floor.
Yelled the fierce Braves with rage and fright,
With fright their bristling war plumes rose:
On these down fluttering, did the night   55
Her jaws sepulchral close.

* Literally 'Evil-child' [JML's note].

These rocks tall-lifted, rent apart,
This Indian legend old
To thee, enchantress as thou art,
A warning truth unfold.   60
Who love, 'mid midnight dangers stand,
To them false fires wink:
Accurséd be the evil hand
That beckons to the brink.

1845.

TALLULAH

RECOLLECT thou, in thunder
How TALLULAH spoke to thee,
When thy little face with wonder
Lifted upwards, rocks asunder
Riven, shattered,   5
Black and battered,
Thou aloft didst see?

Downward stalking through TEMPESTA,
Did a giant shape appear.
All the waters leaping after   10
Hound-like, with their thunder-laughter
Shook the valley
Teocalli,
Hill-top bleak and bare.

Vast and ponderous, of granite,   15
Cloud enwrapt his features were.
In his great calm eyes emotion
Glimmered none; and like an ocean
Billowy, tangled,
Foam bespangled   20
Backward streamed his hair.

On his brow like dandelions
Nodded pines: the solid floor
Rocked and reeled beneath his treading,
Black on high a tempest spreading,   25

Pregnant, passive,
As with massive
Portal, closed the corridor.

Frighted, sobbing, clinging to me
In an agony of dread,   30
Sawest thou this form tremendous
Striding down the steep stupendous
With the torrent:
Night abhorrent
Closing overhead.   35

Then my heart dissembling courage,
That thine own so loudly beat.
Comfort thee, I said, poor trembler:
Providence is no dissembler.
Higher power   40
Guards each flower
Blooming at thy feet.

Flushed and tearful from my bosom
Thereat thou did'st lift thy face.
Blue and wide thy eyes resplendent,   45
Turned upon the phantom pendent,
Whose huge shadow
Overshadowed
All the gloomy place.

Back revolving into granite,   50
Foam and fall and nodding pine,
Sank the phantom. Slantwise driven
Through the storm-cloud rent and riven,
Sunshine glittered
And there twittered—   60
Birds in every vine.

Then sonorous from the chasm
Pealed a voice distinct and loud:

"Innocence and God-reliance
Set all evil at defiance. 65
Maiden, by these,
(As by snow, trees,)
Evil heads are bowed."

1845.

GEORGIA

THOU, like a dove, dost make thy moan,
Although thou utterest no tone,
Nor pleadest with thy voice alone.

The pallid brow beneath thy hair,
Thy gentle uncomplaining air,   5
Make captives of us unaware.

Why art thou armèd otherwise
Than Nature made thee, since thine eyes
An host within themselves comprise?

The axe may do a king's behest,   10
Keen lances pierce the stubborn breast,
Thy eyes—they rob us of our rest!

Ah, weary eyes with watching sore,
And suffering, that evermore
Look back, afraid to look before: 15

And thou who on thy bed forlorn,
In pain, hast often watched the dawn,
Sad sighing—"will it ne'er be morn?"

Take heart: I see thee blooming grow
As erst, where balmy zephyrs blow,   20
And blue waves ripple to and fro.

And like that sea, a tide will wake
In thy young heart, no more to make

The truant blood thy cheek forsake.

No longer wilt thou drooping stand,   25
With thy poor, pale, blue-veinéd hand,
(The costliest gift in all the land!)

Sun warmed thy cheek will grow, and brown.
Health will become thee as a crown,
And light will smile where night did frown.   30

And thou shalt clearly then perceive
That God did only make thee grieve
More elevated faith to leave.

As costly diamonds in their lees,
Washed from beneath the roots of trees   35
By torrents, find the Bengalese.

1845.

TO A LILY

GO bow thy head in gentle spite,
Thou lily white.
For she who spies thee waving here,
With thee in beauty can compare
As day with night.   5

Soft are thy leaves and white: Her arms
Boast whiter charms.
Thy stem prone bent with loveliness
Of maiden grace possesseth less:
Therein she charms.   10

Thou in thy lake dost see
Thyself: So she
Beholds her image in her eyes
Reflected. Thus did Venus rise
From out the sea.   15

Inconsolate, bloom not again
Thou rival vain
Of her whose charms have thine outdone:
Whose purity might spot the sun,
And make thy leaf a stain.   20

1845.

AMY

THIS is the pathway where she walked,
The tender grass pressed by her feet.
The laurel boughs laced overhead,
Shut out the noonday heat.

The sunshine gladly stole between   5
The softly undulating limbs.
From every blade and leaf arose
The myriad insect hymns.

A brook ran murmuring beneath
The grateful twilight of the trees,   10
Where from the dripping pebbles swelled
A beech's mossy knees.

And there her robe of spotless white,
(Pure white such purity beseemed!)
Her angel face and tresses bright   15
Within the basin gleamed.

The coy sweetbriers half detained
Her light hem as we moved along!
To hear the music of her voice
The mockbird hushed his song.   20

But now her little feet are still,
Her lips the EVERLASTING seal;
The hideous secrets of the grave
The weeping eyes reveal.

The path still winds, the brook descends,   25
The skies are bright as then they were.
My Amy is the only leaf
In all that forest sear.

1845.

ENCHANTMENTS

AH! well I call to mind that eve,
That witching eve, thou dear Wihlmene;
The garden seat, the stilly night,
The moon's pale, falling, quivering light,
That stole the leaves between.   5

Fain had I fled, yet could not flee
From thee, Enchantress that thou art:
My will was bound, my tongue was mute,
Thy Upas love took deadly root
Within my fluttering heart.   10

Offtimes thou lookedst into mine,
With thy deep wondrous pleading eyes:
Deceive me not, I said, and smiled:
Where Venus reigns supreme, dear child,
Minerva is not wise!   15

And afterward, when on my hand
Thy cheek soft pressed, what fiery thrill
Leaped through my veins; and, as the sea,
Swept former footprints off—Ah me!
My very heart stood still.   20

Since then, like Scaevola am I—
My left hand all to me remains;
For that thou breathedst on, so great
Has grown in worth, the right, its mate,
No value now retains.   25

TO MY VERY DEAR SISTER

NO need is there of being wise
To read the love within thine eyes;
Thy love thou canst not all disguise.

Thy hair is brown, thy eyes are gray,
And many tender things they say;   5
(Sweet eyes, thus speak to me alway!)

Thy forehead white beneath its veins
Soft throbbing, secret wealth contains,
Fair fruit of fertilizing rains.

For often, lying in the shade,   10
Thy tresses loosened from their braid,
An open book before thee laid,

Thou readest many wondrous things
That give unto thy spirit wings;
And dreamy old imaginings.   15

But more than tress or witching eyes,
Or all that therein hidden lies,
Thy love I infinitely prize.

Thy love is like a joyous rill
That rippling down life's rugged hill,   20
The crevices with gold-dust fill.

Let others covet gold:—for me,
In thy great love great wealth I see,
Nor more endowed I care to be.

1846.

HAW-BLOSSOMS

WHILE yesterevening, through the vale
Descending from my cottage door
I strayed, how cool and fresh a look
All nature wore.

The calmias and golden-rods,   5
And tender blossoms of the haw,
Like maidens seated in the wood,
Demure, I saw.

The recent drops upon their leaves
Shone brighter than the bluest eyes   10
And filled the little sheltered dell
Their fragrant sighs.

Their pliant arms they interlaced,
As pleasant canopies they were:
Their blossoms swung against my cheek   15
Like braids of hair.

And when I put their boughs aside
And stooped to pass, from overhead
The little agitated things
A shower shed   20

Of tears. Then thoughtfully I spoke;
Well represent ye maidenhood,
Sweet flowers. Life is to the young
A shady wood.

And therein some like golden-rods,   25
For grosser purposes designed,
A gay existence lead, but leave
No germ behind.

And others like the calmïas,
On cliff-sides inaccessible,   30
Bloom paramount, the vale with sweets
Yet never fill.

But underneath the glossy leaves,
When, working out the perfect law,
The blossoms white and fragrant still   35
Drop from the haw;

Like worthy deeds in silence wrought
And secret, through the lapse of years,
In clusters pale and delicate
The fruit appears.   40

In clusters pale and delicate
But waxing heavier each day,
Until the many-colored leaves
Drift from the spray.

Then pendulous, like amethysts   45
And rubies, purple ripe and red,
Wherewith God's feathered pensioners
In flocks are fed.

Therefore, sweet reader of this rhyme,
Be unto thee examples high   50
Not calmïas and golden-rods
That scentless die:

But the meek blossoms of the haw,
That fragrant are wherever wind
The forest paths, and perishing   55
Leave fruits behind.

1846.

AHAB-MAHOMMED

A PEASANT stood before a king and said;
"My children starve, I come to thee for bread."
On cushions soft and silken sat enthroned
The king, and looked on him that prayed and moaned.
Who cried again;—"for bread I come to thee."   5
For grief, like wine, the tongue will render free.
Then said the prince with simple truth; "Behold
I sit on cushions silken-soft, of gold
And wrought with skill the vessels which they bring
To fitly grace the banquet of a king.   10
But at my gate the Mede triumphant beats,
And die for food my people in the streets.
Yet no good father hears his child complain
And gives him stones for bread, for alms disdain.
Come, thou and I will sup together—come."   15
The wondering courtiers saw—saw, and were dumb:
Then followed with their eyes where Ahab led
With grace the humble guest, amazed, to share his bread.

Him half abashed the royal host withdrew
Into a room, the curtained doorway through.   20
Silent behind the folds of purple closed,
In marble life the statues stood disposed:
From the high ceiling, perfume breathing, hung
Lamps rich, pomegranate-shaped, and golden-swung.
Gorgeous the board with massive metal shone,   25

Gorgeous with gems arose in front a throne:
These through the Orient lattice saw the sun.
If gold there was, of meat and bread was none
Save one small loaf; this stretched his hand and took
Ahab Mahommed, prayed to God, and broke: 30
One half his yearning nature bid him crave,
The other gladly to his guest he gave.
"I have no more to give"—he cheerly said;
"With thee I share my only loaf of bread."
Humbly the stranger took the offered crumb   35
Yet ate not of it, standing meek and dumb:
Then lifts his eyes,—the wondering Ahab saw
His rags fall from him as the snow in thaw.
Resplendent, blue, those orbs upon him turned:
All Ahab's soul within him throbbed and burned.   40

AHAB MAHOMMED, spoke the vision then;
From this thou shalt be blessèd among men.
Go forth—thy gates the Mede bewildered flees,
And Allah thank thy people on their knees.
He who gives somewhat does a worthy deed,   45
Of him the recording angel shall take heed.
But he that halves all that his house doth hold,
His deeds are more to God, yea more than finest gold.

1846.

ONCE there came a woman weeping,
Weeping to the Savior's feet,
She had left her daughter sleeping
Grievously consumed by heat.
Through the crowd the troubled mother   5
Striving anxiously to see,
Cried unto the wondrous stranger;
Χριστος, ἐλεήσόν με.

When she saw the Lord had passed her
Heeding not, she worshipped near,   10
Saying;—Heal her, gentle Master:
Saying;—Holy Master, hear.
Looking on her, Jesus answered;
Think you it is meet to give
Unto dogs the bread of children,   15
Bread whereby the children live?

But this woman full of sorrow,
Full of *woman's* hope and love,
Trusting earnestly, did borrow
Wisdom from a source above.   20
Truth,—she meekly answered, Master,
Yet they have their own award;
For the dogs are fed with fragments
From the table of their Lord.

Marvelled much our Lord's disciples,   25

Such exalted faith to find
In the kneeling Canaanitess.
Unto her no longer blind,
Then said Jesus; As thou willest
Be it to thee even now.   30
Rise and go unto thy daughter;
Μεγάλη ἡ πἰστις σου

Quick she rose and went rejoicing,
Went rejoicing on her way;
Flew unto the little chamber   35
Where her child had lain the day.
Pale and heavy-eyed no longer,
Healed and beauteous to see,
Came the maiden to the mother,
Sobbing;—Δοξα σοί Κύριε   40

Happy in the dread hereafter,
Threefold happy wilt thou be,
Seeing Christ compassionately,
Meek one, looking upon thee.
Then thy heart will beat with gladness,   45
Saying; Blessedest art thou
Unto whom our Lord has spoken;
Μεγάλη ἡ πἰστις σου.

1846.

ORNITHOLOGOI*

THOU, sitting on the hill-top bare,
Dost see the far hills disappear
In autumn smoke, and all the air
Filled with bright leaves. Below thee spread
Are yellow harvests, rich in bread   5
For winter use; while over-head
The jays to one another call,
And through the stilly woods there fall,
Ripe nuts at intervals, where'er
The squirrel, perched in upper air,   10
From tree-top barks at thee his fear;
His cunning eyes, mistrustingly,

Do spy at thee around the tree;
Then, prompted by a sudden whim,
Down leaping on the quivering limb,   15
Gains the smooth hickory, from whence
He nimbly scours along the fence
To secret haunts.

     But oftener,
When Mother Earth begins to stir,   20
And like a Hadji who hath been
To Mecca, wears a caftan green;
When jasmines and azalias fill
The air with sweets, and down the hill
Turbid no more descends the rill;   25

* Bird-voices [JML's note].

The wonder of thy hazel eyes,
Soft opening on the misty skies—
Dost smile within thyself to see
Things uncontained in, seemingly,
The open book upon thy knee,   30
And through the quiet woodlands hear
Sounds full of mystery to ear
Of grosser mould—the myriad cries
That from the teeming world arise;
Which we, self-confidently wise,   35
Pass by unheeding. Thou didst yearn
From thy weak babyhood to learn
Arcana of creation; turn
Thy eye on things intangible
To mortals; when the earth was still,   40
Hear dreamy voices on the hill,
In wavy woods, that sent a thrill
Of joyousness through thy young veins.
Ah, happy thou! whose seeking gains
All that thou lovest, man disdains   45
A sympathy in joys and pains
With dwellers in the long, green lanes,
With wings that shady groves explore,
With watchers at the torrent's roar,
And waders by the reedy shore;   50
For thou, through purity of mind,
Dost hear, and art no longer blind.

"CROAK! croak!"—"who croaketh over-head
So hoarsely, with his pinion spread,
Dabbled in blood, and dripping red?"   55
"Croak! croak!"—"a raven's curse on him,
The giver of this shattered limb!
Albeit young, (a hundred years,
When next the forest leaved appears,)

Will Duskywing behold this breast   60
Shot-riddled, or divide my nest
With wearer of so tattered vest?
I see myself, with wing awry,
Approaching. Duskywing will spy
My altered mien, and shun my eye.   65
With laughter bursting, through the wood
The birds will scream—'she's quite too good
For thee.' And yonder meddling jay,
I hear him chatter all the day,
'He's crippled—send the thief away!'   70
At every hop—'don't let him stay.'
I'll catch thee yet, despite my wing;
For all thy fine blue plumes, thou'lt sing
Another song!

         Is't not enough   75
The carrion festering we snuff,
And gathering down upon the breeze,
Release the valley from disease;
If longing for more fresh a meal,
Around the tender flock we wheel,   80
A marksman doth some bush conceal.
This very morn, I heard an ewe
Bleat in the thicket; there I flew,
With lazy wing slow circling round,
Until I spied upon the ground   85
A lamb by tangled briars bound.
The ewe, meanwhile, on hillock-side,
Bleat to her young—so loudly cried,
She heard it not when it replied.
Ho, ho!—a feast! I 'gan to croak,   90
Alighting straightway on an oak;
Whence gloatingly I eyed aslant
The little trembler lie and pant.

Leapt nimbly thence upon its head;
Down its white nostril bubbled red   95
A gush of blood; ere life had fled,
My beak was buried in its eyes,
Turned tearfully upon the skies—
Strong grew my croak, as weak its cries."

No longer couldst thou sit and hear   100
This demon prate in upper air—
Deeds horrible to maiden ear.
Begone, thou spokest. Over-head
The startled fiend his pinion spread,
And croaking maledictions, fled.   105

But, hark! who at some secret door
Knocks loud, and knocketh evermore?
Thou seest how, around the tree,
With scarlet head for hammer, he
Probes where the haunts of insects be.   110
The worm in labyrinthian hole
Begins his sluggard length to roll;
But crafty Rufus spies the prey,
And with his mallet beats away
The loose bark, crumbling to decay;   115
Then chirping loud, with wing elate,
He bears the morsel to his mate.
His mate, she sitteth on her nest,
In sober feather plumage dressed;
A matron underneath whose breast   120
Three little tender heads appear.
With bills distent from ear to ear,
Each clamors for the bigger share;
And whilst they clamor, climb—and, lo!
Upon the margin, to and fro,   125
Unsteady poised, one wavers slow.
Stay, stay! the parents anguished shriek,

Too late; for venturesome, yet weak,
His frail legs falter under him;
He falls—but from a lower limb   130
A moment dangles, thence again
Launched out upon the air, in vain
He spread his little plumeless wing,
A poor, blind, dizzy, helpless thing.

But thou, who all didst see and hear,   135
Young, active, wast already there,
And caught the flutterer in air.
Then up the tree to topmost limb,
A vine for ladder, borest him.
Against thy cheek his little heart   140
Beat soft. Ah, trembler that thou art,
Thou spokest smiling; comfort thee!
With joyous cries the parents flee
Thy presence none—confidingly
Pour out their very hearts to thee.   145
The mockbird sees thy tenderness
Of deed; doth with melodiousness,
In many tongues thy praise express.
And all the while, his dappled wings
He claps his sides with, as he sings,   150
From perch to perch his body flings:
A poet he, to ecstasy
Wrought by the sweets his tongue doth say.

Who shouts so loud?—Hallo, hallo!
Who in the pine-top to and fro   155
Rocks gallantly? Ha, brother Crow,
Why cawest thou so loud, below?
"Caw—caw: Last spring good Roger came
And sowed his corn: a tenth we claim.
Look you, I wear a satin hood   160
Blue-black and monkish, reason good

For taking tithe of all we would
According to the good old law.
Caw—caw! quoth I. 'I'll stop your "caw"'
Quoth Roger; 'Ever mortal saw   165
Such a lean, lazy lizzard thing!
No longer will I tatters bring
To fright him off, his neck I'll wring.'
Since then has Roger soon and late,
With rusty barrel lain in wait.   170
I'm twice as old and thrice as wise
As Roger, therefore while he lies,
I dig his corn before his eyes.
This morning Roger came once more,
And sowed a furrow as before.   175
Hey!—muttered I—Here's something strange;
The seasons all ha' made a change,
Unless a bad account I keep!
The fellow's certainly asleep,
He sows in Autumn, when 'ill he reap?   180
Off Roger goes: A feast—I cry,
A feast! From every furrow nigh
The brotherhood their pinions fly.
Now while we single grain from grain
Right busily, adown the lane   185
Creeps Roger stealthily again.
Look to yourselves!—our sentries shriek.
With wings grown wonderously weak
To rise into mid air we seek;
But reeling back, some lie as dead,   190
While others with their pinions spread
Flap in the dust. Amid the din
Of cawing, Roger runneth in:
In either hand around he slings
An anguished trunk with panting wings,   195
Then off the headless carcass flings.

I who had played the host, and fed
But sparingly, in season fled
To pine-top. Never farmer reaped
So cursèd crop; in spirits steeped,   200
His maize a hideous harvest yields,
A malediction on the fields.
No green and waving blade appears,
In place of sweet and golden ears,
Blood soppèd fruit his furrow bears."   205

Although a crafty profligate,
Thou heardest him his grief relate,
With sympathy. Will man abate,
(Thou saidest), nevermore his hate
To these, nor with the helpless share   210
That which without diviner care
Unrecompense of labor were.
Ah, let him give, but cheerfully
To them that now so fearfully
Flit up, and from his presence flee,   215
And he will smiling harvests see
Where indigence was wont to be.
For God loves all, and does not give
Life only, but the means to live.

Stay, stay!—I hear a flutter now   220
Beneath yon flowering alder bough.
I hear a little plaintive voice
That did at early morn rejoice,
Make a most sad yet sweet complaint,
Saying, "my heart is very faint   225
With its unutterable wo.
What shall I do, where can I go,
My cruel anguish to abate.
Oh! my poor desolated mate,
Dear Cherry, will our haw-bush seek,   230

Joyful, and bearing in her beak
Fresh seeds, and such like dainties, won
By careful search. But they are gone
Whom she did brood and dote upon.
Oh! if there be a mortal ear   235
My sorrowful complaint to hear;
If manly breast is ever stirred
By wrong done to a helpless bird,
To them for quick redress I cry."
Moved by the tale, and drawing nigh,   240
On alder branch thou didst espy
How, sitting lonely and forlorn,
His breast was pressed upon a thorn,
Unknowing that he leant thereon;
Then bidding him take heart again,   245
Thou rannest down into the lane
To seek the doer of this wrong,
Nor under hedgerow hunted long,
When, sturdy, rude, and sun-embrowned,
A child thy earnest seeking found.   250
To him in sweet and modest tone
Thou madest straight thy errand known.
With gentle eloquence didst show
(Things erst he surely did not know)
How great an evil he had done;   255
How, when next year the mild May sun
Renewed its warmth, this shady lane
No timid birds would haunt again;
And how around his mother's door
The robins, yearly guests before—   260
He knew their names—would come no more;
But if his prisoners he released,
Before their little bosoms ceased
To palpitate, each coming year

Would find them gladly reappear 265
To sing his praises everywhere—
The sweetest, dearest songs to hear.
And afterward, when came the term
Of ripened corn, the robber worm
Would hunt through every blade and turn, 270
Impatient thus his smile to earn.

At first, flushed, angrily, and proud,
He answered thee with laughter loud
And brief retort. But thou didst speak
So mild, so earnestly did seek 275
To change his mood, in wonder first
He eyed thee; then no longer durst
Raise his bold glances to thy face,
But, looking down, began to trace,
With little, naked foot and hand, 280
Thoughtful devices in the sand;
And when at last thou didst relate
The sad affliction of the mate,
When to the well-known spot she came,
He hung his head for very shame; 285
His penitential tears to hide,
His face averted while he cried;
"Here, take them all, I've no more pride
In climbing up to rob a nest—
I've better feelings in my breast." 290

Then thanking him with heart and eyes,
Thou tookest from his grasp the prize,
And bid the little freedmen rise.
But when thou sawest how too weak
Their pinions were, the nest did seek, 295
And called thy client. Down he flew
Instant, and with him Cherry too;

And fluttering after, not a few
Of the minuter feathered race
Filled with their warbling all the place.   300
From hedge and pendent branch and vine,
Recounted still that deed of thine;
Still sang thy praises o'er and o'er,
Gladly—more heartily, be sure,
Were praises never sung before.   305

Beholding thee, they understand
(These Minne-singers of the land)
How thou apart from all dost stand,
Full of great love and tenderness
For all God's creatures—these express   310
Thy hazel eyes. With life instinct
All things that are, to thee are linked
By subtle ties; and none so mean
Or loathsome hast thou ever seen,
But wonderous in make hath been.   315
Compassionate, thou seést none
Of insect tribes beneath the sun
That thou canst set thy heel upon.
A sympathy thou hast with wings
In groves, and with all living things.   320
Unmindful if they walk or crawl,
The same arm shelters each and all;
The shadow of the Curse and Fall
Alike impends. Ah! truly great,
Who strivest earnestly and late,   325
A single atom to abate,
Of helpless wo and misery.
For very often thou dost see
How sadly and how helplessly
A pleading face looks up to thee.   330

Therefore it is, thou canst not choose,
With petty tyranny to abuse
Thy higher gifts; and justly fear
The feeblest worm of earth or air,
In thy heart's judgment to condemn,   335
Since God made thee, and God made them.

1846.

A PARABLE

I LAY one night and saw a dream
That thus, Irene appeared:
I saw sit shivering by a stream
A maiden silken-haired.

Her tender arms dejectly crossed,   5
Her radiant head bent down;
In melancholy fancies lost,
Her eyelids sought the ground.

"All things in nature harmonize,
And sorrows joys enhance;   10
Why when the sunshine golden lies,
Art thou in mournful trance?"

"Why mournest thou?" I said, and took
Her hands within mine own.
—All calmness straight my soul forsook   15
With tenderness o'erflown.

But lo, while thus the child apart
My arms encircling held,
And pressed against my throbbing heart,
Her bosom throbbed and swelled;   20

My lifted eyes a mocking crowd
Beheld about us stand:
With well-bred air each phantom bowed,
And smiled behind his hand.

202

"Why smile ye, Sirs?"—I briefly cried: 25
"Why come ye here at all?"
"Faith," spoke a Shade, "thy bosom's pride
Hath sat beside us all!

"We, as you see us standing here,
In turn have shared her heart.   30
A new ALCINA charms thy ear,
And thou her ROLAND art.

"Not long its fragrance keeps the rose
That blooms to every gale.
For her who broadcast love bestows,   35
My heart is cased in mail."

Thus spoke in courteous tones the Shade,
Sarcastic smiled and turned.
With blushes burning stood the maid;
For me,—I no more burned!   40

Read me this parable, Irene,
That I may judge aright
If visions such by day are seen,
Or only haunt the night.

1846.

TO ALCINA

CEASE to move me, gentle Venus,
Thou Minerva, spread between us
All thy books: That what is heinous
          In her treating,
          I repeating   5
Once for all may then forget her.
(Banishment than hate is better.)

How is this?—her eyes are tender,
Softly smiles she, white and slender
Are her hands!—The Furies lend her   10
          Charms. Enchanting
          Flies she panting,
To my bosom: Taken,—warmed,
She is to an asp transformed!

Out upon my childish dreaming,   15
Out upon the cheating seeming,
That deceived me! Crafty, gleaming,
          Saw I never
          How for ever
In her hand a blade was holden,   20
Sheath whereof was silk and golden.

Well, despise me if thou choosest:
Nothing by thy hate thou losest.
Heart of mine alone refuseth

　　　To be chided,
　　　To be guided
Into hating where it perished.
(Better, loving, had it perished!)

1846.

TO ANNE

DISCONSOLATE and ill at ease
The heart that is, a future sees
Affording nought to cheer or please.

But she that owns a quiet mind
To good or evil fate resigned,   5
No great unhappiness can find

In any lot. A child in years,
Already have maturer cares
Oppressed thee, and thy eyes to tears

No strangers are. Fair, fresh, and young,   10
Thrice bitterly thy heart was wrung.
For what had they to do with thee,
In thy spring day's despondency,
Or any woful mysteries?

Yet when thy eyes were no more blind   15
With weeping, self-possessed, resigned,
Preëminent arose thy mind.

And resolute in doing well,
Didst henceforth teach thy breast to swell
With nought that maiden will could quell.   20

Thou sawest how man breathes a day

Before re-mingling with his clay:
How feeble in Almighty ken
The most omnipotent of men
Appears: And how the longest life   25
Is one short struggle in the strife
That rocks the world from age to age.

What worthy hand may write the page
Whose Alexandrine words unbind
Thy upwardly directed mind?   30

One beat triumphant of the wings,
And dust no more about thee clings,
And all the galaxy of things

Intangible and vast, expand,
So that thou mayest safely stand   35
On hitherto a quaking sand.

Yet must this excellence be wrought
Not by companionship with thought

Alone: By tracing down the stream
Of life, the glitter of a dream: 40

By repetition vain of creeds:
No,—it is by thy deeds—THY DEEDS,
The flowers will o'ertop the weeds

In thy God's-garden. Cheerfully
Do that allotted is to thee,   45
And fashion out thy destiny;

So that the tomb-doors may not be
Dreaded and dark, but ope to thee
A heaven far as thou can'st see.

1846.

THE TWO GIVERS

EVERY morning, every morrow,
When at noon I cross the river,
Thee I thank right heartily
That thou art so kind a giver.

There it is, we nightly linger,   5
Gazing down into the stream;
It is like a nightly vision,
It is like a pleasant dream.

For we see, in silence standing
With thy fingers locked in mine,   10
In the waters darkly flowing
All the greater planets shine.

From the bridge and from the barges
On the river, redder lights
Gleam: Beyond the sleeping village   15
Others show along the heights.

All the city lies behind us,
Like a hive with busy cells;
And it warns how time is flying,
By the chiming of its bells.   20

All the city lies behind us,
And the toil of human hands:
But the better God-creation
Visible before us stands.

When Diana dimly rising   25
Through the openwork of trees,
On the cliff-sides, on the steeples
Travels down by slow degrees

Silently the pallid splendor,
Till behind our shadows stream,   30
Like the shapes uncouth and dismal
We encounter in a dream.

Then the cool and quiet hour
Tranquillizes all my soul;
I no longer thirst for wisdom   35
And for worldly self-control.

Thee I thank with tenderness,
That thou bearest with my faults;
Knowing thou dost love me truly,
All my better self exalts.   40

And with stronger gratitude
Thank the Universal Giver,
For the cool and quiet evening,
For the woods and flowing river.

Grateful most that he hath planted   45
Pleasure in these hearts of ours,
Not in works and world endeavors,
But the sight and scent of flowers.

1846.

WHY SHE LOVES ME

IT is happiness to be
Loved by one so good as she,
Loved, and that so tenderly.

"Why is it she loves me so?"
Into the deep woods I go   5
Pondering, that I may know.

Underneath the branches spread
Green and tentlike overhead,
Full of happiness I tread.

Soon I find a pleasant seat   10
Hidden from the summer heat,
Leaves and flowers at my feet.

Opposite, around a tree
Climbs a vine, most tenderly
Clasping it and fair to see.   15

Through the fanlike leaves appear
Pendulous like braids of hair,
Slender bunches everywhere.

Truly now I understand
Why, and guided by what hand,   20
I alone her heart command.

Outwardly she sees me rough:
That my heart of better stuff
Is,—she knoweth well enough.

What is it to her or me,⁣ 25
If of all ill-judged I be,
So that understandeth she.

Well, if she can trust me so,
When the winds begin to blow,
Place of shelter shall she know.⁣ 30

During Winters long and drear,
When the fruits all disappear,
Snow and sorrow everywhere,

She shall in my arms remain,
Comforted and quit of pain,⁣ 35
Till the Summers come again.

1846.

THE WELCOME RAIN

THE beating rain
I will with hateful eyes behold again
No more, if it my Love restrain.

In haste she goes;
But rains incessant fall, and like a rose   5
My heart invigorate and fresher grows.

Now must she stay,
Since heaven itself gives reasons for delay;
The long black road and canopy of gray.

She loves me so,   10
It would be misery for her to go
Uncomforted by me, I dare to know.

With mournful eyes
She anxiously regards the sullen skies,
And for the dread of going, not of staying, sighs. 15

Whene'er she sees
The beating drops, they are the swarming bees
That fetch us honey; so her heart decrees.

When I beheld
At dawn the driving clouds, my bosom swelled   20
With bitter thoughts and inwardly rebelled.

For then I thought
That *I* a hateful patience should be taught,

And *she* would sit expectant and unsought;

But now I know,   25
How over sodden graves meek blossoms blow,
Luxuriant the more for what's below.

Henceforth, no rain
To bear, will I ungratefully complain,
If it this once my Love, my Life, detain.   30

1846.

LOQUITUR DIANA

MY temples on my arm I lean,
While glides Diana through the screen
Of tall and overhanging trees,
Until my lifted face she sees,
And book spread idly on my knees.   5

High overhead the leaves are stirred:
From tree to tree, remotely heard
The katydid's incessant call:
Still through the boughs and over all,
The silver shafts of Dian fall.   10

Oh Dian, thou who from thy skies
Dost nightly look into her eyes,
(Her brown eyes unto thee upturned)
Say if her heart hath ever burned
As mine for her hath yearned?   15

Remembers she each summer night
When we beheld thee, from the height,
The silent woods of gloom deliver:
And saw in eddies of the river
Thy arrows fall and shiver.   20

Caressingly I held in mine
Her little hands: No joys of wine,
Or gold, or books in mortal ken,
Can yield such happiness again.

—Ah, Dian, why repeat them then?   25

              (Luna loquitur.)
"Why bring them back?—Oh murmur vain!
Doth not the miser count his gain
In coffers hid?—*Thou safe and fast*
Beneath the lid that shuts the past,
These golden hours hast.   30

"What more would'st thou or any one?
A precious heart thy deeds have won
For thee. Behold how earnestly
With lifted eyes she follows me,
Believing that I look on thee."   35

1846.

THE BOOK OF NATURE

("There are two books," writes Sir Thomas Browne, in the Religio Medici, "from which I collect my divinity; besides that written one of God, another of his servant Nature—that universal and public manuscript, that lies expanded unto the eyes of all." . . . . "Possibly, even the heathens know better how to join and read these mystical letters, than many Christians, who cast a more careless eye on these common hieroglyphics, and disdain to suck divinity from the flowers of nature.")

THE manuscript of Nature's book
Is open spread to every eye,
But few into the leaves will look
That round them lie.

In characters both quaint and old,   5
Yet easy to be understood;
On every hill and vale unrolled,
In every wood.

I see the oaks, like belted knights,
With sturdy sinews gird the land;   10
As Birnam wood besieged the heights
In Malcolm's hand.

The solemn brotherhood of pines,
Like monks slow chaunting in the choir,
Nos miserere: Cypress nuns   15
In sad attire.

But where around the opening glade,
Aslant the golden light descends,
And through alternate sun and shade
The footpath wends;   20

And deeper in, the level sward
With cooler shadows overspread—
(Oh page more worthy of award
Than eye hath read!)

From root to top the haws are crowned   25
With tïaras of snowy bloom,
Through purple violet lips the ground
Exhales perfume.

And there, unto the poet's heart,
Illumined with a thousand dyes,   30
And granite claspings all undone,
The volume lies.

BE PATIENT, poet—say the Haws;
The human heart that flowers bears,
Will ripen fruit in autumn days   35
Of after years.

BE HUMBLE—breathe the Violets;
More worthily is honour won,
If they a pleasing fragrance find
Who looked for none.   40

And if thou—say the Calmias,
A pride in exaltation hast,
See how our bloom that crowns the cliff
Wastes every blast.

LOVE—saith the yellow Jasmine—LOVE!   45
In vain the storm menaces him
Who binds his bosom's tendrils round
A steadfast limb.

And if indeed a poet's heart
Thou hast, who walkest in this wood,   50
Believe that God, in fruit or bloom,
Works out some good.

1847.

DOWN where the river flows between
The city and the dusky screen
Of willow branches long and green
That dim the village lights behind,
With her who is so debonaire,   5
In excellence of heart and mind
So far—so far beyond compeer,
What happiness I find.

There yestereve, with hands in mine
Fast locked as in the olden time,   10
And words more musical than rhyme
To ears that listened wistfully
Yet scarce were satisfied—we stood
The queenly Dian's disk to see
Above the distant cypress wood   15
Soar up triumphantly.

And while we talked of what should be
Our future lot, nor could agree
Therein at first—"Heart's-dearest, see
(I said)—a cloudy fess in twain   20
Divides Diana's silver shield."
And while she gazed, I cried again;
"*Superior* in the azure field,
Behold it ONE again!"

So chid I gently. She is wise,   25

219

And quick to understand; her eyes
Turned to me with a glad surprise,
And such deep love, that I—(I own,)
When on my breast her head she laid,
Found my philosophy all flown.   30
For who hath courage to upbraid
A queen upon her throne?

1847.

FLOWERS IN ASHES

WHERE, with unruffled surface wide,
The waters of the river glide
Between the arches dimly in the early dawn descried;

While musing, Sweet, of thee,—once more
I crossed the bridge as oft of yore,   5
I saw a shallop issue from the shadow of the shore.

With practised ease the boatman stood,
And dipped his paddle in the flood:
And so the open space was gained, and left behind the
      wood.

The dripping blade, with measured stroke,   10
In ripples soft the surface broke;
As once Apollo, kissing oft, the nymph Cyrene woke.

And, fast pursuing in his wake,
I heard the dimpling eddies break
In murmurs faint, as if they said—Herefrom example
      take.   15

Unruffled as this river, lies
The stream of life to youthful eyes;
On either bank a wood and mart, and overhead God's
      skies.

Behind thee slopes the pleasant shore,
The tumult of the town before,   20

And thou, who standest in the stern, hast in thy hand
    an oar.

Oh son of toil, whose poet's heart
Grieves from thy quiet woods to part,
And yet whose birthright high it is, to labor in the mart,

To thee, a child, the bloom was sweet;   25
But manhood loves the crowded street,
And where in closes, loud and clear, the forging
    hammers beat.

But even there may bloom for thee
The blossoms childhood loved to see;
And in the cinders of thy toil, God's fairest flowers be.   30

1847.

A MAY MORN

LAST night the town was close and warm,
But while we slept, arose a storm:
And now how clear
And cool and fresh the morning air.

Between the swarthy trunks I walk,   5
Which she made lovely with her talk,
Saying;—"Dear love,
I see these branches from above;

"And when you are no longer here,
I say—'twas *there* he called me 'dear,'   10
His pride—his pet;—
So, absent, you are with me yet."

How still it is!—the city lies
Behind, half hidden from the eyes;
And from the tops   15
Of trees around the moisture drops.

A bird with scarlet on his wings,
Down in the meadow sits and sings;
Beneath his weight
The long corn-tassels undulate.   20

The thrush and red-bird in the brake
Flit up and from the blossoms shake,

Across the grass,
A fragrant shower where I pass.

Ah, thank God for this peace and rest,   25
But more for that within my breast—
How with a song
The very river ebbs along.

A song indeed most musical
To him who on death's threshold shall   30
Revive to know
The faint and melancholy flow.

Yet still the same as when he stood
With musing eyes bent on the flood,
And smiled to hear   35
The ripples say—"I love thee, dear!"

Not that they said so in good sooth,
But that he—(*I*, in simple truth!)—
Seemed thence to hear
The words that in my bosom were: 40

As once she said them with the braid
That bound her throbbing temples, laid
Against my cheek,
So I could even *feel* her speak.

And when she, blushing, ceased,—and I   45
Was mute with joy—the ripples nigh
Took up the strain,
And said,—"I love thee, Sweet!"—again.

And thenceforth all that once was fair,
Grew fairer:—what unsightly were,   50
Divine, if she
But praised them incidentally.

For she is dearer to me, than

Was ever woman yet to man;
Are one, be sure,   55
Her life and mine for evermore.

1847.
South Carolina.

ILLUSTRIOUS thy name shall be
To all who love in future years:
These little songs I sing to thee,
          Thy tears,
Thy many griefs will I bequeath   5
To uncreated heirs.

Now, hidden are the quiet ways
That bring thee to my bosom nigh;
And when is spent thy term of days,
          Thou'lt die: 10
Then shall thy virtues live in praise
That riches cannot buy.

Night shall descend upon thy eyes,
Thy lips no more repeat my name;
But all the virtuous and wise   15
          Shall claim
Thee for their sister:—*See,* they'll say—
Her whom he raised to fame!

1847.

THE REAPER

HOW still Earth lies!—behind the pines
The summer clouds sink slowly down.
The sunset gilds the higher hills
And distant steeples of the town.

Refreshed and moist the meadow spreads,   5
Birds sing from out the dripping leaves,
And standing in the breast-high corn
I see the farmer bind his sheaves.

It was when on the fallow fields
The heavy frosts of winter lay,   10
A rustic with unsparing hand
Strewed seed along the furrowed way.

And I too, walking through the waste
And wintry hours of the past,
Have in the furrows made by griefs   15
The seeds of future harvests cast.

Rewarded well, if when the world
Grows dimmer in the ebbing light,
And all the valley lies in shade,
But sunset glimmers on the height.   20

Down in the meadows of the heart
The birds sing out a last refrain,
And ready garnered for the mart
I see the ripe and golden grain.

1847.

THE RISING OF THE RIVER

WHILE yestereve, still dark and drear
With driving clouds the heavens were;
And strong and fast
The river through the arches past;

I crossed the quaking bridge alone,   5
Against whose pediments of stone
The surging tide
Swept trunks with arms distended wide.

With waters flowing broad and red,
The level lands were overspread;   10
Their early bloom
All withered in a common tomb.

The path so often trod of yore
No longer traced along the shore,
Before my eyes   15
The gloomy stream, the murky skies.

Oh heart, (I groaned) in such a sea,
Were truth and honor swept from thee,
Which should have been
As rooted forests, firm and green.   20

The flowers in my breast were drowned
By overwhelming passion;—found
My feet no more
A peaceful path along the shore.

But over rising sins and woes,   25
Alike, the simple arches rose
Of faith in God,
So that from shore to shore I trod.

And when, oh Love, serene and fair
The heavens are, and reäppear   30
On every lea,
The fragrant bloom, the steadfast tree;

Then richer for these beating rains
When harvest comes, in golden grains
That heart will be,   35
That trusted in its God and thee.

1847.

A WRECK

WHEN the lost ATLANTIC, drifted
Shoreward, in the surges rolled,
By each wave successive lifted,
Slowly tolled
From the wreck a bell resounding   5
Solemnly across that sounding,
Where lay corpses manifold.

So, when wrecked are my desires
On the everlasting NEVER,
And my heart, with all its fires,   10
Out forever,
These fond words, with sad vibration
O'er your bosom's desolation
Will lament the dead forever.

1847.

ON THE DEATH OF A KINSMAN*

I SEE an Eagle winging to the sun—
Who sayeth him nay?
He glanceth down from where his wing hath won:
His heart is stout, his flight is scarce begun,—
Oh hopes of clay!   5

Saw he not how upon the cord was lain
A keen swift shaft;
How Death wrought out in every throbbing vein,
In every after agony of pain,
His bitter craft!   10

Like old Demetrius, the sun had he
Beheld so long,
Now things of earth no longer could he see,
And in his ear sang Immortality
A pleasant song.   15

Icarus like, he fell when warm and near
The sunshine smiled:
He rose strong-pinioned in his high career—
—*Thy dust remains, thy glorious spirit where,*
Minerva's child?   20

Therefore him Fame had written fair and high

* Hon. Hugh S. Legaré [JML's note].

Upon her scroll,
Who fell like sudden meteor from the sky,
Who strenuous to win at last did die
E'en at the goal.   25

JUNE 21, 1843.

ORTA-UNDIS

Strophe

ORTA virgo resonantem
Vocem auribus undis,
Mihi animo prædulcem
Umbra solitudinis
Audio. Calentes agri   5
Nemoraque muta sunt:
Greges gratam coryleti
Umbram lassi conquirunt;
Umbram cantus insectorum
Sopientes quâ sonant,   10
Aquæ gelidæ saxorum
Fissurisque murmurant.
Mihi fervidis sed horis
Dëest quies nemore
Solo: Æstus nam amoris   15
Oritur in pectore
Vestibus cor palpitare
Solet lætum niveïs
Id tunc speras tu servare
Quod ab omnibus capis?   20
Felix qui cor (evax!) tuum
Palpitare audiat;
Caput cirrisque jampronum
Pectore ut sentiat.

Tuos risus, palpebrasque 25
Jam demissas video—
Cur me pacem spoliasque
Cur me sequeris, Virgo?

ORTA-UNDIS

Translated into English Prose
by
Richard A. Macksey

Strophe

Maiden sprung from the waves, I hear your voice resounding in my ears, the sweetest by far to my spirit, in [my] shadowy solitude. The warm fields and woods are quiet. The tired flocks seek the happy shade of hazel trees, [that] shade where sounds the plundering song of bees, and [where] cool waters murmur among the riven rocks. Yet there is no rest for me through fever- ish hours in this grove alone. For the fiery summer of love starts in my breast [where] a happy heart used to beat beneath snowy garments. Do you really hope to preserve what you snatch from all the rest? Happy is he who hears (O joy!) the beating of that heart of yours, [he whose] curly head is now bending o'er your breast to listen. Your laughter and now your downcast eyelashes I see. Why do you ravish my peace, and why, O maiden, do you follow me?

ORTA-UNDIS

Translated into English Verse
by
Richard A. Macksey

Strophe

MAIDEN risen from the waves,
In shadowy solitude I hear,
Sweet above all else to my soul,
Your voice resounding in my ear.

The warm fields and woodlands sleep   5
In silence and under hazel trees
The weary flocks and grazing sheep
Seek their pleasant shady ease.

And in that shade the plund'ring song
Of countless bees relentless drones   10
While icy waters whisper long
Amid their riven bed of stones.

And yet there is no rest for me
Through feverish hours in this grove alone:
For love's inflaming tyranny   15
Arises in my breast o'erthrown

Where once my heart was wont to beat
With joy beneath white linen bands.
But do you really hope to cheat
All those who seek to grasp your hands?   20

Happy is he who hears (at last!)
The beating of that heart of yours,
His head and ringèd curls pressed fast
To catch that sound your breast immures.

Your laughter rises to the sky,   25
And now your downcast eyes I see.
Why do you steal my peace and why
O Maiden, do you follow me?

TO THE "SWEETEST ROSE
OF GEORGIA"

SWEET, these cares will touch me lightly,
If that gentle face of thine
Wears no shadow. Only brightly
Let the old affection shine
From thine eye, and thou shalt see   5
How strong my heart can be!

Pray thee, dream not that disaster
You and me can come between,
O'er my heart I am no master
When thou art no longer queen.   10
False though to myself I be,
Faithfullest to thee.

If of tears or sorrow, often
I unwitting cause have been,
This thy indignation soften,   15
This, oh love, sufficient screen,
Be, for my offenses such—
That I loved too much!

(Hush! who spoke of indignation?
Was it I upon whose breast   20
She is wont with dear persuasion
In her happy eyes, to rest?
Surely, all that woman may,
She hath given me.)

Were thy lashes wet with weeping,   25
Flushed with joy or pale from fear,
Nay, upon death's threshold sleeping
Even,—drew my footsteps near
Would thy bosom beating faster
Hail its master!   30

Mine, aye mine, for ever!—Only
God can render thee less dear:
He, alone, can make thee lonely,
With a petrified despair
In thy looks—Oh, let us pray,   35
That He never may!

S. Carolina.

MAIZE IN TASSEL

THE blades of maize are broad and green,
The farm-roof scarcely shows between
The long and softly rustling rows
Through which the farmer homeward goes.
The blue smoke curling through the trees,   5
The children round their mother's knees,
He sees, and thanks God while he sees.

He holds one in his sturdy hands
Aloft, when at the threshold stands
(None noticed whence)—a stranger. "Dame,"   10
The stranger said, as half with shame
He made request: "astray and poor,
By hunger guided to your door
I"—"Hush," she answered, "say no more!"

The farmer set the prattler down   15
(Soft heart, although his hands were brown!).
With words of welcome brought and poured
Cool water from the spring: the board
The wife set out. What mellow light
Made the mean hovel's walls as white   20
As snow!—*how sweet their bread that night!*

Long while their humble lot had been
To dwell with Poverty: between
Them all one pallet and a bed
Were shared. But to the latter led   25

The guest in peaceful slumber lay,
While, with what broken sleep they may,
The dame and host await the day.

So passed the night. At length the dawn
Arrived, and showed the stranger gone.   30
To none had e'er been closed their door
Who asked for alms,—yet none before
Had so much lacked in courtesy.
So spoke the wife.—Her husband, he
Sat musing by most anxiously,   35

Of sterner need. A drought that year
Prevailed, and though the corn in ear
Began to swell, must perish all
Unless a kindly rain should fall.
God send it straight!—or toil from morn   40
To eve, the hoard of buried corn,
Aye, food itself, were lost and gone.

Such thoughts now bring him to the door,
Perchance some cloud sails up before
The morning breeze. None—none; in vain   45
His eyes explore the blue again:
With sighs to earth returns his gaze.
Ha!—what is here?—to God be praise!
See, see the glad drops on the maize!

No mist had dimmed the night, and yet   50
The furrows all lay soft and wet
As if with frequent showers; nay
More—all bloom that shuns the day,
And tassel tall and ear and blade,
With heavy drops were downward weighed,   55
And a swift stream the pathway frayed.

Long while might I prolong this strain,
Relating thence how great his gain:

How he who held not from the poor,
Now saw his corncribs running o'er.   60
And how his riches grew amain,
And on his hillside ripened grain
When parched was that within the plain.

But who the guest was of that night
Conjecture thou—I dare not write.   65
We know that angels with the mien
Of men, of men the guests have been:
That he who giveth to the poor
Lends to the Lord. (I am not sure——)
The promise here deep meaning bore.   70

South Carolina.

THE RUSTIC SEAT

COOL twilight shrouds the wooded hill,
As here the narrow street:
Its shadows urge thee from the rill
Meandering at thy feet.

The over-arching branches still   5
Enclose thee in their shade,
Where once my hands, with rustic skill.
A seat of branches made.

A long, long day of happiness,
(Yet scarce begun ere gone,)   10
While you stood by the work to bless
With eyes that smiled thereon.

A pleasant song the streamlet sung;
While in the still retreat,
The gnarled and mossy roots among,   15
We hollowed out the seat.

Quaint oaken boughs, trained to protrude
For arms, and where inclines
The musing head, a cushion rude
Of interwoven vines.   20

With happy eyes that wondered oft,
"When *would* it be complete?"
You knelt upon a couch of soft
Brown foliage at my feet;

Or, seated in the open sun   25
Amidst the holly trees,
With earnest face bent down upon
The book upon thy knees.

Withal, not many leaves that day
Were turned in book of thine,   30
So often went thy looks astray
In loving search of mine!

And when the work was all complete,
And I sat down to rest,
Relinquishing your former seat,   35
You nestled to my breast.

I mind me well—the sun went down
Behind a wooded hill,
The dusky autumn, forest brown,
More dusky grew and chill: 40

And when you shivered with the cold,
Around you, (nothing loth,)
I drew my cloak, whose ample fold
Enclosed and warmed us both.

It was a privilege of eld,   45
Long into habit grown,
That closely to my bosom held,
You should be styled "my own."

And now, so from the world apart,
Thy rest was doubly sweet:—   50
"Thank God!" could only say your heart,
"Thanks! Thanks!" at every beat.

THERE are leaves in the forest,
   And bloom on the plain,
And the swallows return
   To the cottage again.
And my darling and pet   5
   Has forgotten her sighs,
By the blush on her cheek
   And the light in her eyes.

But the blossoms were gone
   And the scent from the gale,   10
And the hawberries hung
   In long clusters and pale,
And the screen of dark firs
   Barred the red in the West,
When last her fair temples   15
   Were leaned on my breast.

From the brow of the steep
   Overlooking the vale,
How blue the far hills,
   And how balmy the gale   20
That rocked the tall pines
   At the feet of my queen;
Like chords of great harps
   Which her voice moved between.

How still were the woodlands!   25
  I heard the wet leaves
Drip fresh from the shower,
  And under the eaves
The tittering swallows,
  And from the cool dells   30
The kine wending homeward
  With tinkling of bells.

"Ah, peace!" my heart said then;
  And "Thanks be to God!"
That this green-fringéd path is   35
  No longer untrod
By the feet I love best.
  Yet the words half belied
The deep joy in my breast,
  When abruptly I cried;   40

"It is *you* with your brown eyes
  That haunt all my dreams!
Do you think I've no joy
  In the flowing of streams,
In the singing of birds,   45
  In the flights of wild-bees,
In the voices that moan
  In the tops of these trees?

"That you move my whole soul
  With the love in your looks,   50
Saying lovelier things
  Than are written in books;
Yes, in all my pet-books.
  Is it so?—that I'm thine
For aye; and thy being   55
  Cöeval with mine?"

And for answer, she only

Drew closer my heart,
So happy, so quiet,
  So loved, so apart   60
From the stir and the tumult!
  Oh happiest fate,
Where the head found a rest,
  And the spirit a mate.

Aiken, S.C., 1848.

ONE sunny day in Angouléme,
　While with an open book on knee,
I sat and mused of love, there came
　A servant of my lord to me.
Sir poet—spake he sans delay,　　　　　　5
My seigneur would thy skill essay.
　Then I went with him willingly.

My lord was in the castle court.
　Quoth he—"My lady here will bide,
And yon unseemly wall and moat,　　　　　10
　To do her pleasure, I would hide
With roses fair, for these have won
Her love of all." It shall be done
　To please my lady, I replied.

I chose to climb the eastern wall,　　　　　15
　A vine whereof the blossoms were
In size the chiefest of them all,
　That from below they might appear
Among their leaves; yet void of scent
Because that thither none e'er went,　　　　20
　Save birds that wanton in the air.

And for the moat a thorny hedge,
　But with gay flowers overspread,
I set along the nearer edge,
　That if unwary hand were led　　　　　　25

To pluck the bloom, the thorns might be
Sufficient guard, lest suddenly
   The slime should swallow up his tread.

Well pleased, my lord surveyed my care,
   Then smiling courteously—"Meseems,"   30
He said, "a lady debonnaire,
   When freshly wakened from her dreams,
She seeks her casement, there should find
The flower most she loves entwined.
   Now choose me that which sweetest seems."   35

Then at my lady's casement low,
   To welcome her and dewy day,
I taught an humble rose to blow,
   Which was not large, nor tall, nor gay,
As choicer bloom, but passing sweet,   40
So that, methinks, the very feet
   That bruised it, fragrant went away.

And when my lady came in state,
   All other flowers passed she by,
And coming to her casement straight,   45
   Led thither by that perfume high,
"This, truly," cried she, "love I best!"
And my meek flower on her breast
   Beneath a jewelled brooch did lie.

This action pleased me, and I said,   50
   In courtly phrase of troubadour,
Aye, lady mine, the highest head
   Is not the dearest loved, be sure—
Nor blooming cheek, nor snowy breast,
Can win a true heart, unpossessed   55
   Of sweetnesses that go before.

For I was thinking all the while
   Of mine own rose, whose soft brown eyes

Of carking care my days beguile.
   And well I know, though these despise   60
Her sweetness as unworth award,
Upon his breast a wiser Lord
   Will bear her fragrance to his skies.

Aiken, S.C.

THE SWORD AND PALETTE
A ROMAUNT

SIR Alvar in the joust no more
Triumphant lifts his lance,
Nor blooming lips, nor bookish lore,
Can win him from his trance.

Lo, through the wood, with heart that grieves,   5
My seigneur paces lone;
He hears the sadly sighing leaves,
The wood-dove's plaintive moan.

Crossed are his arms upon his breast,
Where nestles night and day   10
A vision, blue-eyed, golden-tressed,
That steals his peace away.

"And who is she so debonair,
Beyond our fairest dames,
That yonder page's blunted spear   15
Our seigneur's prowess shames?"

Your courtly dames, like jewels strung,
May courtly praises win:
The sweetest of our songs are sung
To Lilias of the Lynn.   20

Once royal Charles at banquet deigned
To hear my simple lays:
The burthen of my song unfeigned
Was still my Lilias' praise.

But when I sang how lowly born   25
Was she, a limner's child,
Methought with mingled pride and scorn
The jewelled circle smiled.

Oh, be the queenly rose his boast
That bears a haughty crest;   30
I love the lowly blossom most
That suits a russet vest.

II

It was the gray old painter, Mhand,
That stroked her radiant head;
He held his mall-stick in his hand,   35
And painted while she read.

The quaint, black-letter, old romance
She read, propped on her knee,
Of old Sir Hubert's brazen lance
That did the work of three.   40

Of how Sir Guy, with cross on sleeve,
In anger crossed the seas;
And left the faithless Maud to grieve
On penitential knees.

How county Lisle, in witless pride,   45
Misnamed his people "swine,"
And how by swinish tusks he died
When overcome with wine.

And of the tourneys good king John
Held in the open field;   50
And of the couplet Giles of Bonn
Bore ever on his shield.

But more than all these gorgeous dreams
Those legends golden were,
Wherein nor strife nor warlike gleams   55
Disturbed her soul with fear.

Wherein from courts the noble came
To woo the lowly breast;
Her parted lips scarce breathed the name
Her fluttering heart confessed.   60

III
Ofttimes and grim old Maller-Mhand
His mall-staff shook aloft;
"Who rides a tilt to gain thy hand,
Must be no lisper soft.

"Beshrew thy Baron's coat of mail;   65
I love one of mine craft!"
Fair Lilias' cheek waxed red and pale
The while her sire laughed.

Him seeking, haughty Alvar came
As one unused to plea: 70
I wot, from Languèdoc to Maine
No braver was than he!

"Sir Painter," Alvar courteous spoke,
Beneath the painter's roof;
"In vain a heart of stubborn oak   75
I guard with armor proof.

"But yestermorn, in open lists,
My lance achieved the prize;
Their jewelled hands our ladies kissed,
I only sought *her* eyes.   80

"It chafed me sore, my queen should bide
Among ignoble dames:
Let shield-of-eight and courtship wide
Henceforth assert her claims."

IV
Loud laughed in scorn old Maller-Mhand,   85
Loud laughed and curled his beard:

"He comes with mall-stick in his hand
Who woos the Golden-haired.

"Thy breast, steel-clad, is all too cold
To rest such tender head;   90
Pale were thy boasted heaps of gold
Beside its lightest shred.

"I scorn thy braggart deeds of might,
The wolf that slays the lamb.
Blood flecks thy knightly mantle white,   95
And soils thy lordly palm.

"Go,—on thy wrist, in lieu of bird,
A palette perch—then come."
—Amazed the haughty noble heard,
With shame and anger dumb.   100

Then, frowning, spoke: "Are knightly hands
To serve for such as *thou?*
Know, dotard, nobles reap the lands,
Your peasant holds the plough.

"Ill suits thy cloak of clownish red,   105
The pearl it would conceal!"
With scornful insolence he said,
And turned upon his heel.

"Ha! Lilias! what evil chance,
Has led thee to this place?"   110
His rage went out, so piteously,
The tears ran down her face.

The sorrow that her eyes replied
Pierced his stout cuirass through,
And all his panoply of pride   115
Triumphant love o'erthrew.

"Oh Lilias, my only love,
How can I less than yield?

This morn above a mourning dove
At fault my gos-hawk wheeled.   120

"The augury I sought to trace
I gather in thy sighs."
—He held her in a close embrace,
Then vanished from her eyes.

I know some angel, glad and bright,   125
Her chamber entered in,
So joyous were the dreams that night
Of Lilias of the Lynn.

But through the wood, with heart that grieves,
Sir Alvar, pacing lone,   130
Hears overhead the sighing leaves,
And night owl's boding moan.

V

Oh, happy spring-time of the heart,
When love is daily food,
Through which are dangers counted naught,   135
And difficulties woo'd!

Where rose in ancient Roman time
Imperial Caesar's throne,
As stranger from some northern clime
Was lordly Alvar known.   140

No more his knightly deeds command
The lists, his shield advanced:
Before the easel, staff in hand,
The painter stood entranced.

In lieu of hawk, a palette graced   145
His wrist, of polished wood:
In lieu of glittering train, pale-faced,
Behind the MASTER stood.

Much mused the Fra Bartolemè
This marvel to construe,   150
That under cowl of monkish gray
Lurked eyes of tender blue.

And Magdalen within the wood
As northern maids was fair:
And choirs of bright angels stood,   155
Each crowned with golden hair.

Sweet Lilias, the guiding thought,
His pencil still confessed;
While, looking inwardly, he wrought
The vision in his breast.   160

VI

Swift glide the months to years,
Which patient labors claim:
And once again Sir Alvar wears
The recompense of fame.

Now, while the wreath the painting crowned   165
The victor paced apart:
His eyes, fond-musing, sought the ground
While rambling with his heart:

Saw, at the bending of the road,
The blue Rhine reäppear;   170
And how, through trellised vineyards, showed
The roof that held his fair.

"Ah, Lilias, my only love,
How can I less than yield?"
Came sweetly to his ear above   175
The clang of listed field.

"And lives she for his bosom's pride—
To none her charms resigned?"
"Peace, dreamer!" quick his love replied,

And left all doubt behind.   180

While thus his grateful fancies ran,
Like hillside waters sweet—
To thirsty souls that pause to scan
The valley at their feet;

Nearer, along the corridor   185
A maid and sire strayed,
Until the pendant wreath before
Their noiseless feet delayed.

High on the wall the chaplet hung,
And Alvar's toil below;   190
The tale an ancient poet sung,
On canvass taught to glow.

In smiling light Arcadia lay
Green sloping in her hills;
Burst from the mossy rocks and grey,   195
Innumerable rills.

Yet swifter than the brook could flee,
With panting bosom fled
Young Daphnè; supplicatingly
Her little hands she spread.   200

Silenus hears. With laurel bark
Her tender limbs compressed:
The broad and glossy leaves surround
Her palpitating breast.

But through the interlacing shade   205
Of slender stems, appear
Blue eyes, and oft a golden braid
Of long and loosened hair.

Amazed and mute the father spied
His Lilias portrayed;   210

In place of kirtle, white and wide,
In leafy robes arrayed.

Amazed and fluttered stood his child,
And, with a maiden art,
Concealed with folded hands the wild,   215
Loud beating of her heart.

Then, yielding to the inward strife,
Between her falling tears,
She cried aloud, "My lord—my life!"
—*Oh music to his ears!*   220

She stood in garments wide and white,
Blue-eyed and golden-tressed;
She stood and blessed his raptured sight,
Her burning love confessed.

No longer Fatherland had charms   225
To woo him from the South:
He held her in his circling arms,
And kissed her, mouth to mouth.

And as the mariners distressed,
In haven safe, display   230
Their penons all—upon his breast
With smiling face she lay.

—Now out upon that demon owl
That boded in the wood;
That well nigh drove to monkish cowl   235
A noble soul and good!

But said I not some angel bright
Her chamber entered in,
When sweetest visions came that night
To Lilias of the Lynn.   240

TO JASMINES IN DECEMBER

YOUNG jessamines that bloom as sweet
As if it now were May,
Though crisp brown leaves beneath the feet
Hide all the forest way,
I pray you soft my darling greet,   5
And in her bosom say:

Bloom freshly on, thou sister fair,
While pleasant Spring remains,
And while the Autumn's yellow hair
Is plaited thick with grains;   10
For soon will Winter, white and drear,
Encamp upon these plains.

But if thou art not, Love, inclined
To perish with the rest,
When birds may scarce warm shelter find,   15
Then blossom out thy best.
And surely one true heart I'll find
To wear thee on his breast.

And for thy perfume's sake, unstirred
He'll front the icy sleet,   20
The icy sleet of worldly words,
And gather round his feet
In fancy, Spring again, and birds
With carols high and sweet.

Yes, make his winter mild again,   25
And bring him back his May,
And though in prison cell, all men
Will envy him the day.
Not fetters, but a sceptre!—then
The baffled crowds will say.   30

Aiken, S.C., 1848.

A LAUREL BLOSSOM

THE broad and glossy leaves surround
The laurel blossoms fair,
Like ivory young temples bound
With shining bands of hair.
And says the flower naught to thee   5
Who art its sister, dear?

Nay, nay, see, love, the flower's mute,
She uttered with a smile.
Speak thou. My heart with softest lute
Shall answer thee the while,   10
And sure no touching of thy hand
Can any cord defile.

Ah, love, I said, thy loveliness
Will fade away and die.
For see thy little feet they press   15
The bloom that was so high.
Yea, this fair cheek that warms to mine
With meanest things will lie.

Then bending forward to elude
My gaze, I know indeed,   20
She said with utterance subdued,
That through the portals low and yewed
My spirit will be freed.
But is there naught more high and sweet,
My poet, in thy creed?   25

And now her eyes came swiftly up
With brimming love to mine.
Oh friend, as you would drain a cup
Of generous Rhenish wine,
I drank from out those shaded wells;   30
Tarns fringed around with pine.

Then fervently; Yes, thanks to God,
Thou canst not wholly die,
Though underneath the sloping sod,
Meek kisser of the lifted rod,   35
Thy winning ways all lie.
Fade young May bloom; fresh spread the leaves
That brave the wintry sky.

Until the lord of all this wood
With Godlike mouth shall say to thee;   40
"Well done, thou servant wise and good."
Yes, deathless spirit at my knee,
Himself the dear Lord whom we love,
With Godlike mouth shall speak to thee.

Aiken, March 11th.

BALD GRAS ICH

From the Wunderhorn* (German)

I.

"I MOW by the Neckar,
And reap by the Rhine:
I own a heart's treasure
Yet lonely I pine.

"What matters the meadow   5
If scythe I have none:
What matters the treasure
If from me he's gone?

"But if I must mow
By the Neckar and Rhine,   10
I'll throw in the waters
This gold ring of mine.

"It floats down the Neckar,
It drifts down the Rhine;
It shall swim on thereunder,   15
And sink in the brine."

II.

But a fish as it swimmeth

* I can't say whether that graceless little genius, BETTINE BRENTANO [or Arnim,] wrote the original of the above version, although she had somewhat to do with editing the book. What a pity, while one reads of her climbing trees, sitting on Goethe's knee, and all that, it is so difficult to forget it is a respectable old soul,—quite an old soul now,—who is reviewing her eccentric life!

J. M. LEGARE

263

Hath swallowed the ring:—
They serve up the fish
At the board of the king.   20

Spoke out the king thereat,
"Whose ring shall this be?"
Then out spoke my Treasure,
"This ring is for me."

My heart's-dearest, riding   25
Both up hill and down,
Quick brought my ring back
From the court and the town.

Thou mayst reap, said he, darling,
By Neckar and Rhine,   30
But throw not henceforward
Thy plight in the brine.

South Carolina.

THANATOKALLOS

I THINK we faint and weep more than is manly;
I think we more mistrust, than Christians should.
Because the earth we cling to interposes
And hides the lower orbit of the sun,
We have no faith to know the circle perfect,   5
And that day will follow on the night:
Nay more, that when the sun we see, is setting,
He is rising on another people;
And not his face but ours veiled in darkness.
We are less wise than were the ancient heathen   10
Who tempered feasting with a grisly moral.

With higher hope, we shrink from thoughts of dying,
And dare not read, while yet of death unbidden,
As Gipsies in the palm, those seams and circles
And time-worn lineaments in which kings in purple   15
Have trembled to behold, but holy men,
Interpreting aright, like martyred STEPHEN,
In singleness of heart have sunk to sleep;
GOD's children weary us with an evening ramble.
Unthinking custom from our very cradle   20
Makes us most cowards where we should be bold.
The house is closed and hushed; a gloom funereal
Pervades the rooms once cheerful with the light;
Sobs and outcries from those we love, infect us
With strange disquiet, making play unsought   25

Before they take us on the knee and tell us
We must no more be joyful, for a dread
And terrible calamity has smitten one.

And then, poor innocents, with frighted hearts
Within the awful chamber are we led   30
To look on death; the hard impassive face,
The formal shroud, which the stiff feet erect
Into the semblance of a second forehead,
Swathed and concealed; the tumbler whence he drank
Who ne'er shall drink again; the various adjuncts   35
Of a sick room; the useless phials
Half emptied only, on the hearth the lamp,
Even the fly that buzzes round and settles
Upon the dead man's mouth, and walking thence
Into his nostril, starts him not from slumber.   40
All portions of the dreary changeless scene
In the last drama, with unwholesome stillness
Succeeding to the weepings and complaints
Of Heaven's own justice, and loud cries for succor
That fill the dying ear not wholly dead,   45
Distract the fluttering spirit, and invest
A death-bed with a horror not its own.
I thought of these things sadly, and I wondered
If in this thanatopsis, soul as clay
Took part and sorrowed. While I this debated,   50
I knew my soul was loosing from my hold,
And that the pines around, assuming shape
Of mournful draperies, shut out the day.
Then I lost sight and memory for a moment,
Then stood erect beside my usual couch,   55
And saw my longwhile tenement, a pallid
And helpless symbol of my former self.
The hands laid heavily across the breast,
The eyelids down, the mouth with final courage

That aimed a smile for sake of her who watched,   60
But lapsed into a pang and so congealed.
Half sweet, half suffering: Aria to Caecinna.

Poor sinful clod, erewhile the spirit's master
Not less than servant, with desire keen
Alloying love, and oft with wants and achings   65
Leading the mind astray from noblest deeds
To sell it's birth-right for an ESAU'S portion.
I all forgave, for I was all forgiven.
Phosphor had brought a day too broad for twilight
Or mist upon its confines. All the old   70
Sad mysteries that raise gigantic shadows
Betwixt our mortal faces and GOD'S throne,
Had fainted in its splendor; pride and sin,
Sorrow and pain, and every mortal ill,
In the deserted tenement remained,   75
A palace outwardly, a vault within.
And so, because she thought it still a palace
And not a prison with the prisoner fled,
She stood before the gates accustomed. Weeping,
Laid her moist cheek upon its breast, and cried,   80
"My lord! my life!" to what had ceased from living,
And could no more command with word or eyes.
It moved my pity sorely, for these fingers,
Now locked in agonizing prayer, once turned
Gently the pages of his life who slumbered;   85
And this brave mouth, with words of faith and cheer,
Strewed flowers in the path he needs must tread.
That as a conqueror and not a captive,
Dragged at the heavy chariot wheels of Time,
And through an arch triumphal, where for others   90
A narrow portal opens in the sod,
Silent and sad and void of outlet, he
The kingdom of his LORD might enter in.

Thus she made dying sweet and full of beauty
As life itself. There was no harsh transition;   95
He that slept two-fold, woke a single nature,
Beatified and glad. But she who stayed,
Poor little Roman heart, no longer brave
Now that the eyes were shut for evermore,
Which made all virtues sweeter for their praise,   100
Saw not the joy and greatness of the change.
And I drew near her, as a spirit may
Not to the mortal ear, but that the words
Seemed teachings of her bruised and lowly soul.
"Is this the poet of thy summer days,   105
The thoughtful husband of maturer years?
Are these the lips whose kindly words could reach
The deepness of thy nature? If they be,
Let them resume their own, not tarry. Nay,
Thou *knowest,* all that thou didst ever love   110
Is lifted out, and all that thou didst hate
Lived in the flesh, and with the flesh remains.
What matters it to thee, if this decays
And mingling with the sod, is trampled on
Of clownish feet, by gleaming share upturned,   115
Or feeds a rose, or roots a noisome weed?
How canst thou halve thy heart, half to the grave
Half to high Heaven yield? Thank GOD instead,
That he who was so dear to thee, released
From sin and care, at length has found great peace."   120
While she thus mused, her silent tears were stayed,
And kneeling down with her sweet patient face,
Lifted toward Heaven, itself sufficient prayer,
"LORD GOD!" she cried, "thou knowest best how weak
And frail I am, and faithless; give me strength   125
To take the rod thou sendest for a staff,
And falter never more in this lone journey!"

Then she went forth and gathered freshest flowers
And strewed them on the dead: young violets
Upon the breast, verbena round the temples,   130
Loose rose-leaves o'er the mouth, to hide the pang,
And in his hand a lily newly opened,
In token of her faith and his transition.
And in her eyes there reigned such quietude
That those who saw her, said an angel surely   135
Has spoken with her: or, her reason's moved
By sufferings prolonged. But none might say
She loved but lightly, or with levity
Looked forward to the common lot of all.

Aiken, S.C. 1849.

THE TWO KING'S-CHILDREN

This old ballad (translated from the German version in Germanicus Voelkerstimmen) is found in several of the languages having a common origin—such as the Swedish, Danish, Netherlandish or Dutch, and even perhaps in some others.

BEHOLD two children of a king,
Who held each other dear—
They could not each to other come
So deep the waters were.

Thou can'st, my love, right bravely swim,   5
Swim over here to me;—
By night a torch shall lighten up
The way across the sea.

Now there was one false-hearted nun
Crept softly to the sea,   10
And smothered out his light: the prince
Lost in the waves was he.

The daughter to her mother spoke:
"My heart is full of woe—
To wander out along the beach   15
I pray thee let me go."

The mother to the chapel goes,
The daughter seeks the shore;—
She walks all sorrowful and lone,
With grief her heart is sore.   20

"Ah, fisherman, good fisherman!
How ill I am dost see:
Thou can'st and must assist me;—cast
Thy nets along the sea.

"Here have I lost my best beloved
Of all the world around:
If thou can'st fish my treasure up
With gold thou shalt abound."

"For thee this day long will I fish—
God's gifts I'll take, no more."—
He casts his net,—what findeth he?
The prince he drags to shore.

"Now, noble fisher, take thou that
Thy service doth thee gain;
Here is my diamond coronet,
And here my golden chain."

She took her best-loved in her arms,
His wan lips kissed in vain:
"Ah, faithful mouth! could'st thou but speak
My heart would live again!"

She drew him closely to her breast,
The breast so full of woe,
And with him caring naught for life,
Leaped in the waves below.

25

30

35

40

A HUSBAND TO A WIFE

WIFE, my heart is yearning for you,
  For your fond and winning ways.
Come and take this darkness from me,
  Let me find again your praise.
How you love me! Sweet, your kisses   5
  Have not grown more cold or few;
Though in place of sunny meadows,
  Cheerless paths I've led you through.

But my heart I think grows older.
  Once the birds were sweet to hear;   10
Blooming flowers touched me kindly,
  Spring and Fall alike were fair.
Now I scarcely heed a blossom
  Brushing past my cheek, and dim
Strikes the sunshine through the forest,   15
  And the valleys have no hymn.

Books once petted, poor companions
  For a walk. I have no thought
Any more for pleasant rhymings,
  Any more for reading aught   20
Which gave frequent pleasure. Toiling
  Upward hopelessly and long,
Scarcely strength remains for praying,
  And no longer breath for song.

You and I embarked together 25
    When all Earth was full of speech,
And the kiss of every ripple
    Said, "I love thee" to the beach.
Now night broods across the waters,
    Far from sight or sound of shore, 30
And the straining ear is sated
    With the labor of the oar.

Kiss me softly on the forehead:
    Draw me safely to thy breast.
Lest Hereafter's hopes be bartered 35
    For a temporary rest.
Nothing shakes thy strong affection,
    And it is thy joy and pain,
To be loved as never woman
    Was, or can be loved again. 40

Aiken, S.C.

JANETTE

I was the last of all my kin,
My food was scant, my gown was thin.
I would have sooner died than sin.

With cunning words he sought me out.
"My father served him—not without   5
Return." I was too young to doubt.

He took me to his home by stealth:
His wife was there in feeble health;
His wife, who bought him with her wealth.

I knew how much he did despise   10
Her meaner gifts, his loving lies;
I saw it in his scornful eyes.

Her nature, sullen by reproof,
Held him in better moods aloof.
But I was grateful for their roof: 15

And sought by gentleness to teach
The duty each did owe to each;
Her patience, him more kindly speech.

I thawed her heart, I changed her face,
His words partook of better grace;   20
There was more sunlight in the place.

He sat whole hours at her knee.
I was too glad in heart to see

How much it was for love of me.

He spread his cunning wiles so true,   25
I was ensnared before I knew
I loved with every breath I drew.

He read the riddle soon as I.
He stayed me when I thought to fly.
I wept; Oh, was no GOD on high!   30

I would have sooner died than sin:
I fell and lived. All tears within
My scorching eyes were dried therein.

And on my forehead burned a name
That crazed me. Then with cheek aflame   35
I fled into the night for shame.

I hid myself within a wood.
I had laid by my womanhood,
And shared their rustic toil and food.

I hated all things good and pure   40
That mocked me. But I hated more
The heart that loved him at its core.

I trod upon my heart and fate.
Because my love had been so great,
I hated him with cruel hate.   45

I gathered patience in my strife.
I waited. Time removed his wife;
She stood between me and his life.

I waited till his home should be
Stripped of its mourning garb, and he   50
Crossed by no thought of pain or me.

He slew my happiness by craft.
He should be smiling when he quaffed
My hate. I hid myself and laughed.

I took a dagger sharp and bright,   55
I held its flashing from the light,
And that I shaded from his sight.

I turned the lamp upon his cheek;
I saw him lying pale and weak,
As one that from Death's hold did break.   60

His fevered lips, as in unrest,
Moved to my name. What thirsty guest
Held I in hand to probe his breast!

If he had slept in conscious pride
Of strength; if by one smile defied   65
My misery, he then had died.

I thought to find him brave and gay.
I could not strike him as he lay;
I pitied where I thought to slay.

I thrust the weakness from my brain,   70
I trampled on my heart in vain.
A viewless hand on mine was lain.

Look back, a spirit in me said,
My sense of vision turned its head,
And rested on a snowy bed;   75

Wherein a sleeping infant lay.
I knew it was the pleasant May,
Such heavy bloom was on the spray.

I saw the infant grown a maid,
Before the glass her tresses braid,   80
And smiled upon the image made.

And later, kneeling down to smooth
The dying bed of one in sooth,
Who uttered words of grace and truth.

"This life is but a little space.   85
Live purely, love, that by GOD'S grace
We may rejoin in better place."

And have I lived so!—GOD on high,
My spirit hastened to reply,
Knew that thy life had been no lie   90

To him, nor to thy sex untrue,
Until this wronger did undo
Thy weaker nature. Strike him through:

And in his life wash out thy shame.
Men will accord thee fairer name   95
Than now. GOD judges not the same.

More noble this. He did thee harm;
Forgive. Forgiveness self's a charm,
Which may avert GOD'S vengeful arm.

He wronged thee not beyond thy prime.   100
Alas! with what abhorrent crime,
Thou comest here to sear all time.

In one short moment all these things
My spirit showed. The fevered springs
Of life seemed fanned by angel wings.   105

My cool, cool tears were falling fast.
Unconscious what I did, I cast
My dagger down: he woke aghast.

My pallid face, the open door,
The naked weapon on the floor,   110
He saw. "JANETTE!"—he said no more.

I knew in that one startled look
His very soul my crime in-took,
As written in an open book.

Then on a sudden bared his breast.   115
Come strike, he said, so it is best
Thy bitter wrong should be redressed.

Too late I tried to overtake
My sin. My heart did only break
On disappointment for thy sake.   120

I cannot love thee less, Oh sweet!
I will not struggle. At his feet
I bowed down: how my heart did beat!

He called me quick; I raised my head,
He was as pale as one that's dead.   125
"I love you still!" was all he said.

He drew me up, he kissed my face,
My nerveless hands, that in that place
Had slain him but for better grace.

I knew while on his breast I lay,   130
Although no word his mouth did say,
That CHRIST his sin had done away:

And changed to peace of heart my wo,
Despite my penitence was slow.
GOD grant us all our sins to know.   135

Aiken, January, 1850.

THE HEMLOCKS

ALL poets who with thoughtful awe
Walk the green earth, as men advised
Of holy ground, some sweetness draw
From things of other minds despised;

And understand the hidden springs   5
Of love and hate in human kind.
And yet, 'tis said, a linnet sings
The sweetest when its eyes are blind.

The city ladies' eyes were wet,
Or treated with no show of scorn   10
His lines: they touched me nearer yet,
Although I am but country born.

My cheek was pale for lack of life,
And paler for my mourning gown;
And when he came, the winds at strife   15
Had brought my heavy tresses down.

And I was leaning on my hand
In listless mood: The pines below
Made solemn music through the land,
Quite up to where the hemlocks grow.   20

I saw a shadow move across
The cliff, before I met his look,
His noiseless foot was on the moss;
An angler by his rod and book.

The hemlock trunks were rough and tall,　　25
Their fibrous roots, thrust forth to drink
The moisture of the waterfall,
With lichens hid the awful brink.

I would have called in my affright.
My coward tongue was stricken mute.　　30
—It was as swift as thought or sight,
A sudden gap within the root.

And if he cried, the cry was lost,
And I was kneeling on the sod.
And wept to see the chasm crossed,　　35
And in his grasp the broken rod.

There swung a vine with clusters brown,
Between two trunks from each to each;
With all my strength I drew it down,
With all my might I bore it down,　　40
Until it fell within his reach.

And when he thanked me with grave eyes,
And with a pale but gracious lip,
I felt as when a maiden spies
The pennon of her lover's ship.　　45

The ship that from a foreign sea
Brings the true heart of which she dreamed
But yesternight. A Mystery
Grew up between us then meseemed.

I little thought of love before;　　50
I knew he won my heart with ease.
The rustic swains who shunned my door,
Had thought me coy and hard to please.

Their laughter seldom moved my mirth
Because it was as grainless sheaves;　　55

I better love the gala earth
And songs of birds among the leaves.

The dewey sward, the misty height
Slow purpling in the morning gleam,
The copses where with footsteps light   60
He came to angle in the stream.

And sat whole hours at my knee
Repeating from some pleasant book,
While tangled in a stooping tree
His line detained the guiltless hook.   65

And once he read beside the rill
Some verses with a cadence sweet,
And when I praised the writer's skill
He laid the poem at my feet.

And smiled and said the lines were his,   70
And written for a lady fair,
Who loved all Nature as it is
Better than breathing city air;

But that she far excelled his rhymes,
And might have worn a civic crown   75
If she had lived in Roman times;
And how her lovely eyes were brown.

And that he loved her more than life
Itself or fame: this much he said,
When stricken in a playful strife,   80
Sickening, I turned my head—

I turned my foolish head to hide
The tears that would not be repressed;
But when my altered mien he spied,
He drew me blushing to his breast.   85

And I, because I understood
The story, and its purpose then,
In that brief moment,—as he would,
Turned my wet face to his again.

"And do you love me so?! he cried,"   90
"And are you not the lady fine?"
I knew in all the land beside
There was no lighter heart than mine.

Aiken, Dec., 1851.

THE LIGHTHOUSE*

I

ACROSS a league of angry breakers
And three of waste and drifting sand,
With curlews wading in the shadows
And white gulls fishing off the land;

II

A beacon on the far horizon,   5
Nearer a tower worn and white,
A lighthouse half and half a prison,
With rusted gratings round the light;

III

Barren the shore and unfrequented,
And fretted ever by the sea;   10
And these and such were his surroundings,
A hero, and the last of three.

IV

On the long swell from the Bermudas,
While great Orion climbs the sky,
Remote at sea in night and silence,   15
Like sheeted ghosts the fleet go by;

* A version of the above poem having appeared in the July number of
Putnam's Monthly, the author thinks he may show a modest preference for
his unaided composition, by a re-publication of the poem as it stood a few
weeks since in the MS furnished to that Magazine. Whether the Editor of
"Putnam's" in assuming the novel literary powers he has, has exceeded his
ability as far as he has his function of Editor, the public may decide.

J. M. LEGARE.

V

Or surging in the wide Atlantic
Impetuous rolled upon the lee,
When the low coast is lost in drizzle
And white with foam is all the sea.   20

VI

Ah, what endurance and endeavor
Were his who watched between these bars,
On that drear night when wildest tempest
Shut out the earth, the sea, the stars!

VII

Not so had been the autumn morning,   25
Fair skies, light breezes off the shore;
And the two wardens of the tower
Sailed from it to return no more.

VIII

For through the gates of the Antilles
Coastwise there drove a mist that day,   30
And in its wake were frothing waters
And a wild hurricane they say.

IX

In rolled, white capped, the tumbling billows
With bursts of phosphorescent spray,
Fled the wild rack across the heavens   35
And sudden night obscured the day.

X

Shoreward from sea and sedgy marshes
Toiled the sea birds to reach the main,
Drifting aslant before the tempest
Bewildered by the driving rain.   40

XI

Around this tower with cries discordant
Wheeling in oft repeated flight,
They caught on wet and glancing pinions
The gleam of the revolving light.

XII

Through the rain-blurred and beaten casement   45
Each following each in endless chase,
Fled bars of light pursued by shadows
In wider circles round the place:

XIII

Swept over sands and Sound and inlet,
And leagues of sea lashed by the gale,   50
And past the shoal and dangerous headland
In safety guided many a sail.

XIV

And direful wreck had been and drowning
Where wreck had never been before,
Had it but faltered in revolving   55
And seemed some casual light ashore.

XV

Three nights a star on the horizon
By turns illuming sea and sound,—
No mortal hand, sure, fired the beacon
And trailed the glittering lamps around!   60

XVI

For in the first of the tornado,
Just where the seas and currents crossed,
'Whelmed in th' infuriate Atlantic
Both keepers of the Light were lost.

XVII

It was a child of tender years,   65
Kept lonely vigil in their stead,
Nor knew that in the hollow surges
Rolled sire and grandsire stark and dead.

XVIII

He thought of tales of shipwreck dire,
On coasts sea girt and lying low;   70
Of wretches lost in the Atlantic,
And set the glimmering lamps a-row.

XIX

Poised in its well within the tower,
A ponderous weight controls, by night,
Through multiplying wheels and pinions   75
The revolutions of the light.

XX

How he long toiled—a child's endeavor—
At the stiff crank to raise this weight,
While darker rolled the ocean ever,
And wind and rain assailed the grate;   80

XXI

How his great soul remained undaunted
When all his childish strength was vain,
While deeper night involved the ocean,
And wilder beat the wind and rain;

XXII

And how disjoined from wheel and pinion,   85
Studded with lights, a sparkling reel,
Round and around in bright gyrations
He drew at last the cumbrous wheel;

XXIII

And so from shipwreck in the breakers
Saved many a gallant ship, 'tis said,   90
They knew, and wept, who on the morrow
Found him still at his post—but *dead*.

XXIV

'Twas when the furious hurricane
On the fourth day had ceased to blow,
And there were wrecks from Corrientes   95
To the pine shores of Pamlico;

XXV

There came a boat across the seas
In which the keepers twain were drowned,
And found him resting on his knees—
A poor dead child was all they found.   100

XXVI

If 'twas of hunger that he died,
Or thirst, or stress of long fatigue,
Or all conjoined—who may decide?
Witness was none for many a league.

XXVII

Haply it was some angel bright   105
That stood to strengthen all his soul
And helped the feeble hand to write
His name in an immortal scroll.

XXVIII

Give, O blind world, your loud applause
To men renowned through blood and tears—   110
'Twas not for *that* he gave his life
And these are not among his peers.

APPENDIXES

COMMENTARY ON THE POEMS OF JAMES M. LEGARE

My Sister

FIRST PUBLISHED: *The Rambler* (Charleston, S.C.), I (Oct. 23, 1843), 40. REPRINTED: Simms's *Southern and Western Monthly Magazine and Review* (Charleston, S. C.), II (Dec., 1845), 366–67, as "Quae Carior?" (in part); *O-U*, pp. 12–14, as "Quae Carior?" (in part).

JML's only sister was Frances Doughty Legaré (1826–1897). The German couplet derives from the work of Friedrich Leopold, Graf zu Stolberg (1750–1819), and is a slight misquotation of verses 10–11 in his "An die Natur (1775). The meaning may be rendered as, "Ah! it's so good to be with you/ I'll love you forever and ever!" (See the *Gesammelte Werke der Brüder Christian und Leopold Grafen zu Stolberg* [20 vols.; Hamburg: Friedrich Perthes, 1827], I, 113.)

VERSES 7–8 (Quis . . . capitis!). "What shame or limit could there be to the desire/For such a dear person?" (Horace, *Carmina,* I. 24. I.)

Addressing the Philadelphia publishers, Carey & Hart, from Charleston, May 19, 1845, submitting a manuscript volume (an early draft of *O-U*) for their consideration, JML wrote in part as follows: "To any profit resulting I am indifferent, as my desire is chiefly to thus obtain an acceptable offering to the sister, (an only one) to whom I have dedicated the work. A *few* of the articles have been published in magazines, before. The title (I need not mention) is merely *'Belonging to the muse of verse'* (*Erato.*)." (The letter is printed in full in CCD [2], p. 422.)

All Hail the Bride!

FIRST PUBLISHED: *The Orion: or, Southern Monthly: A Magazine of Literature and Art* (Charleston), IV (March, 1844), 27.

VERSE 27 (Jeärus). Presumably a typographical error for Icarus, the youth who, according to Greek mythology, whilst in flight by air from Crete fell into the Mediterranean and drowned when the sun melted the wax with which his wings were fastened to his body. JML refers to him in "On the Death of a Kinsman," verse 16.

Du Saye

FIRST PUBLISHED: *The Charleston Book: A Miscellany in Prose and Verse* [edited by William Gilmore Simms] (Charleston: Samuel Hart, Sr., 1845), pp. 189–99.

VERSE 3 (Congaree). The Congaree River, in the central part of the State, unites with the Wateree to form the Santee River.

VERSE 45 (Condé). Probably Prince Louis II de Condé (1621–1686), Duke d'Enghien, called "the Great," who during the civil wars of the Fronde in France, 1648–1653, allied himself with Spain against his sovereign, Louis XIV.

VERSE 87 (Horry). Col., later Gen. Peter Horry (1747–1815), one of Marion's subordinates in guerrilla operations. As JML's meter suggests, the name is pronounced o-*ree*. His "Journal," ed. A. S. Salley, has been published in the *South Carolina Historical and Genealogical Magazine* over the period 1937–1947.

In his letter to Carey & Hart (see commentary under "My Sister," above) JML concluded: "I believe it would be better to place the verses to 'my sister' *before* the uninteresting DuSaye."

Quae Pulchrior?

FIRST PUBLISHED: *Southern and Western Monthly Magazine and Review* (Charleston, S.C.), I (Jan., 1845), 25–26. REPRINTED: *O-U*, pp. 25–29.

The Latin title means, "Who Fairer?" In the 1848 version JML omitted the dedication to Miss Mary C., and the month at end. Textually he increased each stanza by one verse at its close, made a variety of minor punctuational alterations throughout, and revised the first two stanzas, which originally stood as follows:

> I woo thee, thou bright one,
> With soul and with song.
> Thy praise from my bosom
> Flows fervid and strong.
> How faint to thee, matchless!   5
> Earth's beautiful are:
> I worship and woo thee,
> Bright maid, from afar.
>
> I seek not, as Danae,
> Jove captured of old,   10
> I seek not to win thee
> With showers of gold.
> I bring thee no jewels,
> No titled renown;
> What wealth hath the scholar   15
> Whose wreath is a crown!

VERSE 63 (Bayard). Pierre du Terrail, Seigneur de Bayard (*ca.* 1473–1524), French soldier renowned as the "chevalier sans peur et sans reproche." The appearance of his name only with the 1848 version of this poem may reflect JML's reading of W. G. Simms's *The Life of the Chevalier Bayard* . . . (New York, 1847).

VERSE 76 (Sylla). Lucius Cornelius Sulla [*sic*] (138–78 B.C.), Roman general and politician, was dictator during 82–79. (See E. Badian, "Waiting for Sulla," in his *Studies in Greek and Roman History* [New York: Barnes & Noble, Inc., 1964], pp. 206–34.)

"The reviewer would like to quote all of 'Quae Pulchrior?,' if only to show his readers how trippingly it goes but also to ask the poet what a 'carcanet mind' is [verse 22]?" (*Southern Literary*

Messenger, XIV [June, 1848], 388–89.) The epithet applies to an ornamental collar or necklace, or to a band for the head.

Quae Carior?

FIRST PUBLISHED: *Southern and Western Magazine and Review* (Charleston, S.C.), II (Dec., 1845), 366–67. REPRINTED: *O-U,* pp. 12–14.

The Latin title means, "Who Dearer?" In the 1848 version JML inserted six minor punctuational alterations.

Georgiana

FIRST PUBLISHED: *Southern and Western Magazine and Review* (Charleston, S.C.), II (July, 1845), 17, as "Miserere." The title was doubtless taken by JML, in common with many other poets and artists, from the opening words of the Psalm 51, "Miserere mei Deus," or, "Have mercy upon me, O God." REPRINTED: *O-U,* pp. 5–7. In this version JML omitted the year date at end, and did not retain an indention of the third and sixth verses in each stanza. He also made nineteen minor textual alterations, mostly punctuational, and changed the title to commemorate the death of Emma Georgiana Maxwell (see n. 14, chap. III, above).

VERSE 31 (Niobé). In Greek legend this daughter of King Tantalus was so proud of the beauty of her sons and daughters that she challenged their comparison with the children of Leto, by whom Zeus had sired Apollo and Artemis. Piqued at such audacity, the latter pair shot down all of Niobe's offspring, with the result that her heart became as stone. She was transformed into a rugged rock down which her tears trickled silently.

VERSES 34–36 (TU . . . SOLATIUM). The first two verses are verbatim from the Eucharistic sequence, "Lauda, Sion, salvatorem . . .," composed by St. Thomas Aquinas (*ca.* 1225–1274), Italian scholastic philosopher and theologian in the Dominican order. The entire sequence may be found in the *Analecta Hymnica Medii Aevi,* ed. Clemens Blume und Guido M. Dreves (Leipzig: O. R. Reisland, 1886–1922), L, 584–85. In *O-U* verse 35 was misprinted as: "QUI NOS PACIS HIC MORTALES." The final verse, not in Aquinas, since it completes the poem's rhyme and is in a rather uncommon hymn meter, is doubtless by JML himself. The translation reads: "You who know all things and prevail,/ Who feed us mortals here below,/ Jesus, grant solace."

Toccoa

FIRST PUBLISHED: *Southern and Western Magazine and Review* (Charleston, S.C.), II (Nov., 1845), 303–05. REPRINTED: *O-U*, pp. 55–58; Longfellow (1879, 1882).

In the 1848 version JML deleted an enumeration of the poem's eight stanzas, his signature at end, and the two-paragraph preface. He substituted for the preface a briefer footnote and made numerous minor punctuational and stylistic alterations to the text.

In the glossary to his *Myths of the Cherokees,* 19th Annual Report, Bureau of American Ethnology (Washington: Government Printing Office, 1900), p. 533, James Mooney renders "Toccoa" as "Taguâ 'hi," but gives no derived meaning. In *ibid.,* p. 418, he offers a legend concerning the Falls. See also "The Old Legend of Toccoa," in T[homas] Addison Richards, *American Scenery, Illustrated* (New York: Geo. A. Leavitt [*ca.* 1854]), pp. 106–08. (A copy of the Penfield, Ga., 1842, edition of Richards' work is in JJL Coll.)

VERSE 36 and n. (PE-RO-KAH). Mooney does not list this term.

Tallulah

FIRST PUBLISHED: *O-U,* pp. 59–62. REPRINTED: Longfellow (1879, 1882); Clarke (1896, 1913); Alderman and Harris (1909, 1929); Hungerpiller (1931).

"The word [Tallulah] is of uncertain etymology," says James Mooney, *Myths of the Cherokees,* p. 533. He writes it, "Talŭlŭ," and offers myths about the Falls (pp. 346, 417–18, and 481). "The name can not be translated. A magazine writer has rendered it

'The Terrible,' for which there is no authority" (p. 417). One Barnard, of Augusta, Ga., appended to his acrostic poem, "Tallulah," *Augusta Mirror*, III (June 19th, 1841), 94, a note stating that the word meant "terrible."

VERSE 13 (Teocalli). "I was much taken by that stanza on Tallulah Falls. Sounds like the meter in 'Hiawatha,' and it must have been written before Longfellow's poem [published Nov., 1855]. If I had known it, I would have put it in my article.

"I cannot locate the name Teocalli. It must be a made-up name. I have looked in that long list of names (Cherokee) in Mooney's glossary, but cannot find it." (E. Merton Coulter [Athens, Ga., July 21, 1964, to CCD].)

"But it would be unjust to create the impression that Legaré cannot, at times, strike a deeper note. This he usually does when he attains that originality of technique which he alone possesses of all the minor Carolinian writers of verse. Thus, his stanzas on the Tallulah Falls are vigorous and imaginative . . . ." Ludwig Lewisohn (1909).

Georgia

FIRST PUBLISHED: *O-U,* pp. 15–17.

To a Lily

FIRST PUBLISHED: *O-U,* pp. 10–11. REPRINTED: Stedman and Hutchinson (1889–1890, 1894); Stedman (1900); Weber (1901); Trent (1905); Holliday (1908); Alderman and Harris (1909, 1929); Wauchope (1910); Stockard (1911); Fulton (1917); Bartlett (in part) (1929, 1938, 1948, 1955); Kreymborg (1930, 1941); Hungerpiller (1931); Parks (1936).

VERSES 11–15. "Have we not here a defective picture from the misuse of a preposition? The maiden does not see 'her image' reflected *in* but *to* her eyes, in the lake." (*Southern Literary Gazette* [Athens, Ga.], I [Aug. 26, 1848], 127.)

VERSES 6–10. JML "wrote lines in *Orta Undis and Other Poems* obviously experimental in nature. In 'To a Lily' the angularity of the lines is somewhat subdued by the inner rhythms and cross alliteration . . ." (Charmentz S. Lenhart [1956]). "With its dainty conceits and delicate phrasing, this poem serves as another good example of the higher poetry of the South" (Carl Holliday [1908]). " 'To a Lily' has a . . . French grace" (Alfred Kreymborg [1930]). "In 1934 or 1935 when I began work on the eleventh edition of Bartlett, I left in the 'To a Lily' stanzas—you'll smile at my 'woman's reason'—because John Bennett, the Charleston, S.C., author, lives on Legaré Street, and I wanted to keep Legaré's memory green" (Louella D. Everett [Boston, Mass., Aug. 26, 1948, to CCD]).

Amy

FIRST PUBLISHED: *The Opal: A Pure Gift for the Holydays,* ed. John Keese (New York: J. C. Riker, 1847), pp. 189–90. RE-PRINTED: *O-U,* pp. 8–9; Duyckinck (1855); Stedman (1900); Stockard (1911).

In the 1848 version, from the original eight stanzas, JML deleted two, substituting for the earlier the present third (verses 9–12), and did not retain an indention of the second and fourth verses throughout. He made six minor textual alterations, all but one punctuational. The deleted stanzas read as follows:

> More joyously the stream leaped up
> > To lave her small and snowy hands;   10
> To glide between her fingers, left
> > The timid fish their sands.

> We heard our beating hearts within   21
> > That solitude of woods and stone;—
> How pleasant with the one beloved,
> > To wander on alone!

Enchantments

FIRST PUBLISHED: *The Opal: A Pure Gift for the Holydays*, ed. John Keese (New York: J. C. Riker, 1847), pp. 227–28.

VERSE 21 (Scaevola). Gaius Mucius Scaevola "according to some authors originally bore the *cognomen* Cordus, which he subsequently changed for Scaevola. . . . Now *scaevola* was an amulet worn by Roman children, but popular etymology wrongly connected it with *scaeva*, the left hand; thence arose the story of the brave Roman who, having failed to kill Porsenna, showed his indifference to physical pain by holding his right hand in fire. . . ." (*The Oxford Classical Dictionary*, 2nd edit., ed. N. G. L. Hammond and H. H. Scullard [Oxford: The Clarendon Press (1970)], p. 957.)

To My Very Dear Sister

FIRST PUBLISHED: *O-U*, pp. 3–4.
See commentary under "My Sister," p. 291, above.

Haw-Blossoms

FIRST PUBLISHED: *O-U*, pp. 18–21. REPRINTED: Trent (1905); Alderman and Harris (1909, 1929); Wauchope (1910); Gill (1916); Fulton (1917); Hungerpiller (1931); McDowell (1933); Parks (1936).

VERSE 5 (calmïas). The calico bush, or laurel (*Kalmia latifola*).

VERSES 5–8. " 'Haw-Blossoms,' an appealing lyric, also forces a moral. Before the moral intrudes, it moves to such charming measures as . . ." (Alfred Kreymborg [1930]).

Ahab-Mahommed

FIRST PUBLISHED: *O-U*, pp. 22–24. REPRINTED: Stedman (1900); Weber (1901); Holliday (1908); Coussens (1908); Alderman and Harris (1909, 1929); Stockard (1911); Gill (1916).

"*Ahab Mahommed* may be designated as a miniature of Lowell's *Vision of Sir Launfal*. It is not lacking in beauty of thought and grace of expression." (Carl Holliday, *A History of Southern Liter-*

ature [New York and Washington: Neale Pub. Co., 1906], p. 219.)
"A didactic note, via New England, mars some of the poems: the
ballad, 'Ahab Mahommed,' sounds like one of Longfellow's" (Alfred Kreymborg [1930]). ". . . an oriental legend . . . in the manner of Leigh Hunt's 'Abou Ben Adhem'" (Edd W. Parks [1936]).

Woman of Canaan

FIRST PUBLISHED: *O-U,* pp. 30–32.

Canaan, the Land of Promise or Promised Land, was that which
the Lord promised to Abraham because of his obedience. (See, for
example, *Exod.* 12:25, *Deut.* 9:28.)

VERSE 8. The Greek means, "Christ, have mercy on me!" The
Greek refrains in the poem derive from the account of the healing
of the Woman of Canaan in *Matt.* 15:22–28, and perhaps also
from that of the Syro-Phoenician woman in *Mark* 7:25–30.

VERSE 32. The Greek means, "Great is thy faith." JML has
rearranged the word order from the original in order to guarantee
his rhyme.

VERSE 40. The Greek means, "Glory to Thee, O Lord!"

VERSE 48. A repetition of verse 32.

Ornithologoi

FIRST PUBLISHED: *O-U,* pp. 33–49. REPRINTED: *Graham's
American Monthly Magazine of Literature and Art* (Philadelphia,
Pa.), XXXIII (July, 1848), 1–3.

JML subjected the later version of the poem to numerous alterations of punctuation and language, mostly minor. (His employment of quotation marks, originally somewhat confused, has been
regularized.) The four most significant changes appeared as follows
in *O-U*:

> Are breast-high harvests, and the red   5
> Wide fallow fields:

> But thou, where roar
> The pine woods in long corridor,   20
> Sonorously and evermore,
>
> When through the budding shrubs descried
> Green slope the fields on every side;
>
> Of grosser mould; bird-voices, deer   33
> Bleets, the innumerable cries
>
> For Nature, through thy purity   51
> Is open as a book to thee.

VERSES 53, 56 (CROAK!, raven's) : In *O-U* the capitalization of these words was reversed. It may or may not be significant that Edgar Allan Poe's poem, "The Raven," was first published in the New York *Evening Mirror* in its issue of Jan. 29, 1845, and appeared in book form there as *The Raven and Other Poems* in early November, 1845.

VERSES 154–219: For some reason, perhaps the requirements of space, this section was omitted from the magazine version of the poem. It is herewith restored from *O-U,* pp. 41–44. Therein verses 218–19 were italicized. The emphasis is now deleted, since in the magazine version the poem's final line, originally in capital letters, stands in lower case, thus suggesting that JML's general intent was toward de-emphasis.

"Yet only if one wishes to consider verses of the lowest artistic merit—the kind of thing which appears in 'The Poet's Corner' of newspapers or in second-rate periodicals—is the subject especially large. The truth is that American poetry has few good bird verses to show. There is almost nothing in it comparable to the great bird poems of Shelley, Wordsworth, or Keats. . . . American birds are richly represented in prose; in poetry, generally, they are slighted or ignored." (Robert W. Welker, *Birds and Men: American Birds in Science, Art, Literature, and Conservation, 1800–1900* [Cambridge: Belknap Press of Harvard University Press, 1955], pp. 136–37.)

A Parable

FIRST PUBLISHED: *O-U,* pp. 50–52.

VERSE 31 (Alcina). In the Italian epics dealing with the adventures of Orlando or Roland, such as Ariosto's *Orlando Furioso* (1516) or Boiardo's *Orlando Innamorato* (1495), she is Carnal Pleasure personified, enjoying her lovers for a season but then transforming them into trees, stones, wild beasts, etc., as her fancy chooses.

VERSE 32 (Roland). In Italian "Orlando," he was the nephew, and most famous of the paladins, of the Emperor Charlemagne. Slain by the Saracens at the battle of Roncesvalles in the Pyrenees, Roland is the hero of the epics above noted as well as of the 11th-century *Song of Roland.*

To Alcina

FIRST PUBLISHED: *O-U,* pp. 53–54.

For explanation of title see commentary under "A Parable," above.

To Anne

FIRST PUBLISHED: *O-U,* pp. 65–68. REPRINTED: Alderman and Harris (1909, 1929); Wauchope (1910).

"The love poems, most of them apparently inspired by his wife, Anne (Andrews) Legaré, show sincere feeling with rare traces of the sentimentality which marred the work of the many Southern imitators of Thomas Moore. Occasionally one finds a conceit worked out so elaborately as to suggest artificiality." (Jay B. Hubbell [1954].)

The Two Givers

FIRST PUBLISHED: *O-U,* pp. 69–72.

VERSES 28–35. "Again, in a very sweet poem, we find a passage in which we are perplexed to get at the author's meaning . . ."

(*Southern Literary Messenger* [Richmond, Va.], XIV [June, 1848], 388–89).

Why She Loves Me

FIRST PUBLISHED: *O-U*, pp. 73–75.

The Welcome Rain

FIRST PUBLISHED: *O-U*, pp. 76–78.

Loquitur Diana

FIRST PUBLISHED: *O-U*, pp. 79–81. REPRINTED: *The Literary World* (New York), III (May 13, 1848), 283–84 (last five stanzas); *Holden's Dollar Magazine* (New York), I (June, 1848), 375–76 (last five stanzas).

The Latin title means, "Diana Speaks."

The Book of Nature

FIRST PUBLISHED: *Southern and Western Literary Messenger and Review* (Richmond, Va.), XIII (June, 1847), 342. REPRINTED: *O-U*, pp. 86–89. In this version the only alteration from the original occurs in verse 18, which first read, "Like Cretan gold the light descends,".

The quotation in JML's preface, from the *Religio Medici* ("A Doctor's Religion") (1642) of the English physician Sir Thomas Browne (1605–1682), derives from Part I, Section 16. (See Browne's *Works*, ed. Geoffrey Keynes [London: Faber & Gwyer; New York: William E. Rudge, 1928–1931], I, 21.)

VERSES 11–12 (Birnam, Malcolm). Shakespeare, *Macbeth*, IV, i, 92–94.

VERSES 13–16. "That stanza is perfect, looked at from any angle. Has the wistful music of a pine-grove or the quiet solemnity of a group of cypresses ever been struck off more vividly or with more originality in four lines?" (G. Croft Williams [*ca.* 1922], p. 7.)

Love's Heraldry

FIRST PUBLISHED: *Southern and Western Literary Messenger and Review* (Richmond, Va.), XIII (July, 1847), 422. RE-PRINTED: *O-U*, pp. 97–98. In this version the only alterations from the original are a change of title (from "Heraldry of Love") and a readjustment to the left margin of verses 5 and 7 in each stanza, which had been indented.

Flowers in Ashes

FIRST PUBLISHED: *Southern and Western Literary Messenger and Review* (Richmond, Va.), XIII (Aug., 1847), 471–72. RE-PRINTED: *O-U*, pp. 90–92; Augusta, Ga., *Daily Constitutionalist*, June 2, 1848, p. 2, col. 4; Alderman and Harris (1909, 1929); Wauchope (1910); Hungerpiller (1931). In the *O-U* version the only alteration from the original is a deletion of quotation marks beginning at verse 15, "Herefrom. . . ," and repeated at the head of each stanza thenceforth.

"Here Legaré's technique seems almost modern, and in such lines as [verses 3, 6, and 27] he has a distinction of movement that is quite admirable" (Ludwig Lewisohn [1909]). In "The Reaper," "Haw-Blossoms," and "Flowers in Ashes" JML reveals a "mastery of technique that is distinctly modern" (George A. Wauchope, "Literary South Carolina . . . ," *Bulletin of the University of South Carolina* [Dec. 1, 1923], pp. 41–42).

A May Morn

FIRST PUBLISHED: *Southern and Western Literary Messenger and Review* (Richmond, Va.), XIII (Sept., 1847), 547. RE-PRINTED: *O-U*, pp. 93–96. In this version JML substituted the date, 1847, for the location, at the end, and made some thirty-two alterations, mostly punctuational. Verses 9–10 first read—

"And when you go I murmur—'here,
Beneath these leaves he called me *dear*,

Verse 32 first read—
> The melancholy plaint and low.

VERSES 1–4, 13–24. "These four stanzas from 'A May Morn' are highly consonant to nature" (*Southern Literary Messenger* [Richmond, Va.], XIV [June, 1848], 388–89).

VERSES 17–20. "And always he is severely simple, charming with a reluctant charm, plain and clear, as in this stanza . . ." (Ludwig Lewisohn [1909]).

Last Gift

FIRST PUBLISHED: *O-U*, pp. 99–100. REPRINTED: Hubbell (1954).

"'Last Gift,' presumably addressed to his wife, shows us the Southern poet trying his hand at the old Petrarchan convention of the power of poetry to immortalize a woman's beauty and goodness . . ." (Jay B. Hubbell [1954]).

The Reaper

FIRST PUBLISHED: *O-U*, pp. 1–2. REPRINTED: *Southern Literary Messenger* (Richmond, Va.), XIV (June, 1848), 388–89; *The Knickerbocker Magazine* (New York), XXXII (Aug., 1848), 179; *Southern Literary Gazette* (Athens, Ga.), I (Aug. 26, 1848), 124; *Southern Quarterly Review* (Charleston, S.C.,), XVI (Oct., 1849), 228–29; Alderman and Harris (1909, 1929); Wauchope (1910); Hungerpiller (1931); Parks (1936); Davis (1952).

VERSE 14 (hour). "We are sorry to see so clever a writer as Mr. Legaré making two syllables of 'hour.' Has *flour* two syllables? It is a common but grievous error to eke out these and kindred words. They have but one syllable and but one sound." (*The Knickerbocker Magazine* [New York City], XXXII [Aug., 1848], 179).

The Rising of the River

FIRST PUBLISHED: *O-U*, pp. 82–84.

A Wreck

FIRST PUBLISHED: *O-U*, p. 85.

On the Death of a Kinsman

FIRST PUBLISHED: *O-U*, pp. 63–64. REPRINTED: *DeBow's Review* (New Orleans, La.), VI (Aug., 1848), 159–60; Alderman and Harris (1909, 1929); Parks (1936); Davis (1952).

See page 26, above. In reprinting the piece J. D. B. DeBow remarked that he had "always thought [it] very fine."

VERSES 1–5: "His poems reveal a more careful and competent workmanship than those of all but three or four of his Southern contemporaries. 'On the Death of a Kinsman' . . . has an admirable opening stanza, rather above the level of the four which follow. . . ." (Jay B. Hubbell [1954].)

VERSE 11 (Demetrius). This allusion remains unexplained. Of the one hundred and thirty individuals by that name in classical antiquity, none seems to fit the case. The least unlikely would be the Cynic philosopher who flourished at Rome *ca.* A.D. 60. He is cited by Lucian, Epictetus, and several times by Seneca.

VERSE 16 (Icarus). See commentary under "All Hail the Bride!," verse 27.

"It is apt, chaste, solemn, as should be the description of a great man that lies dead. In it also are a sweet language and a startling conceit that seem to echo out of Elizabeth's great time. Not that the author was Elizabethan in power or in range, but his verse shows that he knew how English was written at one time." (Rev. G. Croft Williams [*ca.* 1922], p. 7.)

Orta-Undis

FIRST PUBLISHED: *O-U*, pp. 101–102.

The Latin title means, "Sprung [born] from Water" or from the waves.

VERSE 10 (*Sopientes*). Probably a typographical error for *Spoliantes*.

VERSE 23 (*cirrisque*) : Probably a typographical error for *cirrusque*.

"The title of the book is taken from the name of a clever specimen of Latin versification on the last two pages of the volume" (*Southern Literary Gazette* [Athens, Ga.], I [Aug. 26, 1848], 127).

"He was also, it would seem, a classical scholar. The poem which gives the title to his volume—placed at the end in the modern fashion—is in Latin. Legaré and Walter Savage Landor, who also wrote verse in Latin, come near the end of a long English tradition which goes back through Milton to the medieval poets." (Jay B. Hubbell [1954].)

"The author probably intended the second fourteen lines to stand as the strophic responsion of the first fourteen, after the Greek system of metrical repetition. In this sense, the second half of the poem should be designated 'Antistrophe.' The latter does not, however, represent a change in voice, since there is no answer to the poet's cry, and the two units are syntactically bound together. . . . The verse translation is a little mushy (but so is the poem: he may have been reluctant to put the old topos of unrequited love into English). As you can see from a comparison with the prose version, it stays fairly close to the text. I used a loosely slung tetrameter, which suggests for me the pace of a continuous passage in iambic dimeter. The Latin, incidentally, strikes me as rather forced and at times faulty; I am at a loss to account for the poem's place in the book save on grounds of personal attachment." (Richard A. Macksey [Baltimore, Md., Feb. 4, 1965, to CCD].)

To the "Sweetest Rose of Georgia"

FIRST PUBLISHED: *Literary World* (New York), III (May 6, 1848), 266.

The title refers to JML's wife, Anne. *O-U* was itself dedicated to her in the language of the title.

Maize in Tassel

FIRST PUBLISHED: *Literary World* (New York), III (May 13, 1848), 287. REPRINTED: Charleston, S.C., *Mercury*, May 18, 1848, p. 2, col. 1; R. W. Griswold (1855, 1856, 1873).

"The original poem under his signature, in our present number, is a fair specimen of his chaste and flowing style of dealing with natural objects . . ." (*Literary World*, III, 283).

"As you said in your last [letter] 'Maize in Tassel' anticipates somewhat Lanier—and Lanier may have seen it! Except for last stanza, I find it a very fine poem." (John Gould Fletcher [Little Rock, Ark., April 22, 1950, to CCD].)

The Rustic Seat

FIRST PUBLISHED: *Southern Literary Gazette: An Illustrated Weekly Journal of Belles-Lettres, Science and the Arts* (Athens, Ga.), I (June 17, 1848), 41.

A Song for "The Rose"

FIRST PUBLISHED: *Southern Literary Gazette* (Athens, Ga.), I (Sept. 9, 1848), 137.

VERSE 53 (pet-books). For JML's favorites see page 76, above. For another reference to "pet-books" see "A Husband to a Wife," verse 17.

The Trouvére's Rose

FIRST PUBLISHED: *Southern Literary Gazette* (Athens, Ga.), I (Jan. 20, 1849), 281.

VERSE 1 (Angouléme). The ancient Iculisma, Angoulême is today the capital of Charente department, on the River Charente, in western France, some sixty-four miles north-northeast of Bordeaux.

The Sword and Palette

FIRST PUBLISHED: *Richards' Weekly Gazette* (Athens, Ga.), II (May 12, 1849), 52. (File in Washington Memorial Library,

Macon, Ga.) REPRINTED: In *The Prize Articles Contributed to Richards' Weekly Gazette* (Athens, Ga.: William C. Richards, 1849), pp. 19–21. (Copy in Henry E. Huntington Library, San Marino, Cal.)

For this "romaunt" JML won the second prize of ten dollars in a contest announced in the issue of the *Gazette* for Oct. 14, 1848 (I, 182). First prize of twenty dollars was won by Mrs. C. W. DuBose for a descriptive piece, "Wachullah." "It is with pleasure, and with pride, too, that we call the attention of our readers to the original poetry appearing in the new series of the Gazette. In today's paper there will be found two charming lyrics from [W. Gilmore] Simms and [Henry Rootes] Jackson—and our two prize poems by Mrs. DuBose and Mr. Legare, have been received with warm admiration. We venture to say that poetry of a higher order has not made its appearance in the columns of any contemporary Journal during the same period." (Editorial, "Our Southern Poets," *Richards' Weekly Gazette,* May 19, 1849 [Second Year, No. 3 . . . Whole No. 53].)

VERSE 199 (Daphnè). In Greek mythology, one of the nymphs attendant upon Artemis, or Diana, who, as chastisement for not remaining in the single state, transformed her into a laurel tree.

VERSE 201 (Silenus). In some of the Greek myths he is represented as a son of Hermes, or Mercury; in others, of Pan and a nymph. Usually described as the oldest of the Satyrs and their paternalistic guardian, to the Greek mind he appeared particularly as a companion of Dionysus, knowledgeable in how to press the grapes for wine but so fond of that liquid as readily to indulge in it to excess.

To Jasmines in December

FIRST PUBLISHED: *Literary World* (New York), IV (May 26, 1849), 456. REPRINTED: Davis (1952); Hubbell (1954).

A Laurel Blossom

FIRST PUBLISHED: *Literary World* (New York), V (July 21, 1849), 50.

Bald Gras Ich

FIRST PUBLISHED: *Southern Literary Messenger* (Richmond, Va.), XIV (Oct., 1848), 596–97. REPRINTED: *Wheler's Southern Monthly Magazine* (Athens, Ga.), n.s. I (July, 1849), 17.

The German title means, "Now I'm Mowing" by the Neckar, and now by the Rhine. In the later version JML changed his title from "The Golden-Ring. *From the German of Bettine Brentano's* WUNDERHORN"; added the footnote to the title; divided the eight quatrains into two parts; made some twenty-five punctuational and stylistic changes, mostly minor; and at the end deleted the phrase, "South Carolina."

The collection of German folk songs known as *Des Knaben Wunderhorn,* or "A Child's Cornucopia," was first published by its compilers, Ludwig Achim von Arnim (1781–1831) and Clemens Maria Brentano (1778–1842), in 1806–1808. Elisabeth, or Bettine, von Arnim, born Brentano (1785–1859), biographer and social critic, wife of Clemens Brentano, is best-known today for her quasi-fictional *Goethes Briefwechsel mit einem Kinde* (1835). JML's poem is a close translation of a piece entitled, "Rheinischer Bundesring," said by the compilers to have been "contributed by Mrs. von Pattberg." (See *Des Knaben Wunderhorn: Alte Deutsche Lieder* [Heidelberg: Mohr und Zimmer, 1808] II, 15–16.)

Thanatokallos

FIRST PUBLISHED: *The Knickerbocker Magazine* (New York), XXIV (Sept., 1849), 204–06. REPRINTED: *Russell's Magazine* (Charleston, S.C.), V (July, 1859), 370–72; Griswold (1855, 1856, 1873).

The Greek title means "Beauty in Death" or "The Beauty of Death." Though readily intelligible, the word is probably a made-up one by JML, since no such noun compound exists in the language.

From Aiken, July 5, 1849, JML addressed Evert A. Duyckinck in part as follows (from the original in the Duyckinck Collection, New York Public Library) :

I yesterday afternoon received your pleasant note,—pleasant despite the little disappointment contained, for the trait I have so often admired in your critical notices, that of differing without hurting, is, I now find, not peculiar to your public style. * * *

In regard to Thanatokallos, there *is* one other magazine I would like it to appear in, and one only; although when I wrote to you I was quite honest in what I desired, and still think as then indeed, but the temptation of the credit to be gained by a *re*publication in the best journal in the country, is rather too much to be resisted. Will you send the enclosed note and the MS poem to the Editor of the Knickerbocker, and if it pleases you say what you can to advance my wishes in that quarter? *Should* Mr [Lewis Gaylord] Clark decline, pray receive the poem gratuitously for your own columns again. With best wishes and truly yours

J. M. Legaré

P.S. Before sending the MS, will you be so kind as to make the following corrections in the text—my writing is easily imitated. For—"How can'st thou halve thy heart" [verse 117] read "Canst thou divide thy heart". And fourth line from end—for

"or her reason's shaken"

read   "or her reason's (moved"

(frayed"

However as an author frequently corrects his composition for the worse, if you differ from me in regard to one or more of these correction[s], pray omit them.

J. M. L.

The earlier correction was rejected, the latter used; and the poem appeared, not in the Duyckincks' *The Literary World,* but in the Clarks' "Old Knick," which is the version here given.

VERSE 17 (Stephen). Stephen "Protomartyr," deacon and preacher, died *ca.* A.D. 35. Denounced to the Sanhedrim as a heretic, he was by them stoned to death outside Jerusalem.

VERSE 62 (Aria, Caecinna). Arria (*sic*) Major, the wife of Caecina Paetus, professed Stoicism. When her husband was condemned by Claudius for his part in a conspiracy, she stabbed herself, then handed the dagger to Paetus, saying, "Paete, non dolet" ("Paetus, it doesn't hurt"). (See Pliny, *Epistles,* III. 16, and Martial, I. 13.) This pair had appeared elsewhere this year in JML's work. (See page 39, above.)

VERSE 68 (Esau). In the Old Testament, the son of Isaac, who sold his birthright for a mess of pottage (a dish of boiled vegetables and meat). His name is a Hebrew word meaning "rough," or "covered with hair."

" 'Thanatokallos,' possibly suggested by Bryant's Thanatopsis, contains a vivid picture of death, though the details used are rather repellent to the sensitive reader. The blank verse . . . moves with dignity and self-control." (Sidney E. Bradshaw, *On Southern Poetry prior to 1860* [Richmond, Va.: B. F. Johnson Co., 1900], p. 95.)

The Two King's-Children

FIRST PUBLISHED: *Wheler's Monthly Magazine* (Athens, Ga.), n.s. I (Nov., 1849), 101.

JML has made a fairly close translation of this ballad, though in eleven quatrains as contrasted with the thirteen of the German. For one version see "Edelkönigs-Kinder," which was "contributed by Mr. Schlosser," in von Arnim's and Brentano's *Des Knaben Wunderhorn* (Heidelberg, 1808), II, 252–54. There are two versions from a later edition of the *Wunderhorn,* both entitled "Die Königskinder," in von Arnim's *Sämmtliche Werke* . . . (Berlin: von Arnim's Verlag, 1857), XI, 336–41. One was "communicated from South Germany"; the other, in dialect, was "communicated from Westphalia" in 1837. A variant version, entitled "Zwei Königskinder" and attributed to "oral" origins, appears in *ibid.,* XIV, 308–10.

A Husband to a Wife

FIRST PUBLISHED: *Southern Literary Messenger* (Richmond, Va.), XVI (Jan., 1850), 6–7.

Janette

FIRST PUBLISHED: *The Knickerbocker Magazine* (New York), XXXV (March, 1850), 245–46.

The Hemlocks

FIRST PUBLISHED: *Southern Literary Messenger* (Richmond, Va.), XVIII (Feb., 1852), 115–16.

Writing to John R. Thompson, editor of the *Messenger,* from Aiken, Feb. 1, 1850, JML declared that the present poem "so far as it is written (the whole is *sketched* out) is very far superior to any work, long or short, hitherto attempted: and this is not *my* judgment solely. . . . So I repeat this is not *my* opinion merely, but that of the only eyes [his wife Anne's] possessing the freedom of all my MSS, and which seldom judge erroneously, because they are part of a pretty head, in intellect both much clearer and better than mine. . . .

". . . I also pledge myself to give you the request of 'The Hemlocks'—(the poem above-referred to) when completed, which will not be for some months, as I never write a word of it when not in the humor; it was begun before 'Janette' and others even: and that at your own price of $4. [per page] of course. Do you like all this?—I hope you *do*—you should, I think! Although I dislike the practise and have never before done it, I will enclose a few verses of the 'Hemlocks,' that you may judge at least the *style* so far as written."

(Printed in full in CCD [1], pp. 226–27.)

The Lighthouse

FIRST PUBLISHED: Anon., "The Boy of the Light-House," *Putnam's Monthly Magazine* (New York), VIII (July, 1856), 40–42. REPRINTED: *Southern Literary Messenger* (Richmond, Va.), XXIII (Aug., 1856), 150–53.

JML's footnote: The editor of *Putnam's* was Charles F. Briggs (1804–1877), a seaman turned journalist and story writer, often using the pseudonym of "Harry Franco." His associate editors were George William Curtis and Parke Godwin.

In the earlier version of the poem stanzas IX, XXIII, and XXVII were omitted, while eight other stanzas suffered stylistic changes.

The poem may well have been stimulated by a real occurrence. "The winter of '55–6 will stand out in all future almanacks as 'that cold season.' Throughout the entire continent, the snow has been heavier, and more universal than was ever known before. The 'sunny South,' heretofore exempt from the terrors of Jack Frost, has this season suffered from his chilling influence. . . . The record of naval disasters daily swells in calamities, and hourly accumulates with horrors." (Editorial, *Frank Leslie's Illustrated Newspaper* (New York), I [Apr. 5, 1856], 262.) This type of reaction to disaster is seen as a phase of the Romantic attraction toward the themes of death and mortality, by John B. Harcourt, "Themes of American Verse, 1840–1849 . . ." (Ph. D. dissertation, Brown University, 1952), pp. 732–33.

VERSE 95 (Corrientes). Either Cape Corrientes, Argentina, extending into the Atlantic Ocean at a point southeast of Buenos Aires province, or a cape of the same name on the southwest coast of Pinar del Río province, western Cuba.

VERSE 96 (Pamlico). Pamlico Sound, lying between the mainland of eastern North Carolina and islands off the coast.

WORKS REPRINTING VERSE
BY JAMES M. LEGARÉ

1845 [Simms, William Gilmore (ed.)]. *The Charleston Book: A Miscellany in Prose and Verse*. Charleston, S.C.: Samuel Hart, Sr.

"Du Saye. A Legend of the Congaree" (pp. 189–99)

1855 Griswold, Rufus W. (ed.). *The Poets and Poetry of America*. 16th edition. Philadelphia: Parry & McMillan.

"Maize in Tassel," "Thanatokallos" (pp. 577–78)

Reprinted in 17th edition (Philadelphia, 1856) and in reissue supervised by Richard Henry Stoddard (New York, 1873)

1855 Duyckinck, Evert A., and George L. Duyckinck (eds.). *Cyclopaedia of American Literature*. 2 vols. New York: Charles Scribner.

"Amy" (II, 720)

Reprinted in revised edition (New York, 1866) and in reissue edited by M. Laird Simons (Philadelphia, New York, and London, 1875)

1879 Longfellow, Henry Wadsworth (ed.). *Poems of Places*. . . . 31 vols. Boston: Houghton, Mifflin & Co., 1876–1879.

"Tallulah," "Toccoa," XXVII (. . . *America. Southern States*), 215–17, 219–21

Reprinted in *Poems of America . . . Southern States.— British America* (Boston, 1882)

1889 Stedman, Edmund C., and Ellen M. Hutchinson (eds.). *A*
1890 *Library of American Literature.* . . . 11 vols. New York:
Charles L. Webster.

"To a Lily" (VIII, 149–50)

Reprinted in New Edition (New York, 1894)

1896 Clarke, Jennie T. (ed.). *Songs of the South* . . . , intro.
Joel Chandler Harris. Philadelphia: J. B. Lippincott Co.

"Tallulah" (pp. 86–88)

Reprinted in 3rd edition (Garden City, N.Y., 1913)

1900 Stedman, Edmund C. (ed.). *An American Anthology,*
1787–1900. New York: Houghton Mifflin.

"Ahab-Mahommed," "Amy," "To a Lily" (pp. 266–67)

1901 Weber, William L. (ed.). *Selections from the Southern*
Poets. New York: Macmillan.

"Ahab-Mahommed," "To a Lily" (pp. 115–18)

1905 Trent, William Peterfield (ed.). *Southern Writers.* New
York: Macmillan.

"Haw-Blossoms," "To a Lily" (pp. 291–92)

1908 Holliday, Carl (ed.). *Three Centuries of Southern Poetry*
(1607–1907). Nashville and Dallas: Publishing House of
M.E. Church, South.

"Ahab-Mahommed," "To a Lily" (pp. 130–32)

1908 Coussens, Penrhyn W. (ed.). *Poems Children Love.* New
York: Dodge Publishing Co.

"Ahab-Mahommed" (pp. 279–80)

1909 Alderman, Edwin A., and Joel Chandler Harris (eds.).
Library of Southern Literature. 16 vols. New Orleans, Atlanta, Dallas: Martin & Hoyt, 1908–13.

"Ahab-Mahommed," "Flowers in Ashes," "Haw-Blossoms,"

"On the Death of a Kinsman," "Tallulah," "To a Lily," "To Anne," "The Reaper" (VII, 3193–3203). Selections and prefatory sketch by Ludwig Lewisohn.

Reprinted in Popular Edition (Atlanta, 1929, 16 vols. in 9)

1910 Wauchope, George A. (ed.). *The Writers of South Carolina.* Columbia: State Publishing Co.

"Flowers in Ashes," "Haw-Blossoms," "On the Death of a Kinsman," "Tallulah," "The Reaper," "To Anne," "To a Lily" (pp. 249–58)

1911 Stockard, Henry J. *A Study in Southern Poetry.* New York and Washington: Neale Publishing Co.

"Ahab-Mahommed," "Amy," "To a Lily" (pp. 119–22)

1916 Gill, Henry M. (ed.). *The South in Prose and Poetry.* New Orleans: F.F. Hansell & Bro.

"Ahab-Mahommed" (pp. 368–69), "Haw-Blossoms" (pp. 247–49)

1917 Fulton, Maurice Garland (ed.). *Southern Life in Southern Literature: Selections of Representative Prose and Poetry.* Boston and elsewhere: Ginn & Co.

"Haw-Blossoms," "To a Lily" (pp. 216–19)

1929 *Bartlett's Familiar Quotations,* ed. Nathan H. Dole. 10th edition, Boston: Little, Brown.

"To a Lily," 1st and 3rd stanzas (pp. 755–56)

Reprinted in 11th, 12th, 13th editions (Boston, 1938, 1948, 1955, respectively)

1930 Kreymborg, Alfred (ed.). *Lyric America . . . 1630–1930.* New York: Coward, McCann.

"To a Lily" (p. 141)

Reprinted in 2nd revised edition (New York, 1941)

1931 Hungerpiller, J[ohn] C. (comp.). *South Carolina Literature, with Biographical Notes and Critical Comments.* Columbia: R. L. Bryan Co.

"Flowers in Ashes," "Haw-Blossoms," "Tallulah," "The Reaper," "To a Lily" (pp. 95-7)

1933 McDowell, Tremaine (ed.). *The Romantic Triumph: American Literature from 1830 to 1860.* New York: Macmillan.

"Haw-Blossoms" (p. 704)

1936 Parks, Edd Winfield (ed.). *Southern Poets: Representative Selections, with Introduction, Bibliography, and Notes.* New York and elsewhere: American Book Co.

"Flowers in Ashes," "Haw-Blossoms," "On the Death of a Kinsman," "The Reaper," "To a Lily" (pp. 94-99)

1952 Davis, Curtis Carroll. "The Several-Sided James Mathewes Legaré: Poet," *Transactions of the Huguenot Society of South Carolina,* No. 57 (Charleston, S.C.: . . . Waverly Press, Inc.), pp. 5-12.

"On the Death of a Kinsman," "The Reaper," "To Jasmines in December" (pp. 9-11)

1954 Hubbell, Jay B. *The South in American Literature, 1607-1900.* ([Durham, N. C.:] Duke University Press).

"Last Gift," "To Jasmines in December" (pp. 563-64)

WRITINGS BY
JAMES M. LEGARÉ

FICTION

Catalogued in CCD (3), pp. 526–27.

"Miss Peck's Friend: A Novel in Ten Chapters," *Putnam's Monthly Magazine of American Literature, Science, and Art,* I-II (May-July, 1853), 539–46, 618–29, 45–60. Unsigned.

"JOURNAL OF LITERATURE: EUROPEAN AND AMERICAN"

Printed prospectus, one page. Dated Augusta, Ga., August, 1847. Signed: J. D. Legare and J. M. Legare. John C. Calhoun Papers, Clemson College Library, Clemson, South Carolina.

LEGARÉ GENEALOGY

"Discovery of an interesting Document containing the Genealogy of the Legare Family," Charleston, S.C., *Courier,* March 15, 1844, p. 2, col. 3.

Summary and translation, from the Latin, of an unlocated hoax manuscript. Reprinted in part:

Boston, Mass., *Daily Advertiser,* March 23, 1844, p. 1, col. 7.

Baltimore, Md., *Republican & Daily Argus,* April 3, 1844, p. 2, col. 6.

Baltimore, Md., *Baltimore Patriot & Commercial Gazette,* April 4, 1844, p. 2, col. 1.

"Interesting Discovery," Charleston, S.C., *Mercury,* March 15, 1844, p. 2, col. 3.

LETTERS (TO AND FROM)

Boston Public Library

JML to Carey & Hart, Charleston, May 19th, 1845. (Chamberlain Collection.)

JML to Revd R. W. Griswold, Aiken, May 31st [1846]. To same, N York [*ca.* autumn, 1851]. JML to Thomas Powell, Aiken, Nov. 16th, 1849. (Griswold Collection.)

Charleston Library Society, Charleston, S.C.

Anon. to JML, Esq. [Charleston, n.d.]. (JJL Coll.)

Clemson College Library, Clemson, S.C.

JML to Hon. John C. Calhoun, Aiken, S.C., Sept. 14th, 1847. To same, Aiken, S.C., Oct. 26th [1847]. Calhoun to JML, Fort Hill, Sept. 18th, 1847. (Calhoun Collection.)

Columbia University Library, New York, N.Y.

JML to W. G. Simms, Esqr, Charleston, May 6th, 1845. (Special Collections.)

Duke University Library, Durham, N.C.

Henry Wadsworth Longfellow to JML, Cambridge, Oct. 2nd, 1849. (Paul Hamilton Hayne Collection.)

Harvard University Library, Cambridge, Mass.

William D. Ticknor & Co. to JML, Boston, May 5th, 1848. To same, Boston, May 19th [18]49. (Ticknor Account- and Letter-Books, Houghton Library.)

JML to Prof. H. W. Longfellow, Aiken, Sept. 22nd, 1849. To same, April, 1850. To same, June 9th, July 18th, 1851; N. York, Sept. 7th, [Sept.] 20th, 1851. To same, Aiken, May 19th [1852]. To same, Jan. 15th [1853]. To same, July 3rd, 1854. Longfellow to JML, Cambridge, March 15th, 1853. (Longfellow Papers, Harvard College Library.)

Historical Society of Pennsylvania, Philadelphia, Pa.

JML to Hon. J. C. Spencer, Charleston, Feb. 16th, 1844. (Gratz Autograph Collection: American Poets.)

Library of Congress, Washington, D.C.

JML to James H. Hammond, all from Aiken, S.C. Sept. 6th [1849]. March 22nd, June 16th, Nov. 24th [1858]. May 15th, 1859. (James Henry Hammond Papers, vols. 16, 23–24, 25–26.)

National Archives, Washington, D. C.

JML to the Commissioner of Patents [Joseph Holt], all from Aiken, S. C. March 27, March 30, April 28, May 4, 1857, Feb. 23, 1858. (Records of the United States Patent Office, Case File nos. 18,980, dated Dec. 9, 1857, and 20,569, dated June 15, 1858, Record Group no. 241.)

National Library of Scotland, Edinburgh.

JML to Prof. [William Edmondstoune] Aytoun, Aiken, S. carolina, U.S., March 23rd, [18] '52. (Blackwood Papers.)

New York Public Library

JML to J. R. Thompson, Aiken, Feb. 1st, May 16th, and May 22nd, 1850. (Anthony Collection.)

JML to the *Literary World* and/or Evert A. Duyckinck, Esq., all from Aiken, S.C. May 8th [1848?], June 11th, July 5th, 1849. To same, Feb. 15th, 1850; March 26th [1850?]. To same, July 14th, 1851. To same, Jan. 1st [1852?]. (Duyckinck Collection.)

Pierpont Morgan Library, New York, N.Y.

JML to Fletcher Harper, Esquire, N York (No 7 London Terrace, W 23rd St), Oct. 6th [1853]. To same, Aiken, S.C., Feb. 16th, 1854. Fletcher Harper to JML [New York, Oct. 8th, 1853], draft.

South Caroliniana Library, University of South Carolina, Columbia, S.C.

JML to Gen. Geo. P. Morris, Aiken, S.C., Dec. 22 [1854].

University of Virginia Library, Charlottesville, Va.

JML to John R. Thompson, Aiken, Nov. 13th, 1849. JML to Revd R. W. Griswold, N York, Thursday morng. [*c.* autumn, 1851]. (C. Waller Barrett Collection.)

"Magazines of the Day," Charleston, S.C., *Mercury,* Oct. 11th, 1849, p. 2, col. 4. Unsigned. (File in Charleston Library Society.)

ORTA-UNDIS, AND OTHER POEMS. Boston: William D. Ticknor & Company, M DCCC XLVIII. Pp. viii, 102.

WORKS MENTIONING
JAMES M. LEGARÉ

BIOGRAPHICAL

Adams, Oscar F. *A Dictionary of American Authors.* 5th edition. Boston and New York: Houghton Mifflin Co. [1904].

Allibone, S. Austin. *A Critical Dictionary of English Literature and British and American Authors Living and Deceased.* . . . 3 vols. Philadelphia: J. B. Lippincott Co., 1891.

[Bragg, Laura M.]. "Cotton Furniture," *Bulletin of the Charleston Museum,* XV, No. 8 (Dec., 1919), 76–77.

Burke, W. J., and Will D. Howe. *American Authors and Books: 1604 to the Present Day.* Revised by Irving R. Weiss. New York: Crown Publishers, Inc. [1962].

Davis, Curtis Carroll. "The Several-Sided James Mathewes Legaré: Poet," *Transactions of the Huguenot Society of South Carolina,* No. 57 (Charleston, S.C., 1952), pp. 5–12.

——— (ed.). "Poet, Painter, and Inventor: Some Letters by James Mathewes Legaré, 1823–1859," *NCHR,* XXI (July, 1944), 215–31.

Death Notices

Charleston, S.C., *Daily Courier,* June 2, 1859, p. 2, col. 2.

Charleston *Mercury,* June 2, 1859, p. 2, col. 6.

"Editor's Table," *Russell's Magazine,* V (July, 1859), 370–72. Probably by editor Paul Hamilton Hayne.

Herzberg, Max. *The Reader's Encyclopedia of American Literature.* New York: Thomas Y. Crowell Co. [1962].

Morgan, Catherine W. "Life of James Mathews Legare," Aiken, S.C., *Standard and Review*, May 2, 1923, p. 1. Reprinted in Teague (see below).

National Cyclopaedia of American Biography, XII, 284. 44 vols. New York: James T. White & Co., 1893–1962.

Salley, Alexander S., Jr. "James Mathewes Legare," Charleston, S.C., *Sunday News and Courier*, Nov. 1, 1903, pt 2, p. 1, cols. 3–5.

[Simms, William Gilmore]. "Domestic Resources," Charleston *Mercury*, Nov. 29, 1861, p. 1, col. 2.

Teague, Elizabeth C. "Aiken Hi Alumni Place Marker at Poet's Grave," Aiken, S.C., *Standard and Review*, Feb. 13, 1942, p. 5. Summarized in Charleston *Sunday News and Courier*, Apr. 5, 1942, p. 11.

Wallace, W. Stewart (comp.). *A Dictionary of North American Authors Deceased before 1950*. Toronto: Ryerson Press [1951].

Williams, Rev. George Croft. "James Matthewes Legare and His Poetry." Typescript, 15 pp., Columbia, S.C., *ca.* 1922. In possession of grandson, Edward B. Borden, Columbia, S. C.

CRITICAL

(in addition to certain titles in Appendix I)

Bradshaw, Sidney E. *On Southern Poetry prior to 1860*. (University of Virginia Studies in Southern Literature.) Richmond: B. F. Johnson Co., 1900.

Davis, Curtis Carroll. "A Letter from the Muses: The Publication and Critical Reception of James M. Legaré's 'Orta-Undis, and Other Poems' (1848)," *NCHR*, XXVI (Oct., 1949), 417–38.

———. "Fops, Frenchmen, Hidalgos, and Aztecs: Being a Survey of the Prose Fiction of J. M. Legaré of South Carolina (1823–1859)," *NCHR*, XXX (Oct., 1953), 524–60.

————. "Mr. Legaré Inscribes Some Books: The Literary Tenets, and the Library, of a Carolina Writer," *Papers of the Bibliographical Society of America,* LVI (Second Quarter, 1962), 219–36.

Hart, John S. *A Manual of American Literature.* Philadelphia: Eldredge & Brother, 1872.

Lewisohn, Ludwig. "J. M. Legare." (The Books We Have Made.) Charleston, S.C., *Sunday News and Courier,* Aug. 16, 1903, p. 20, cols. 4–5.

Parks, Edd Winfield. *Segments of Southern Thought.* [Athens: University of Georgia Press], 1938.

Shaw, John MacKay (comp.). *Childhood in Poetry.* 5 vols. Detroit, Mich.: Gale Research Co. [1967].

Wauchope, George Armstrong. "Literary South Carolina: A Short Account of the Progress of Literature and the Principal Writers and Books from 1700 to 1923," *Bulletin of the University of South Carolina,* No. 133 (Dec. 1, 1923), pp. 41–42.

MISCELLANEOUS

Brewster, Lawrence F. *Summer Migrations and Resorts of South Carolina Low-Country Planters.* (Trinity College Historical Society Papers, Series XXVI.) Durham: Duke University Press, 1947.

Eidson, John O. *Tennyson in America: His Reputation and Influence from 1827 to 1858.* Athens: University of Georgia Press, 1943.

Flanders, Bertram H. *Early Georgia Magazines: Literary Periodicals to 1865.* Athens: University of Georgia Press, 1944.

[Griswold, R. W.]. "The Correspondence of R. W. Griswold," *Boston Public Library Quarterly,* I (July, 1949), 72.

Harcourt, John B. "Themes in American Verse, 1840-1849: A Survey of the Volumes from That Period in the Harris Collection of American Poetry in Brown University." 2 vols. Unpublished Ph.D. dissertation. Brown University, 1952.

Ingle, Edward. *Southern Highlights: A Picture of Social and Economic Life in the South a Generation before the War.* (Library of Economics and Politics, Number Ten.) New York: Thomas Y. Crowell & Co. [1896].

Jackson, David K. (comp.). *The Contributors and Contributions to the "Southern Literary Messenger" (1834–1864).* Charlottesville, Va.: Historical Publishing Co., Inc., 1936.

Lenhart, Charmentz S. *Musical Influence on American Poetry.* Athens: University of Georgia Press [1956].

Literary History of the United States, eds. Robert E. Spiller, et al. 3rd edition, revised. 2 vols. New York and London: Macmillan Co., 1963.

Meriwether, R. L. "The Papers of John C. Calhoun," *Autograph Collectors' Journal,* V (Winter, 1953), 52–53.

Miller, Joseph Roddey. "John R. Thompson: His Place in Southern Life and Literature; a Critical Biography." Unpublished Ph.D. dissertation. University of Virginia, 1930.

Moses, Montrose J. *The Literature of the South.* New York: Thomas Y. Crowell & Co. [1910].

The New-York Historical Society's Dictionary of Artists in America: 1564–1860, eds. George C. Groce and David H. Wallace. New Haven: Yale University Press, 1957.

Parks, Edd Winfield. *William Gilmore Simms As Literary Critic.* (University of Georgia Monographs, No. 7.) Athens: University of Georgia Press, 1961.

Rutledge, Anna Wells. *Artists in the Life of Charleston: Through Colony and State from Restoration to Reconstruction.* (Transactions of the American Philosophical Society, n.s. XXXIX, pt. 2.) Philadelphia: American Philosophical Society, 1949.

Ryan, Frank W., Jr. *"The Southern Quarterly Review,* 1842–1857: A Study in Thought and Opinion in the Old South." Unpublished Ph.D. dissertation. University of North Carolina, 1956.

[Simms, William Gilmore]. *The Letters of William Gilmore Simms,* eds. Mary C. Simms Oliphant, Alfred T. Odell, and T. C. Duncan Eaves. 5 vols. Columbia: University of South Carolina Press, 1952–56.

South Carolina: A Guide to the Palmetto State. (American Guide Series [Work Projects Administration].) New York: Oxford University Press [1941].

Tryon, William S., and William Charvat (eds.). *The Cost Books of Ticknor and Fields and Their Predecessors, 1832–1858.* New York: Bibliographical Society of America, 1949.

Who Was Who in America: Historical Volume, 1607–1896 (Chicago: Marquis/Who's Who, Inc., 1963). Revised edit., 1967.

INDEX

INDEX